Database Management Systems

Database Management Systems

Practical Aspects of Their Use

Edited by R. A. Frost

McGRAW-HILL BOOK COMPANY

New York   St. Louis   San Francisco   Montreal   Toronto

Library of Congress Cataloging in Publication Data
Main entry under title:

Database management systems.

Includes index.
1. Data base management.   2. Information storage and
retrieval systems.   I. Frost, R. A. (Richard A.)
QA76.9.D3D35866   1984   001.64   84-3864
ISBN 0-07-022564-8

First published in Great Britain by Granada Publishing, 1984.

1234567890   DOC/DOC   8987654

ISBN 0-07-022564-8

Typeset by Cambrian Typesetters, Aldershot, Hants, Great Britain.
Printed and bound by R. R. Donnelley & Sons Company.

Contents

Preface

The aim of this book is to complement existing literature rather than compete with it. At present, there are many well-written books on database theory, several on database system design, and a few which survey the various proprietory database management systems (DBMSs) which are available. There is, however, a noticeable lack of literature covering the practical issues of database work. In particular, there is little reading material available to help the potential DBMS user acquire a 'feel' for what it is like to use such systems. This book is intended to go some way towards filling this gap.

It is assumed that the reader has some experience of computing and is reasonably familiar with terms such as 'sequential file', 'hash table', 'lock', 'transaction processing', 'back-up', 'query' and the like, although brief definitions are given in the text when such terms are first used. It is also assumed that the reader has been introduced to the basic architecture of a database system and has some knowledge of the various DBMSs which may be purchased. If this is not the case, then it is recommended that such knowledge be acquired through reference to some suitable book on data structures and database system design (e.g. Cardenas, A.F. (1979) *Data Base Management Systems*, Allyn and Bacon) together with reference to some book in which proprietory DBMSs are described (e.g. Wiederhold, G. (1983) *Database Design*, 2nd edn. McGraw-Hill Book Company).

The text, after the introduction, is divided into three parts:

1. Fundamentals
2. Case studies
3. In conclusion

The purpose of the fundamentals part is to set the scene for the case studies which follow and includes: definitions of essential terms; a description of the database system design process; and a discussion of the part played by the database management system with examples of four of the most common types. We describe the steps which are taken in the design of a database system from scratch (i.e. without the aid of a DBMS). We do this in order to remind the reader of what is involved in database system design. In general, we recommend that database systems should not be designed from scratch since the process is too complex. An appropriate DBMS should be used to facilitate the task. The description of the four common types of DBMS which follows is of a pragmatical rather than a theoretical nature. We describe those characteristics of the four types which affect their practical use. For example, we illustrate the limitations of *hierarchical* DBMSs and indicate when it may, or may not be appropriate to use such systems.

The case studies which are presented in part 2 all refer to real applications. Each study was written by the person who was responsible, or partly responsible, for the application described. The cases were chosen to represent a reasonably broad cross-section of database work. Each author was asked to describe his experience with particular emphasis on a given aspect of database system design.

The concluding section, part 3, summarises the points which have been raised in the preceeding text. Checklists are given which could be employed by naive database system designers to help avoid some of the pitfalls which might otherwise hinder their progress.

R.A. Frost

The Contributors

Richard Frost originally studied Physics and Physiology at the University of London graduating in 1971. For the following two years he taught Physics and Mathematics at a high school in Nigeria. His involvement with computers began in 1973 while studying for an MSc degree in Medical Physics at the University of Aberdeen. After graduating, he worked with computers in both commercial and medical environments. In 1976, he moved to the University of Strathclyde as a senior research fellow in hospital computing and subsequently joined the staff as a lecturer in Computer Science maintaining his contact with non-academic computing through consultancy work. He is the author of several papers on database theory and is currently involved in the design of a novel type of database management system.

Sam Dunnachie entered the field of management services at a Clydeside engineering company with whom he had originally trained and worked as a mechanical engineer. After a period in Organisation and Methods, he moved to a large engineering group where he worked as a programmer and systems analyst on manufacturing systems before entering the database field as Group Database Co-ordinator. In this position he helped to establish the use of the Burroughs DMS II database management system in order processing and marketing systems. He then moved to BNOC (subsequently Britoil) as Senior Systems Analyst on database applications and after initially working on HP3000s, he organised and co-ordinated the exercise to select the company's IBM mainframe database software. This resulted in the decision to purchase IDMS, FOCUS and STATUS and he is now responsible as database manager for a number of applications using this software.

Sam Tannahill started his career in engineering where he was employed as a draughtsman. In 1959, however, he turned his attention to mathematics and commenced studies in Glasgow where he subsequently qualified for Associateship of the Royal College of Science and Technology. He then practised mathematics for several years before returning to studies in 1968 at the University of London where he obtained an MSc in Mathematics. His involvement in computers began in 1969 when, as a Scottish Education Department Research Fellow, he was involved in a project concerned with the use of computers for school timetabling. Since 1972 he has been a lecturer in Maths and Operational Research at various colleges and universities throughout Britain. He is currently a lecturer at the University of Strathclyde where he is involved in research on the use of database management systems in schools.

David Crabtree entered data processing in 1963 after leaving Brasenose College, Oxford. His career began with a thorough grounding in programming and systems analysis. This included, later, the management through to implementation of projects in manufacturing and commerce. In 1973 he turned to consultancy and was engaged in many special tasks, including the strategic overview of computing directions, DBMS selection, data dictionary and data administration. For the past few years he has been engaged full-time in MRP2 (manufacturing resource planning). He is a keen advocate of evolutionary systems and database development in this area.

George Berrich studied Systems Science at Michigan State University in 1968. Since then he has been involved in operations, technical support and database system software with a number of companies. He is currently database manager with the Stakis plc.

George McLeod began his career in computing with the Health Service in 1975 when he worked in medical computing as a programmer and systems designer. This involved the use of database systems as a means of implementing the complex data structures in the medical field. As Senior Systems Designer with the Grampian Health Board, he was responsible for supporting database management systems and other systems software. He then moved to the Grampian Police in 1983 as Senior Systems Analyst/Programmer and is currently implementing a number of new systems. He gained an MSc in Computer Studies from Essex University in 1977.

Patrick Prosser graduated from the University of Strathclyde in 1977 with a degree in Computer Science. His career began with Burroughs Machines Ltd in Cumbernauld where he was involved in the software development of intelligent cheque encoding equipment. His next position was with Alcan Plate Ltd where he was responsible for the development of a shop floor reporting system. He is currently a systems analyst with Britoil and is involved in systems support on a distributed computing network consisting of six HP3000's.

Ray Welland began his career in computing at the University of Reading where he gained a degree in Maths and Computer Science. His first job was in applications programming at the Computer Centre of UCL. He returned to Reading in 1972 as lecturer in Computer Science and has since taught at the University of Glasgow and at the University of Strathclyde. He is the author of several publications including four books on commercial computing and is currently involved in research in software engineering.

Alex Gray originally studied Mathematics and Natural Philosophy at Edinburgh University, graduating in 1964. He continued his studies at the University of Newcastle upon Tyne obtaining an MSc in Automatic Computing and Numerical Analysis in 1965. After graduating, he remained at Newcastle as a senior research associate and worked on the MEDUSA project which was concerned with the development of an on-line information retrieval system for the MEDLARS database. Since 1972 he has been a lecturer in the department of Computing Mathematics at University College, Cardiff. During this time he has directed several research projects concerned with information retrieval and database theory, and between 1979 and 1981 he was on secondment while holding the SSRC senior research fellowship in database management. He is currently involved in the SERC funded PROTEUS project which is establishing a homogenous distributed database system linking several sites throughout Britain.

Acknowledgements

My appreciation extends to many more people than can be named here. Special thanks are due to S. Dunnachie, S.C. Tannahill, D. Crabtree, G. Berrich, G. McLeod, P. Prosser, W.A. Gray and R.C. Welland, all of whom contributed to the latter part of this book.

I am also grateful to the University of Strathclyde for allowing much of the preparation of the manuscript to be carried out using university time and resources. I am particularly grateful to the secretaries in the department of Computer Science who patiently typed and retyped many drafts before the final version was ready.

No book can be written in a vacuum and I would like to thank my colleagues for the time which they have spent in discussion with me on matters relating to database management.

Finally, I am very grateful for the help which my wife, May, has given me in drawing diagrams and in proof-reading and for the encouragement which she and our parents, Mr & Mrs Frost and Mr & Mrs Henderson have given me during the time I have been involved with this book.

Introduction

Man needs information for survival. Without sensing danger, he cannot run from it and without knowledge of food, he cannot eat. In the early stages of his evolution, man relied on his own senses of sight, hearing, touch, taste and smell to furnish him with the information necessary for his survival. Later on, he developed the ability to share information with his companions, communicating and receiving knowledge by gestures and speech. After that he began to supplement the transitory data of speech with data of a more durable kind. As early as 30 000 B.C., the semi-nomadic men of Europe, who hunted and gathered food with tools made of flint, bone and wood were representing their environment by data which would last for a long time. Examples of Palaeolithic art have been found in the caves of France, Spain and Africa.

By 3000 B.C., the Egyptians were painting pictorial hieroglyphics on rolls of papyrus to represent and record religious themes and events. Concurrently, the people of the Mesopotamian valley were also developing a system of writing based on pictographs. These people, unlike the Egyptians, had no papyrus so they used flat tablets of baked clay to store their data. The cuneiform characters were imprinted in the clay before baking by means of sharp pointed sticks. However, it was more the use of relatively permanent records rather than the invention of such writing which was to influence civilisation. The written word is only one form of storing data. Other forms such as photographs, films and magnetic recordings can be just as effective and more so in certain circumstances. The media is unimportant. What is important is the semi-permanence of the data.

The value of recorded data was recognised in Ancient times. Hammurabi, the king of the first dynasty of Babylonia (2285—2242 B.C.), issued a decree requiring agents selling goods for merchants to give the merchants sealed memoranda quoting prices. It was customary for every business transaction to be put in writing and signed by the contracting parties and witnesses. The temples and government offices of Babylonia employed hundreds of scribes and administrators to record and manage data relating to sales, rents, loans, wages, taxes and so on. These records were kept in central locations and subjected to royal examination and audit.

In the ensuing period, proper libraries came into being. The library of Ashur-Banipal (668—630 B.C.) at Ninerva contained 30 000 tablets including receipts, levy lists, official and private correspondence, poems, prayers, lists of dates, dictionaries and tables of weights. Libraries were often housed in religious temples or the palaces of royalty. The greatest library of the ancient world grew up at Alexandria in Egypt around 200 B.C. Thanks to its royal patrons, this library consisted of between 200 000 and 700 000 rolls of papyrus.

Management of these large collections of literary and commercial data had its problems. Records had to be validated and some had to be translated. All had to be organised for access and the *databases* had to be protected from damage and theft. In the library of Ashur-Banipal, access to data was facilitated by the use of registers. Tablets were arranged by subject in chests on shelves and were sometimes put in earthern jars for protection. At Alexandria, many texts were edited and reduced to a canonical form before being stored. Rolls were organised in various ways to ease access, some were put in buckets and portrait medallions of writers were used to aid location of their works.

These techniques of ancient times may be thought of as constituting an early form of *database management*. Some are analogous to techniques used today. The positioning of portraits to aid users to locate data is similar to the use of indexes in indexed-sequential files. The major difference between ancient and modern databases is in the media on which the data is stored. The problems are very much the same and include:

- deciding what data to store
- obtaining the data
- validating the data before input
- reducing the data to some common canonical form
- organising data to ease multi-user access
- protecting data against unauthorised access
- protecting data against damage in storage

Fortunately, we have increased our understanding of database management over the last 2000 years and have developed a few additional techniques and tools to help us overcome some of these problems. For example, the use of hashing techniques for direct access to data and the use of locking strategies to prevent errors due to concurrent update are fairly recent inventions which are independent of storage media. However, many problems still remain and the reader is cautioned against thinking that database management is now a well-defined discipline which he or she will easily learn. It is not well enough understood to be well-defined. The techniques and tools which have been developed are generally only applicable under certain conditions. Often, techniques are described with reference to small unrealistic examples. In such a context, a technique appears to be more powerful than it really is. In this book, this is avoided by tempering theoretical description of modern database management techniques with accounts of what happens in practice. To enable the reader to obtain a deeper appreciation of these practical issues, seven accounts of real applications are included, each of which concentrates on a particular aspect of database management. It is hoped that, when the reader studies this material, he or she will not be too dismayed by the complexity of the database management task or by the shortcomings of the techniques and tools described. Advances have been made. For example, 2000 years ago, it probably took several minutes if not hours to locate one of the 200 000 odd rolls in the Alexandrian library. An equivalent data retrieval operation can now be performed in a fraction of a second.

PART 1
Fundamentals

By R.A. Frost, (University of Strathclyde)

In this first part, some of the concepts and terminology which are currently used in database work are revised, beginning with definitions for the terms *database*, *database system* and *database management system*. Advantages which derive from the use of databases are described and the steps involved in the design of database systems are discussed to show how this process can be facilitated by use of database management systems. In conclusion a brief review is given of the various types of database management systems which are currently available.

The aim here is to set the scene for the case studies which comprise part 2, therefore discussion of the database system design process is oriented towards practical rather than theoretical considerations. What may be regarded as an ideal approach to database system design is presented, but tempered by reference to what, in practice, generally happens.

This part, by virtue of its purpose, covers the subject at a rather superficial level. However, where appropriate, references to other works have been included so that more detailed discussions may be found.

CHAPTER 1

Databases

A *database* is a collection of data which is accessed by more than one person and/or which is used for more than one purpose.

The database might be a large collection of similar data such as that relating to airline seat reservations, or it might consist of various related data such as that used in an integrated accounting system.

There are several advantages of using a single shared database in which the data is generally stored only once, as opposed to maintaining several separate, possibly non-disjoint, files:

(a) Resources may be saved if the data is collected and stored without duplication. In addition, economies of scale might apply if all of the data is stored in one place under one management.

(b) The data may be put to more use than if it were stored separately. If a new user or new application requires use of data which is already in the database, then in many cases, such a requirement can be readily met. If, on the other hand, the required data is stored at several locations under various managements, then a great deal of time and effort might be required to gain access to it.

(c) The data is likely to contain fewer errors. In particular, inconsistencies in the data are likely to occur less frequently. One of the problems of keeping several separate non-disjoint sets of data is that some copies might be updated whilst other copies are overlooked. A similar problem might occur if you keep two diaries. When two supposedly identical files contain contradicting data they are said to be inconsistent. This problem occurs to a lesser extent if a database is used since, in general, there is less redundancy (duplication) of the data.

Of course, it could be argued that there are several disadvantages of using databases. For example: (i) the data must be transmitted from the sources to the central database and from the central database to the end-users, (ii) security and privacy constraints must be enforced on access to the database to prevent unauthorised reading or changing of data. This is likely to be more complicated than if the data were held in several separate files and (iii) standard data formats need to be created and adopted by all users of the database.

However, it could also be argued that these last two considerations are not really disadvantages but are practices which should be adopted whether a database is used or not. If this view is taken, then an additional advantage of using a database is that it compels organisations to adopt worthwhile practices.

Irrespective of whether or not the above tasks are regarded as disadvantages, they still need to be carried out if a database is to be used. In addition, several other tasks arise as a consequence of using a database. They are collectively known as database management tasks and are carried out by a system called a *database system*.

CHAPTER 2

Database Systems

DEFINITION

A *database system* is a set of resources whose collective responsibilities include the following:

(a) Storing the database.
(b) Maintaining database security by enforcing privacy and integrity constraints and by providing the necesssary back-up for recovery from hardware/software breakdown.
(c) Providing users/uses with the necessary input/output routines so that the database can be accessed as required.

In this book, it is assumed that a major component of the database system is a computer and that the database resides in some form of computer storage. However, database systems can be built which do not use computers and many of the concepts discussed are equally applicable to this case.

AN IDEAL DATABASE SYSTEM ARCHITECTURE

In fig. 2.1 is shown what might be regarded as an ideal architecture for a database system. It consists of nine modules the functions of which are briefly described below. (A more comprehensive description of each module is given later.)

CONCEPTUAL SCHEMA
The conceptual schema is a description of the application area. That is, it is a description of those things which are to be modelled by data in the database. It typically includes a list of the types of entity which are of interest, a list of the relations between these entity types and a list of the integrity constraints which apply to these relations. The conceptual schema can be used, for example, to introduce potential users to the database system thereby resolving any misunderstandings which they might have about the application area. It is also used during the design and construction of other parts of the database system as discussed in later sections.

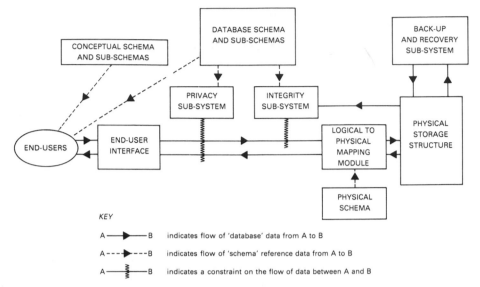

Fig. 2.1 An ideal architecture for a database system.

That part of the conceptual schema which is of interest to a particular end-user or group of end-users is called the *conceptual sub-schema*. Ideally, sub-schemas should be presented to end-users in a form which is most appropriate for them. For example, some end-users might prefer a diagrammatical description such as that illustrated in fig. 2.2. Others might be more at home with a record-like notation such as that shown in fig. 2.3. Sub-schemas have similar functions to schemas, however, their use is oriented more to end-users rather than to database system designers.

DATABASE SCHEMA
This is a description of the data which is stored in the database and specifies what data elements are stored and what access paths are provided between these elements. The database schema also contains specifications of privacy as well as integrity constraints. It is somewhat similar to the conceptual schema, *but is a description of data rather than of reality*. Some aspects of reality which are described in the conceptual schema will not be represented by data in the database schema. Note, however, that the database schema does not specify how the data is actually stored or how access paths are provided. (Ideally it should *not* refer to files, records, sets or the like.) It is, therefore, an implementation independent description and for this reason is sometimes referred to as *logical schema*.

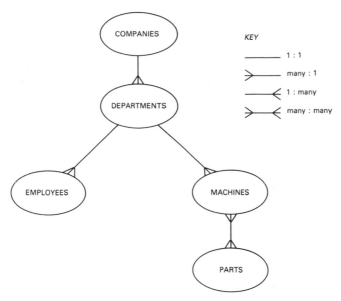

Fig. 2.2 A diagrammatical schema.

Companies	
Departments	
Employees	Machines
	Parts

Fig. 2.3 A record-oriented notation for a conceptual schema.

That part of the database schema which is of interest to a particular end-user or group of end-users is called a *database sub-schema*. Ideally, a sub-schema should be specified using a notation which is most appropriate for the use to which it is being put. Database sub-schemas have several uses: (i) they can be referred to by application programmers to see what access paths are available in that part of the database in which they are interested, (ii) similarly, they can be referred to by the end-users when they are using a report program generator or formulating queries etc. using a query language provided (see *end-user interface* below) and (iii) they can be used to divide the database into units for the specification of privacy constraints. For example, a sub-schema could be defined for which all users have read access but only one specified user has write (update) access.

PHYSICAL SCHEMA

The physical schema is a description of the physical structure of the database. If, for example, conventional indexed-sequential files are used to store the database, then this will be stated in the physical schema. It will also contain details of record formats, blocking factors etc. The physical schema is constructed as an essential part of the design process. However, it may also be used as an integral part of the operational database system as discussed below. The physical schema is sometimes called the internal schema.

PHYSICAL STORAGE STRUCTURE

The structure in which the database actually resides is termed the physical storage structure. It typically consists of disc files, tapes, mainstore indices and programs to manipulate these components.

BACK-UP AND RECOVERY SYSTEM

The back-up and recovery system is the module which rebuilds the database after corruption due to hardware or software failure.

END-USER INTERFACE

The software which is part of the end-user interface typically consists of application programs, report program generators and query languages. The application programs when executed allow the end-users to enter, retrieve and update data in the database. Application programs can be written to present data to the users in a form which is most appropriate for them. No knowledge of the database is needed to use an application program. The end-user need only be aware of the integrity constraints which apply to the data and the meaning of the 'prompt' messages which are issued by the application program. Use of the report program generators and query languages, however, does require a knowledge of database contents and access path provision. A report program generator (RPG) is a utility program which helps end-users create 'reports'. The end-user specifies the data content and format of the report required and the RPG creates a report program which, when executed, obtains the necessary data from the database and displays it according to the format specified. Whenever an up-to-date report is required, the end-user simply re-runs the report program. The RPG is often used to generate programs for outputting reports which are required on a regular basis. Query languages, on the other hand, are often used to meet 'one-off' requests for data or to provide a *browsing* facility with which the end-user can navigate his or her way round the database. Before a query language can be used, the user needs to know what access paths are available in the database. This information can be obtained by reference to the relevant database sub-schema. Similarly, application programmers need to refer to relevant database sub-schemas when they construct application programs.

LOGICAL TO PHYSICAL MAPPING MODULE
Ideally, the application programs, RPG programs and query languages request data packages using some *logical* language which is based on the structures as specified in the database schema. That is, a language which is independent of the physical storage structure. The conversion of logical requests to physical commands which manipulate the physical storage structure is then carried out automatically by the *logical to physical mapping module*. This module refers to the physical schema in order to perform its task. One advantage of this approach is that modification to the physical storage structure, due for example to the introduction of a new computer or operating system, has minimal impact on the database system. The logical language remains the same, therefore, the application programs are not affected. The only program requiring change is the logical to physical mapping program. Systems which have this architecture are said to be more *data-independent* than ones which do not. Note, however, that data-independence is also related to other factors which are discussed later.

PRIVACY SUB-SYSTEM
The privacy sub-system protects the database from unauthorised access. Ideally, privacy constraints are expressed in the same logical language as that used by the application programs and are then incorporated into the database schema. When end-users attempt to input or output packages of data (via the application programs) the privacy sub-system refers to the database schema to see if such access is allowed and then acts accordingly.

INTEGRITY SUB-SYSTEM
The integrity sub-system protects the database from the input of certain types of erroneous data. Ideally, integrity constraints such as 'no employee can work in more than one department' are expressed in the logical language and are then incorporated into the database schema. When end-users attempt to input packages of data (via the application programs) the integrity sub-system refers to the database schema and to the database itself to see if such input is allowed.

ADVANTAGES OF THIS ARCHITECTURE

The advantages of the architecture as described above are felt in all stages of the system life-cycle. For example: (i) the design stage is facilitated by the modular structure and by the fact that the application programs and the integrity and privacy sub-systems all refer to the database in logical terms. Each of these modules can be designed independently and the designers need not be concerned with the implementation details of the physical storage structure used, (ii) use of the system is facilitated by the presence of the conceptual and database schemas. End-users can refer to these schemas to clarify their understanding of the application area and to find out what data is stored in the database and (iii) maintenance of the system is facilitated to a large extent by the logical to physical mapping module. As mentioned, the introduction of new hardware and/or operating system has minimal impact on the system if this module is present.

PRACTICAL CONSIDERATIONS

In practice, few systems conform to the ideal architecture. This is largely due to the difficulty in designing the logical to physical mapping module. In general, application programs communicate with the data storage structure directly and privacy and integrity controls are embedded in these application programs. However, to simplify the following description of database system design, the design process is divided into stages which bear some relation to the modules of the ideal architecture as described above.

CHAPTER 3

Database System Design

When the need for a database has been established, someone, or some persons, must design and implement a database system to support it. The design process may be thought of as consisting of eight stages:

- specification of the conceptual schema
- specification of the input/output requirements
- specification of the database schema
- specification of the physical storage structure
- design of the privacy sub-system
- design of the integrity sub-system
- design of the back-up and recovery sub-system
- design of the input/output application programs and RPG and query languages

Two points should be made: Firstly, the ordering which is implied above is somewhat misleading in that it is an over-simplification to suggest that the physical storage structure can be designed before thought is given as to how privacy, integrity and back-up are to be provided. The last four tasks tend to be carried out in parallel.

Secondly, tradition is broken in recommending that the conceptual schema should be constructed before the input/output requirements are specified. The reason for this is straightforward: although the input/output specification fully defines what the system is required to do, it only defines what is required at a particular point in time. Experience has shown that this requirement is likely to change as time progresses. Therefore, using the traditional approach, where the input/output requirements are regarded as the most important part of the system specification, can result in the design of a database system which could become obsolete very quickly. On the other hand, the conceptual schema is relatively stable and its use as the focal point for system specification should result in longer lasting database systems.

A conceptual schema is simply a description of the application area. That is, it is a description of that part of the universe which is to be represented by data in the database. No mention is made, in the conceptual schema, of how this data is to be stored or *how it is to be used*. For this reason the conceptual schema is more stable than the input/output requirements.

Each of the stages of database system design is now discussed in more detail, starting with the specification of the conceptual schema. Notice that in this chapter, the design of a database system is described from scratch assuming that no database management system (DBMS) is available to help the designer with this task.

SPECIFICATION OF THE CONCEPTUAL SCHEMA

WHAT IS A CONCEPTUAL SCHEMA?

As mentioned earlier, the *conceptual schema* is simply a description of the application area. For example, it might contain (i) a list of the types of *entities* involved: employees, departments, machines, parts, etc., (ii) a list of the interesting *relations* between these entity types: employees work in departments, machines are built from parts, etc. and (iii) a list of the *integrity constraints* which apply: e.g. 'if employee A manages employee B and employee A works in department D, then employee B must also work in department D'.

The conceptual schema is a description of reality and not of data. Consequently, it does not refer to access paths, privacy constraints and the like. Information about this part of the system is contained in the *database schema* which is described later.

USE OF THE CONCEPTUAL SCHEMA

The conceptual schema has several uses in the context of database system design:

(a) It can be used at the start of the design process to integrate the interests of the various end-users.

(b) It is a useful description for communication with non-technical end-users. The application area is described without reference to access requirements or physical storage considerations and is therefore free of technical jargon.

(c) It helps the designer to build a more durable database system. By looking at the conceptual schema, the designer can identify those access paths which, although not required now, may be required at some time in the future. The database system can then be designed such that these access paths could be easily accommodated if required.

(d) Once the database system has been designed, the conceptual schema may be used to introduce potential users to it. This is particularly important if the system is being considered for transfer to, and use at, another site. The conceptual schema may help identify any fundamental differences between the organisation at the new and original sites. Such differences might require extensive alterations to be made to the system before it can be used at the new site and are best identified early.

FORMAL SPECIFICATION

Conceptual schemas are generally written in English, if at all. Often, the database system designer keeps such information in his head. However, there are good reasons why a more formal approach should be used:

(a) The meaning of the resultant conceptual schemas would be less ambiguous.

(b) The logical consistency of the schemas could be determined if the conceptual schema definition language were 'decidable' in the strict mathematical sense. This would allow some types of mistakes in the designer's perception of the application area to be identified.

(c) It might be possible to use formally defined constraints to maintain the semantic integrity of the database *automatically*. Even if this were not possible, it should be easier to write programs to enforce each individual constraint if the constraints are specified in some standard way.

Unfortunately, work on formally defined conceptual schema definition languages is still at the research stage. No really useful language has yet been developed. However, some informal notations are being used. These include the conceptual schema definition language, CSDL, (Roussopoulos, 1979) and the binary-relational notation (Shave, 1980) which regards the universe as consisting of entities related by binary-relationships. As an example, consider the conceptual schema shown in fig. 3.1. This schema is specified using a modified binary-relational approach and describes an application area comprising employees, companies, departments, machines and parts. Relations between these entity types are depicted by named arcs in the schema. The 'cardinality' of the relations is given by the label underneath (or to the right of) the arc. For example, an employee is allowed to manage up to 20 employees but an employee may not have more than one manager.

PROBLEMS IN CREATING CONCEPTUAL SCHEMAS

One of the most difficult problems in creating the conceptual schema is in obtaining the agreement of all the potential users of the system that the schema represents the application area correctly. This is

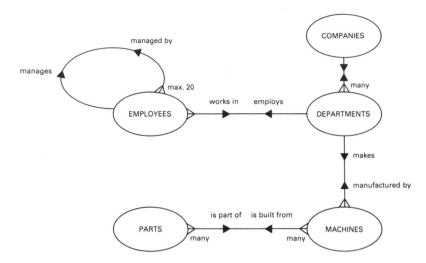

Fig. 3.1 A simple conceptual schema (incomplete).

largely due to the many exceptions which are often allowed to override the general rules which govern organisational structures. For example, it might be true that in most cases an employee is only allowed to have one manager but this might be overruled in the case of secretaries. Although such exceptions complicate the specification of the conceptual schema, it is better that they are identified early on in the design process. Failure to do this could result in the need to introduce ad hoc extensions to the system at some later date.

SPECIFICATION OF THE INPUT/OUTPUT REQUIREMENTS

IDENTIFYING REQUIRED DATA

Now that a common terminology has been established for the application area, the designer can embark upon the task of identifying which parts of the application area should be represented by data, and when and how this data should be presented to the users. In other words he/she is in a position to specify the function of the *end-user interface*. The art of doing this falls within the scope of *systems analysis*. It involves a thorough understanding of the application area and an ability to determine the real value of the data to the organisation for which the database system is being built. Many books have been written on this subject, however, it should be noted that systems analysis is not yet a science but is a skill that may only be acquired through practical experience in conjunction with extensive reading. A good reference to start with is (Gane and Sarson, 1977).

DATA ANALYSIS

Once the required data has been identified, the next step involves the definition and classification of this data. This task may be facilitated by use of methods which are gaining acceptance as comprising a well defined discipline called *data-analysis* of which much has been written e.g. (BCS, 1978), (King, 1977) and (Gradwell, 1975). The result of the first stage of data analysis is a *data dictionary* which is a description of all data items which are to be processed by the system.

The data dictionary might consist of a manually supported set of forms, or it might be maintained by a computer-based system such as DATAMANAGER (see later). A typical data dictionary allows the designer to record the following properties of each data-item:

- name
- synonyms
- definition, i.e. a description of the real world entity which it represents
- type, e.g. string, integer, real, etc.
- format
- access constraints
- integrity constraints
- relationship to other data-items
- source
- usage

Discussion of the use of data dictionaries can be found in (BCS, 1976), (Canning, 1981), (Lomax, 1978) and (Van Duyn, 1982).

INPUT/OUTPUT PACKAGE SPECIFICATION

After the data dictionary has been constructed, the next step in the specification of the end-user interface is to determine how groups of data items should be *packaged* for input to and output from the system. Most techniques which are used for data analysis also provide facilities for such specification. However, many of the techniques describe the packages in terms of the data structures which are to be used for the physical storage of the database. For example, packages are often described as records or files. Such an approach confuses what the system is required to do (i.e. what packages of data are to be made available to the users) with how the system is to do this (i.e. how the data is to be stored e.g. as files of records or relations etc.). Ideally, at this stage, the designer should be able to specify the required packages with as little reference to implementation detail as possible. For example, instead of stating that 'package A consists of an employee record, printed on paper, which is generated by the user entering an employee number at a terminal', a better specification would be that 'package A consists of an employee number, name and salary, on human readable hard copy media, which is generated by the user entering an employee number at one of several specified locations'.

This method of specification gives the designer more freedom when designing other aspects of the system. A few techniques have been developed which support this approach and an example of the use of one is given in fig. 3.2, (Warnier, 1971). However, none of these techniques has yet gained wide acceptance, although some are recommended in recent books on systems analysis e.g. (Couger, Colter, Knapp, 1982).

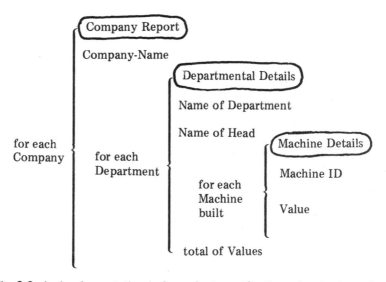

Fig. 3.2 An implementation independent specification of output required.

DETERMINING PACKAGE CONTENT
We have not really said much about how the contents of the input/output packages are identified. In general, it is not a simple matter of asking the users what packages they want. This might provide a starting point but should not be regarded as a means of achieving a final input/output specification. The designer needs to rationalise the user's requirements in order to construct a minimal set of requirements. This process involves three stages:

- determine users' input/output requirements
- construct the data dictionary
- determine what minimal set of input/output packages would meet the total set of user requirements

Such minimisation would, in general, require a degree of compromise. For example, some users might be provided with packages containing more data than was strictly necessary whereas others might have to use two packages with cross-referencing to obtain the data they require. In many cases, however, users may be quite tolerant of such a compromise and the designer should always consider minimisation of input/output packages since this would normally result in fewer application programs.

Another factor which must be taken into account when deciding on the input/output package structure concerns data privacy. This is discussed later.

APPLICATION PROGRAMS

The actual generation of input/output packages is carried out by programs commonly called *application programs*. These programs are not considered until the data storage structure has been designed. In addition, the media on which the packages are presented depends upon factors which are not yet known, e.g. what hardware configuration is to be used etc. These considerations are returned to later.

SPECIFICATION OF THE DATABASE SCHEMA

At this stage, the designer will have created three 'documents': (i) a description of the application area (the conceptual schema), (ii) a definition and classification of the data items which are to be manipulated by the system (the data dictionary) and (iii) a specification of the characteristics of the various packages of data which are required by the users. The designer will also have gathered information concerning the privacy and integrity of the data and this will have had some influence on the choice of the input/output package contents.

The next step is to specify the total data content of the database and the characteristics of the access paths required through this data. This specification is called the *database schema*. It is similar to the conceptual schema but differs in that it is a description of data rather than of reality.

Like conceptual schemas, database schemas are often written in English. However, some data dictionary sytems are sophisticated enough to be used for database schema definition. Care must be taken to distinguish between data analysis and database schema definition. Data analysis is concerned with the definition and classification of the data which is to be manipulated by the database system. Database schema definition is concerned with the use of this data: what access paths are required, what privacy constraints should be imposed and so on.

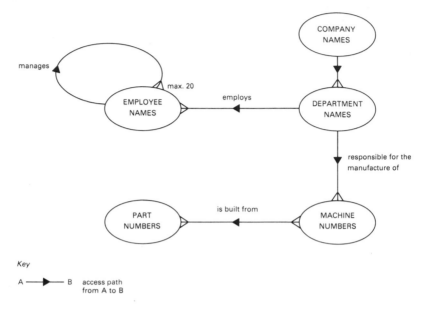

Fig. 3.3 A simple database schema (incomplete).

Irrespective of what notation is employed for specification, it is useful to think of the database schema as a network such as that shown in fig. 3.3. The nodes represent types of data, and the directed arcs represent access paths between data types. In a complete schema the nodes would contain information which might include:

- the data type name
- a definition of the data type or a reference to the data dictionary where the definition may be found
- a list of the various formats in which the data is required by the various input/output packages
- a list of the users and/or packages which are allowed access to the data type
- a list of the integrity constraints which apply to the data type, e.g. 'age of employee cannot exceed 70'

The arcs of the network are labelled with information which might include:

- the name of the access path or relation which the arc represents, e.g. 'is built from'

- a definition of the relation or a reference to the data dictionary where the definition can be found
- a list of the uses of the access path, e.g. 'package # 15 uses each access path of this type twice per week in employee order, package # 57 uses one random path of this type once per week'
- a summary of the access path use
- a list of the users/packages which are allowed to follow the access path and the mode (read/write) allowed
- a list of the integrity constraints which apply, e.g. 'an employee may not be related to more than one department'

When creating the database schema, the designer should refer to the conceptual schema as well as the input/output package specification. This will aid prediction of what access paths might be required by future applications. For example, although the current input/output package specification might not indicate a need for an access path from machine to department, the system designer should establish whether or not such a requirement might arise in the predicted lifetime of the system. If such a requirement is likely, then this should be mentioned in the database schema.

In many ways, the database schema may be thought of as a specification of what the database system is required to do. It describes what data is to be stored and what access paths are to be provided. Notice, however, that no mention is made of how the access paths are to be implemented. It is for this reason that the database schema is sometimes referred to as the *logical schema* to distinguish it from the physical or internal schema which is described next.

DESIGN OF THE PHYSICAL STORAGE STRUCTURE

CHOOSING THE COMPUTER CONFIGURATION
The designer is now in a position to decide how the data should be stored physically. This decision involves many factors in addition to the requirements as given in the database schema and end-user interface specification. The characteristics of the available computer hardware, operating systems and programming languages must be taken into account as well as factors concerning staff expertise, management preference and so on.

The choice of computer hardware is often dictated by political as well as financial considerations and the decision as to what computer configuration should be used is not always taken by the database system designer. Choice of hardware is considered further in Chapter 5.

DATA STRUCTURES

Assuming then, that the hardware configuration has been chosen, the next step is to specify how the data is to be stored and accessed within this configuration. This specification is called the *physical schema* or *internal schema* and consists of a description of one or more *data structures* based on combinations of structures taken from a set which includes:

- sequential files
- indexed sequential files
- transposed files
- inverted files
- hash tables
- trees
- relations
- networks using pointers

Each of these structures has its own relative advantages and disadvantages and these must be taken into account by the designer when choosing an appropriate structure. For example, sequential files are readily available in most programming languages, are ideal for sequential processing but do not support random access. Hash tables, on the other hand, provide very fast random access but generally need to be programmed for the particular data which is to be stored and they do not provide sequential access. In order to make the choice, the designer must have a thorough knowledge of such performance characteristics. Fortunately, several studies have been carried out which contribute to our understanding of these factors. For example:

- sequential files (Schneiderman and Goodman, 1976)
- indexed sequential files (Wiederhold, 1977)
- transposed files (Batory, 1979)
- inverted files (Claybrook and Yang, 1978)
- hash tables (Severence and Duhne, 1976)
- B-trees (Nakamura and Mizoguchi, 1978)
- relations (Chamberlin, 1976)

EXAMPLES OF PHYSICAL STORAGE STRUCTURE

For a simple database schema a single data structure might suffice. For example, given the database schema in fig. 3.4, an appropriate physical storage structure might consist of a single sequential file of employee records sorted into employee name order.

For more complicated database schemas, more complicated physical storage structures are likely to be required. It might be

Fig. 3.4 Example of a simple database schema (incomplete).

necessary to use more than one type of data structure and it is frequently necessary to duplicate data in order that sufficiently efficient access paths are provided. Even database schemas which are only marginally more complicated than the example above require careful design. For example, consider the database schema shown in fig. 3.5. This schema might have been constructed for a system in which a telephone directory is to be stored and used to find numbers for given names *and* names for given numbers. (Notice that these example schemas are incomplete. Details which are irrelevant to the present discussion have been omitted.) An indexed sequential file of records containing name and number might suffice for access from name to number. However, access from number to name would be hopeless. For a successful search, 50 000 records on average, would have to be scanned. For an unsuccessful search, all 100 000 records would require to be examined. A reasonable solution to this particular problem requires the data to be duplicated thereby providing fast access in both directions. For example, two hash tables, one using the name as hash key and the other using the number as hash key, might constitute an appropriate physical storage structure.

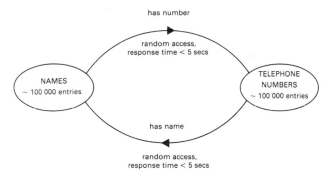

Fig. 3.5 Telephone directory database schema.

DATA-INDEPENDENCE

A very important aspect of physical storage structure design which we have not yet discussed in detail is concerned with *data-independence*. This term is used to describe the extent to which the physical storage structure is independent of the application programs which access it and vice-versa. A completely data-independent system displays the following properties:

(a) All relations between entities which are specified in the conceptual schema are represented by equally efficient access paths in the physical storage structure.

(b) All access requests which are issued by application programs to the physical schema are couched in terms of some *logical* language which is independent of the actual data structures which comprise the physical storage structure. Such requests are then converted by the *logical to physical mapping module*, into implementation dependent commands. For example, the logical request 'retrieve salary of 'J Smith'' would be converted to commands meaning: retrieve a record from employee file using 'J Smith' as key and deliver the value of the second field of this record.

The advantages of having a data-independent database system are two-fold: (i) new application programs can be added with minimal effort. If the necessary access paths are already available then there is no need to modify or extend the physical storage structure to accommodate them and (ii) the implementation environment can be more easily changed. If a new computer is purchased and a different type of data structure is to be used in the physical storage structure then this change can be made without modifying any of the application programs. The only program requiring modification is the logical to physical mapping program.

In practice, physical storage structures are often designed with only a limited amount of built-in flexibility. New applications are accommodated by ad hoc extensions to the storage structure resulting in database systems which eventually become unwieldy and have to be replaced by new systems.

DESIGN OF THE PRIVACY SUB-SYSTEM

Database *privacy* is defined as a property of the database which reflects the extent to which the data is protected against unauthorised access.

Privacy requirements are first identified during the construction of the conceptual schema. If English is the language used then the schema might contain statements such as: '*A* and *B* are the only employees who are allowed to know the salaries of other employees'. During the subsequent design of the database schema, such statements are converted into *access constraints* which are couched in terms of data elements and access paths, i.e. in the ideal case, in terms of the nodes and arcs of the database schema. For example, the requirement above might be converted to the constraint: 'users A and B are the only users who are allowed to follow the access paths linking employees to salaries'.

The access constraints are then taken into account when the physical storage structure is designed, however, the actual mechanisms for enforcing the constraints are best contained in a separate module or sub-system called an *arbiter*.

Two advantages derive from this approach:

(a) The design process is facilitated. All access control mechanisms reside in one module and a single standard approach may be used for their implementation.
(b) The resulting system is more data independent than it would be if the access control mechanisms were built into the physical storage structure or application programs.

Ideally, complete data independence may be achieved since the access constraints need never be couched in terms of physical data structures (i.e. files, records, relations and so on). If access requests are issued by input/output application programs in some logical language as discussed previously, then the arbiter can enforce the constraints, as expressed in the database schema, without any reference to the physical storage structures (see fig. 2.1). The arbiter would be a relatively simple program which would perform the following functions:

(a) Identify the user.
(b) List the nodes and/or arcs of the database schema which correspond to that part of the database which the user is trying to access.
(c) Consult the access constraints to see if such access is allowed. If so, then permit access else take some action as defined in the database schema.

Design of the privacy sub-system involves decisions concerning how users/uses are to be identified, for example, by user names and passwords or by machine readable identity cards, how access rights for an identified user are to be stored and retrieved and what actions should be taken when an attempt is made at unauthorised access to data.

The actual mechanics of access control might involve the use of a *security matrix* (Conway, Maxwell and Morgan, 1974) or of an *access matrix* (Fernandez, Summers and Coleman, 1975). In both of these techniques the columns of the matrix represent data elements and the rows represent users. The element $M [i, j]$ of the matrix specifies access rights of user i to data j.

In practice, most privacy sub-systems are not designed to exhibit the data independence as discussed above. Application programs tend to issue access requests in terms of physical rather than logical data structures and the columns of the access matrix, if one is used, tend to represent physical storage structures such as files, records, relations and so on. In many cases not even this level of modularisation is used and access constraints are implemented in an ad hoc manner as follows:

(a) Privacy constraints are specified in terms of individual user's rights to access specific parts of the physical storage structure, e.g. employee file, manager record, salary field.

(b) Some of the constraints are implemented by restricting access to relevant input/output programs and/or data files. This might be achieved by use of the privacy controls in the operating system. In general, such controls are based on the use of passwords to gain access to programs or files.

(c) Other constraints might require ad hoc procedures to be written to reside within the input/output application programs. Such procedures are used to constrain access to those parts of the database which are not regarded as 'units of data' by the operating system. For example, if a particular user is allowed to read some but not all of the fields in a certain type of record, then such control cannot be enforced by use of passwords in a file oriented operating system, and an ad hoc procedure would have to be written.

Although much has been written on the subject of database privacy, most of this material is concerned with the social implications of insecure data. However, some publications do consider the mechanics of privacy control and these can be referred to by the system designer when building the privacy sub-system e.g. (Denning and Denning, 1979).

DESIGN OF THE INTEGRITY SUB-SYSTEM

We define database *integrity* as a property which reflects the extent to which the database is an accurate model of that part of the universe which it represents.

The integrity sub-system is responsible for maintaining integrity by protecting the database against invalid (as opposed to unauthorised) alteration or destruction. Errors in the data occur for a number of reasons and protection must be provided for each, for example:

(a) Parts of the universe are observed incorrectly before they are represented by data, e.g. a thermometer might not be calibrated correctly. Incorrect input data results.
(b) Observations are not made frequently enough, e.g. an employee might be represented as working in department M when in reality the person has been transferred to department N.
(c) Data is corrupted in coding, transcription, and/or transmission.
(d) Errors are introduced through concurrent update, e.g. user 1 reads balance B at time $T1$, adds X to B and overwrites the original balance at time $T2$. User 2 repeats the process, reading at time $T3$, adding Y to the balance, and writing at time $T4$. If $T1 < T3 < T2 < T4$ and $X \neq 0$ then the balance will be in error.
(e) Data is corrupted in storage through hardware faults.

Various techniques have been developed to reduce the occurrence of such errors, or to detect them when they occur. Many of these techniques are well understood and their use is common practice. For example, parity checks are used to detect errors in data transmission, and locks are used to reduce errors due to concurrent update. A concise description of these methods is given by Wiederhold (1983). Some aspects of the problem are very poorly understood. For example, the problem of 'out-of-date' data has not received much attention in the literature. However, Klopprogge (1981) has addressed this question in a recent publication and makes some interesting suggestions as to how the time dimension might be taken into account.

SEMANTIC INTEGRITY

Other aspects of the problem are poorly understood although some progress has been made. One of these aspects is concerned with *semantic integrity*. By semantic integrity, we mean the compliance of the database with constraints which are derived from our knowledge about what is and what is not 'allowed' (or sensible) in that part of the universe which is represented by data in the database. The maintenance of semantic integrity involves preventing data which represents a disallowed state of the universe from being inserted into the database. The procedures which maintain semantic integrity detect semantic errors, inform the user that an error has taken place, and prevent data from being inserted into the database. The design of these procedures is similar to the design of the security sub-system:

(a) Integrity constraints are identified during construction of the conceptual schema which might contain statements representing knowledge such as 'no employee may have two salaries' and 'it is unlikely that anyone has an age greater than 110'.

(b) These constraints are then couched in terms of data elements and access paths and constitute part of the database schema, e.g. 'only one access path between an employee and a salary is allowed' and 'no element of type age may be greater than 110'.

(c) The constraints are then taken into account when designing the physical storage structure.

(d) Mechanisms are designed for the enforcement of the integrity constraints.

INTEGRITY CONSTRAINT ENFORCEMENT

Ideally, the enforcement mechanisms should be grouped together into a single program similar to the privacy arbiter. In practice, however, this is rarely done. The reason for this is that semantic integrity constraints can be of varying degrees of complexity and the subject is not yet well enough understood for a general purpose integrity checking algorithm to have been developed. Consequently, ad hoc procedures tend to be written and embedded in the application programs which handle the data input packages. For example, the application program which allows users to enter new employee data might have a procedure for checking that the entered age is not greater than 110.

The disadvantage of this ad hoc approach is that the code for checking a single integrity constraint might appear in many different application programs. This is particularly undesirable if the integrity check requires the database to be interrogated. However, if this is not the case, then there is an advantage in the approach: some integrity checking can be done 'off-line'. Input packages may be generated and checked at remote locations before being batched for input.

The maintenance of integrity is a difficult and poorly understood subject. However, it is of crucial importance that the database system is designed such that the required level of confidence in the accuracy of the data can be maintained. Notice that we have not said that the database should be completely correct. This is unrealistic. What is important is that the database is sufficiently accurate for the use for which it is intended. The designer must remember that integrity checking can be expensive. One of the decisions is to find the right compromise between correctness and cost.

DESIGN OF THE BACK-UP AND RECOVERY SUB-SYSTEM

One aspect of integrity which we have omitted from the discussion so far concerns the protection of the database against errors which occur through system failure. Such failure may be due to hardware breakdown or software bugs. Whatever the cause of data corruption, the system must be capable of *recovering* from the disaster. This may be achieved in a variety of ways by use of locking strategies, transactions, back-up files and recovery routines.

THE LOCKING STRATEGY

The *locking strategy* determines how the database should be partitioned into units for update. The units might be fields, records, files or some larger sections of the database. While a copy of the unit is being updated, the original is locked to prevent any access to it. When the update is complete, the new version of the unit replaces the old version and the update is thereby committed. Should the system fail during update, then the original remains intact. In many cases, the unit might not be copied, but locked for exclusive use by the transaction which updates it directly (rather than updating a copy of it). If the system fails during update in this case, then the old version is reinstated by use of back-up files and recovery routines as explained later.

The locking process also serves the purpose of preventing errors due to concurrent update (see Chapter 10).

TRANSACTIONS

The use of *transactions* is closely related to integrity. A transaction is a collection of database accesses which are regarded as comprising a unit of processing as far as integrity checking is concerned. The choice of transaction size is determined by other factors in addition to integrity. For example, the 'logical' units of work as seen by the user will have some influence on the choice of transaction content.

BACK-UP FILES

The *back-up files* typically consist of a *journal file* and *dump files*. The journal is normally a sequential file held on tape which contains copies (or images) of database units before and/or after they are updated, together with copies of the transactions which update them. The dump files consist of copies of the whole or parts of the database which are taken periodically. For example, a copy of one-seventh of the database may be taken every day, or a copy of the whole database may be taken once a week.

RECOVERY ROUTINES

The *recovery routines* determine how a correct version of the database may be reinstated after system failure. Ideally, the database should be returned to the state it was in just before the failure. Various techniques have been developed, two of which may be simply described as follows:

(a) *Roll-back* or *backward recovery*: the journal file is scanned to identify the before-images of the units which were being updated when the system failed. These before-images are reinstated.

(b) *Roll-forward* or *forward-recovery*: a copy of the database (or that part of the database which has been corrupted) is obtained from the most recent dump file and loaded. The journal file is then used to bring the database up to the state it was in just before the failure. After-images can be used directly or transactions which occurred since the dump can be automatically rerun.

Roll-back can be used to deal with deadlock resolution (where two transactions lock units of the database required by each other and thereby prevent each other from completion), run-unit failure (where a transaction terminates prematurely), and communication/write errors which corrupt a single locked unit of the database.

Roll-forward is generally used when the failure has affected a large section of the database and the extent of corruption is not restricted to the units which were active at the time of the failure. This occurs, for example, with disk-head crash.

DESIGN OF THE RECOVERY SUB-SYSTEM

Design of the recovery sub-system involves decisions concerning how often dumps should be taken, how big the locked units and transactions should be and what information should be recorded on the journal file. To a large extent, the recovery sub-system is dependent on the physical storage structure, and the design of these two parts of the system should be carried out concurrently.

DESIGN OF THE APPLICATION PROGRAMS

The final stage of the design process concerns the design of the *application programs*. These programs provide two facilities:

- they allow the user to build packages of data for input to the system
- they access the database and generate packages of data for output from the system

A simple application program might provide only one of these facilities. For example, a program which generates a departmental report may access the database and create this report without any form of user input. In some cases, however, a single application program will handle both input and output packages of data. For example, an application program which is used for a payroll might allow the user to input a package of data comprising an employee's name and hours worked, and might output a package consisting of payslip data. As can be seen from this example, not all of the data which constitutes an output package is necessarily obtained from the database. In general, some of the data might be generated by the application program itself after reference to data held in the database.

The specification of an application program includes descriptions of

- package(s) of data which are to be input by the user
- package(s) of data which are to be output to the user
- privacy constraints which are to be applied to use of the application program
- integrity constraints which are to be applied to the input packages
- response characteristics required. For example, the maximum time which can be tolerated between user input and system output

Ideally, the last three need not be specified since the rest of the system should already have been designed to accommodate these requirements. The privacy sub-system should impose any privacy constraints defined for a given user irrespective of what application program is being used. The integrity sub-system should prevent any inconsistencies from arising in the database irrespective of where the input data came from. Also, the data storage structure should have been configured to give the required response for all output packages for which the system was designed.

In addition, if the system has been designed to be data-independent, then the person constructing the application programs need not be concerned with details of the physical schema. All requests for data from the database can be couched in the 'logical' terms of the database schema and then converted automatically to physical storage commands by the logical to physical mapping module as described earlier.

In practice, however, the above is rarely achieved and a typical application program is generally a mixture of security and integrity validation routines together with procedures for the manipulation of the physical storage structure.

COMMENTS ON DATABASE SYSTEM DESIGN

So far the steps which would be involved in the design of a database system from scratch have been described. That is, it has been assumed that no database management system is available to assist the designer in this process.

The recommended approach requires the designer to:

- describe the application area and construct the conceptual schema
- identify the user's input/output requirements
- construct the data dictionary
- specify a minimal set of input/output packages
- specify the database schema
- design the physical storage structure
- design the privacy sub-system
- design the integrity sub-system
- design the back-up and recovery sub-system
- design the application programs

In practice, however, very few systems are designed in this way. Frequently, as mentioned earlier, the conceptual schema exists only in the designer's mind. The input/output packages are specified without the use of a data-dictionary and the physical storage structures are chosen without the intermediate construction of a database schema. This results in database systems which are data-dependent. That is, they are highly dependent on the physical storage structures used and consequently are difficult to modify when these structures are changed due to the introduction of a new computer and/or operating system. In addition, such systems generally require extensive modification to accommodate new application programs.

Corners are cut for a number of reasons:

- no widely accepted formal languages exist for conceptual or database schema specification
- computerised data dictionary systems are not available for all computer systems
- data storage structures are difficult to design, and the designer is often limited in choice of data structures to those which are available in the computing environment of the database system to be implemented
- the privacy and recovery mechanisms which are available in the operating system which is being used are often thought to be good enough for the database system itself

Of more importance is the inherent complexity of the process. From the last few pages, the reader will have gathered that database system design from scratch involves many factors and requires a great deal of expertise in a number of areas of computer science.

Fortunately database systems need not be designed from scratch. The designer can use a *database management system* to assist in the task. A database management system (DBMS) is a collection of procedures, documentation aids, languages and programs to facilitate the design and implementation of database systems.

Typically, a DBMS is based on a general purpose storage structure which can be tailored to meet the requirements of various database systems. The DBMS generally comes equipped with privacy, integrity and recovery sub-systems which can also be tailored for particular requirements. More sophisticated DBMSs provide facilities for the generation of application programs from specifications written in very high-level languages. Much of the designers work is done for him.

Ideally, it should be possible to use a single DBMS to implement many various database systems. For example, it should be possible for one person to use a DBMS to implement a shop floor reporting system and for another person to use the same DBMS to implement an integrated accounting system. However, this ideal has not yet been achieved. Some DBMSs are better suited to certain types of application than others. In the next chapter, four common types of DBMS are discussed.

REFERENCES

Batory, D.S. (1979) 'On searching transposed files', *ACM Trans. Database Systems* 4(4), 531—544.

BCS (1976) *Interim Report of the Data Dictionary Systems Working Party*, British Computer Society, London.

BCS (1978) *Proceedings of BCS Conference on Data Analysis for Information Systems Design*, British Computer Society, London.

Canning, R.G. (1981) 'A view of data dictionaries', *EDP Analyser*, Vista, CA.

Chamberlin, D.D. (1976) 'Relational data base management: a survey', *Computing Surveys* 8(1).

Claybrook, B.G. and Yang, C.S. (1978) 'Efficient algorithms for answering queries using unsorted multilists', *Information Systems* 3, 93—97.

Conway, R.W., Maxwell, W.L. and Morgan, H.L. (1972) 'On the implementation of security measures in information systems', *CACM* 15(4).

Couger, J.D., Colter, M.A. and Knapp, R.W. (1982) *Advanced System Development/Feasibility Techniques*, John Wiley and Sons.

Denning, D.E. and Denning, P.J. (1979) 'Data Security', *ACM Computing Surveys* **11**(3).

Fernandez, E.B., Summers, R.C. and Coleman, C.D. (1975) 'An authorization model for shared data base', *Proceedings of the 1975 ACM SIGMOD International Conference on the Management of Data.*

Gane, C. and Sarson, T. (1977) *Structured Systems Analysis*, NY: IST Data Books.

Gradwell, J.L. (1975) 'Why data dictionaries', *Database* **6**(2), 15—18.

King, P.J.H. (1977) 'Information analysis for database design', *On line Database Conference*, London.

Klopprogge, M.P. (1981) 'Term: an approach to include the time dimension in the entity-relationship model', *Entity-Relationship Approach to Information Modelling and Analysis*, ed. P.P. Chen, 477—512.

Lomax, J.D. (1978) *Data Dictionary Systems*, NCC Publications, England.

Nakamura, T. and Mizoguchi, T. (1978) 'An analysis of storage utilization factors in block split data structuring scheme', *Proc. 4th Int. Conf. Very Large Data Bases*, West Berlin, IEEE, New York, 489—495.

Robinson, H.M. (1981) *Database Analysis and Design*, England: Chartwell-Bratt, 223—226.

Roussopoulos, N. (1979) 'A conceptual schema definition language for the design of data base applications', *IEEE Transactions on Software Engineering* SE-5, 481—496.

Severance, D.G. and Duhne, R. (1976) 'A practitioner's guide to addressing algorithms', *Commun. ACM* **19**(6), 314—326.

Shave, M.J.R. (1981) 'Entities, functions and binary relations: steps to a conceptual schema', *The Computer Journal* **24**(1), 42—45.

Shneiderman, B. and Goodman, V. (1976) 'Batched searching of sequential and tree structured files', *ACM Trans. Database Systems* **1**(3), 268—275.

Van Duyn, J.V. (1982) *Developing a Data Dictionary System*, Englewood Cliffs, NJ: Prentice-Hall Inc.

Warnier, J.D. (1974) *Logical Construction of Programs*, Leiden, Netherlands: H.E. Stenfert Kroese BV.

Wiederhold, G. (1983) *Database Design*, 2nd edn. McGraw-Hill Book Company, 91—120.

CHAPTER 4

Database Management Systems

CHARACTERISTICS OF AN IDEAL DBMS

A DBMS has been described as a collection of procedures, documentation aids, languages and programs which can be used to facilitate the design and implementation of database systems. Ideally, the components of a DBMS would include:

- a *conceptual schema definition language* which is powerful (allowing any organisational structure to be described), natural to use and decidable (that is, the consistency of schemas written in it can be determined)
- a *data dictionary system* together with guidelines for data analysis
- an implementation independent *input/output package specification language* which could be used to describe useful packages of data
- an implementation independent *database schema definition language* which can also be used to specify privacy constraints, security requirements and access path requirements
- a general purpose *symmetrical data storage structure*. By symmetrical it is meant that all access paths which are provided in the structure have equal efficiency
- a *logical to physical mapping module*
- a general purpose *privacy sub-system*
- a general purpose *integrity sub-system*
- a general purpose *back-up and recovery sub-system*
- an *application program generator*
- a *report program generator*
- a general purpose *query language*.

Given such an ideal DBMS, the creation of a database system would simply involve the following steps, as illustrated in fig. 4.1:

(a) Construct the conceptual schema using the language provided. This would include a definition of integrity constraints and inference rules.

(b) Perform a data analysis study and create a data dictionary. This would involve definition of the meaning and format of data items and the specification of useful packages of data-items. For example, a package $P1$ may be specified as:

$$\underline{P1}$$
$$\left\{\begin{array}{l} \text{customer-name} \\ \text{address} \\ \text{balance} \end{array}\right.$$

(c) Describe the privacy and back-up and recovery requirements in the logical language provided.

(d) Specify some of the application programs using the high level language provided in the application program generator module. For example, an application program specification may include statements such as:

> display 'please enter customer name';
> read cname;
> retrieve $P1$ with customer-name = cname;
> display 'please enter amount to be credited or debited';
> read amount;
> add amount to balance of $P1$;
> replace $P1$;

The data storage structure and general purpose integrity and recovery mechanisms would then be configured automatically as would the

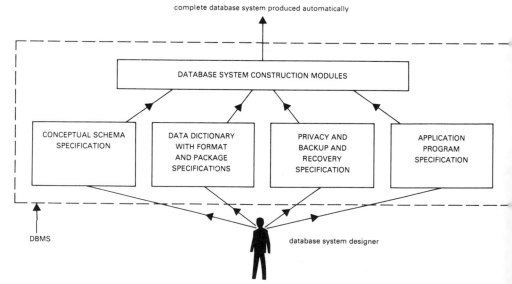

Fig. 4.1 An ideal DBMS architecture.

application programs. The designer would not need to know how the data was stored since all communication with the physical storage structure would be carried out by the logical to physical mapping module.

Notice also, that the designer need not specify the database schema in full since, in the ideal DBMS, all relations in the conceptual schema would be implemented as access paths with equal efficiency in the storage structure, therefore the conceptual schema and the database schema would be identical in this respect.

The ideal architecture as described above also displays a high degree of data-independence. Since all relations in the conceptual schema are represented by access paths with equal efficiency in the data storage structure, any new end-user requirements can be accommodated by simply specifying the new input/output packages and the application programs which use them. If the required data is there, then it can be readily accessed.

LIMITATIONS OF EXISTING DBMSs

Unfortunately, currently available DBMSs are not ideal. Although researchers are developing fully automatic components, e.g. (Frost and Whittaker, 1983), no single DBMS has yet been produced which can automatically generate a complete database system from its specification. In general, the DBMS user must become involved with implementation details as well as system specification, fig. 4.2. In particular, the DBMS user must be fully conversant with the data storage structure underlying the particular DBMS being used (due largely to the common absence of a logical to physical mapping module). Integrity constraints, privacy controls, input/output requirements and so on are typically specified in terms of the underlying storage structure. Two important consequences of this are:

(a) The database system designer's task is complicated by the need to be conversant with the terminology of the data storage structure used by the DBMS.
(b) The expressive power of the various specification languages provided by the DBMS (e.g. schema specification language, query language, etc.) tend to be limited to correspond to the limitations of the underlying data storage structure.

The second point is very important and deserves further explanation. Suppose that we have a DBMS which is based on a hierarchical storage structure (such a system is described in more detail later). It is probable that the specification languages which are provided by that DBMS are limited in their expressive power such that they can

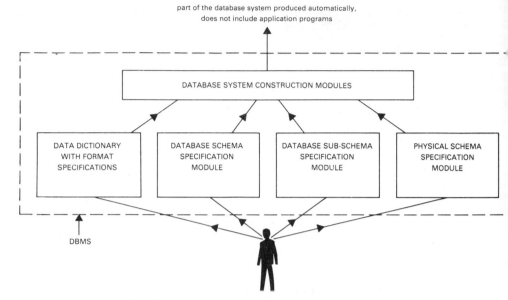

Fig. 4.2 A typical commercial DBMS architecture.

only be used to describe hierarchical organisations and hierarchical access paths. In order to use such a DBMS, the designer and the end-users must perceive the application area as consisting of a set of hierarchical structures. That is, they must use a hierarchical *view of the universe*. This may not be the most natural view to use and, of more importance, it may not be powerful enough to accommodate all those parts of the universe which the user wants to model in the database.

Before discussing views of the universe in more detail, three other shortcomings of currently available DBMSs are mentioned:

(a) They do not provide data-independence to the extent outlined for the ideal system. In general, when a database system has been designed and implemented using a commercial DBMS, it is relatively inflexible. Any new input/output requirements which crop up may often only be accommodated by major re-organisation of the database and physical schemas followed by extensive modification or re-compilation of existing application programs. This is a consequence of two factors: firstly, the views of the universe which underly most commercial DBMSs are asymmetrical, resulting in asymmetrical conceptual schemas, asymmetrical database schemas, and asymmetrical physical storage structures. The effect is that some access paths are implemented more efficiently than others and some access paths are not implemented at all. New input/output requirements may require the application area to be viewed in a different way and new access paths to be provided by modification to the data storage structure. Secondly, the absence in most currently available DBMSs of a central logical to physical mapping module means that modification to some part of the data storage structure may have an impact on many existing application programs which use that part.

(b) Yet another way in which currently available DBMSs do not match up to the ideal as described concerns the extent to which they automate the implementation of database systems. In general, the data storage structure is automatically configured from the database schema and the necessary back-up and recovery sub-systems are provided. However, in most cases the construction of application programs is left to the DBMS user. High level database commands such as INSERT, FIND and DELETE may be provided but the programs in which these commands appear must be constructed by the user. Integrity constraints and sometimes even the privacy controls are typically implemented as ad hoc procedures embedded in application programs.

(c) One final criticism of currently available DBMSs concerns their architecture. In many systems, the distinction between conceptual, database and physical schemas is not clear. Often, only two schemas are used: the database (or logical) schema and the physical schema, and these tend to overlap. One consequence of this is that a designer using a DBMS to help implement a database system, must immediately start thinking in terms of the data structure used by that DBMS. Often, the designer commences by performing a data analysis study and then goes on to specify the database schema using a notation which refers to components of the DBMS data storage structure. Integrity and privacy constraints are also specified using this notation. The result is that no implementation independent specification of the application area or of the user requirements is ever constructed. If a new DBMS is introduced at some later date then the whole system may have to be re-specified as well as re-designed. This is most likely if the new DBMS uses a different view to the one being replaced.

Notwithstanding the shortcomings discussed above, the use of a DBMS can simplify design and implementation of database systems. Perhaps not to the extent which one would ideally like, but at least their use is a vast improvement on designing database systems from scratch.

VIEWS OF THE UNIVERSE

WHAT IS A VIEW OF THE UNIVERSE

It was mentioned in the previous chapter that use of a hierarchical DBMS requires the database system designer to view the application area as consisting of a set of hierarchical structures. In general, the use of any DBMS requires the user to perceive the application area in a way which is dictated by the view of the universe on which the DBMS is based. What is meant by these statements is now clarified.

A *view of the universe* is defined as a set of concepts which can be used to formulate and rationalise our perception of parts of the universe. Such rationalisation is necessary to model and analyse parts of the universe in a consistent way. Different views are used to build different models for different purposes as shown in fig. 4.3(a). For example if some part of the universe is to be analysed using Newtonian mechanics then an appropriate view is one which requires that part to be regarded as consisting of objects whose positions in space can be accurately defined. On the other hand, if that part of the universe is to be analysed using quantum mechanics then the view will require that part to be regarded as consisting of objects whose positions in space are given by probability distributions.

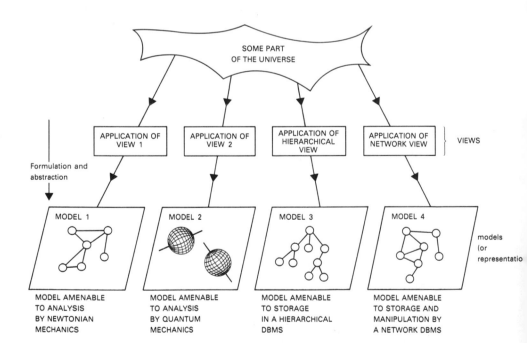

Fig. 4.3(a) Application of views of the universe.

Views of the universe are similar to what some physicists call 'systems of axioms' and what some mathematicians call 'abstraction functors'. A view consists of a notation together with a set of rules for the application of this notation. The rules help us name, classify and model the components and processes which constitute that part of the universe in which we are interested.

VIEWS OF THE UNIVERSE IN DATABASE WORK

In database work, a view helps the designer to build a database which represents parts of the universe in a consistent way. For example, a view can help the designer distinguish between *entities* and *relationships*. Entities may then be represented, for example, by records and relationships can be represented by access paths between these records. However, a more important use is that a view helps the designer perceive the universe in such a way that its data representation (model) can be easily stored and manipulated by the DBMS being used. In this respect, the view must reflect the limitations of the DBMS. For example, the hierarchical view requires the universe to be regarded as consisting of *entities* which are related in hierarchical structures such as that shown in fig. 4.3(b). It cannot be used, for example, to build models of *many to many relations* such as that which links machines to parts. Machines may be built from many parts and a single part may be used in the construction of many machines. If the hierarchical view is used, then one might think that this situation could be modelled as shown in fig. 4.3(c). This model is not really acceptable since each 'real' entity is represented by two or more data elements. This limitation of the hierarchical view reflects the fact that hierarchical data structures are the only storage structures which are readily supported by hierarchical DBMSs.

In general then, the view of the universe on which a DBMS is based is necessarily dependent on the storage structure used by that DBMS. In fact, the idea of a view is relatively new. In the past, the potential DBMS user would ask two questions, amongst others, when choosing a DBMS:

(a) Is the DBMS capable of storing a data model of all those parts of the universe in which we are interested? If not, then it is of limited use.

(b) How difficult is it for us to model those parts of the universe in which we are interested such that the model can be readily stored in the available storage structures?

By introducing the concept of a view, these two questions can now be replaced by two others which should be easier to answer:

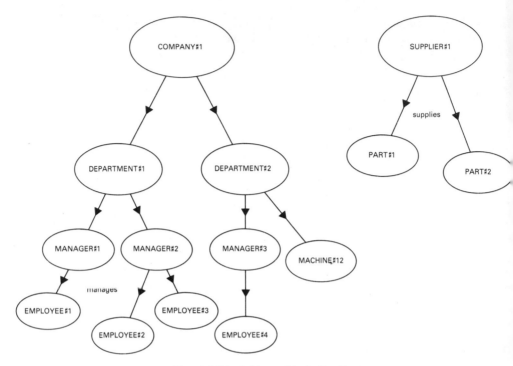

Fig. 4.3(b) A hierarchical situation.

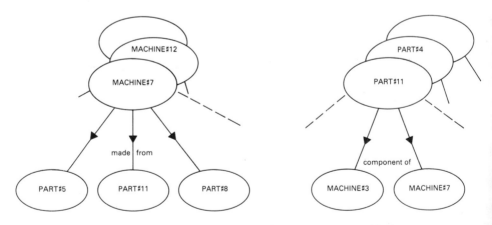

Fig. 4.3(c) A hierarchical view of a many to many relation.

(c) Can the DBMS view be used to model that part of the universe in which we are interested?

(d) How difficult is it to model that part of the universe in which we are interested using the view available?

These questions should be easier to answer than (a) and (b) since they do not refer to storage structures and therefore do not require the potential user to learn about such structures. It is for this reason that the concept of a view of the universe has been introduced.

Four views which are commonly used in database work are now described: the hierarchical, network, DBTG network and relational views. DBMSs are normally classified according to which of these four views they use. Knowing the limitations of the view used by the DBMS under consideration, it is therefore possible to perform at least an initial appraisal of the usefulness of that DBMS without going into any technical details of its construction.

Descriptions of views which are given in this chapter are not definitive. The aim is to present simple descriptions of each view which conform to the widest (most general) interpretation of their meaning rather than the particular meanings which they are given when used in the context of a particular DBMS. For example, the following description of the hierarchical view refers to the generally accepted features of this view rather than the specific features in IMS terminology. (IMS is an acronym for 'Information Management System' which is a widely used 'hierarchical' DBMS.)

The reason for this approach is that the discussions which follow are of general applicability and should enable the reader to appreciate some of the limitations and strengths of the four different types of DBMS. Specific limitations and strengths of a particular DBMS may only be identified by reference to literature which contains a detailed (and usually lengthy) description of that DBMS.

THE HIERARCHICAL VIEW

The hierarchical view regards the universe as consisting of *entities*, *attributes* and *relationships*. Entities are related to other entities in tree structures such as those shown in fig. 4.3(b). The nodes of the trees are entities and the arcs (or branches) are relationships between entities. Entities at the top of the tree are called *roots*. Roots may be related to any number of lower level 'dependent' entities and each of these may be related to any number of lower level dependents and so on. If entity X is a dependent of entity Y, then Y is called the *father* of X and X the *son* of Y.

An *entity set* is a set of entities and a *relation* is a set of relationships. All relationships from a given relation must link father entities, from at most one entity set, to son entities from at most one different entity set. For example, all relationships of type 'manages' must link a father entity, from the 'manager' entity set, to a son entity from the 'employee' entity set. This means that this view cannot be used to model the situation in which managers manage other managers. The user would have to perceive such a situation as shown in fig. 4.4.

The major constraint of the hierarchical view is that entities may be related to at most one father entity. This means that the hierarchical view cannot be used to build models of situations such as those illustrated in fig. 4.5.

We now consider *attributes*. An attribute is regarded, in the hierarchical view, as a property of an entity (e.g. height, age, address) which has no meaning (or more correctly, no interest) on its own. Unfortunately, no clear definition has ever been given of the terms 'entity' and 'attribute' and the user of the hierarchical view must refer to examples for guidance.

An entity may be related to many attributes and an attribute may be related to many entities. Therefore, the single father restriction governing the relationship between entities does not apply. Situations such as that shown in fig. 4.6, can be modelled by the hierarchical view. However, such relationships between entities and attributes are normally depicted as shown in fig. 4.7.

Notice that there is no attempt to give formal definition of the terms 'entity' and 'attribute'. A rough guideline is that if ever it is necessary to find out something about an object then it should be

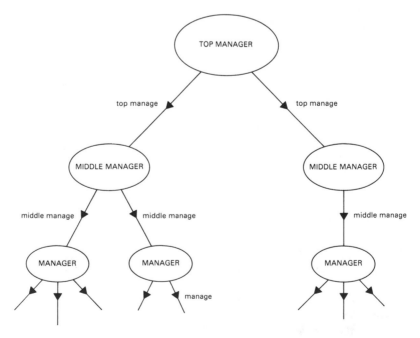

Fig. 4.4 A hierarchical view of management.

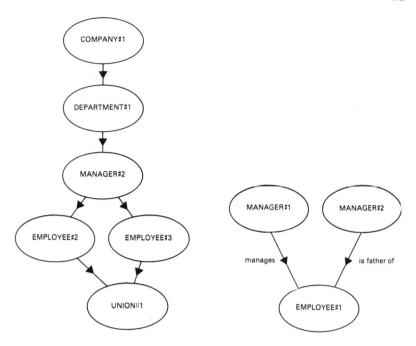

Fig. 4.5 Situations which cannot be readily accommodated by the hierarchical view.

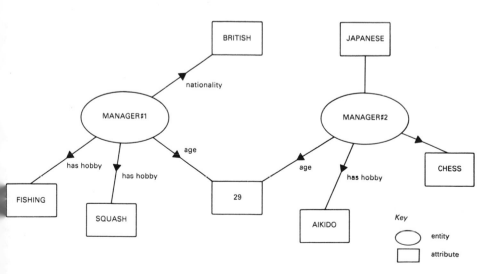

Fig. 4.6 Relationships between entities and attributes.

Name	Age	Nationality	Hobbies
Manager 1	29	British	Fishing
			Squash
Manager 2	29	Japanese	Squash
			Aikido
			Chess

Fig. 4.7 The usual representation of entity/attribute relationships.

regarded as an entity, otherwise it is an attribute. For example: if you want to use the data model to produce a list of all managers who are aged 29, then 'age 29' should be regarded as an entity and not an attribute.

SHORTCOMINGS OF THE VIEW

The hierarchical view leads to an assymetrical perception of the universe in two respects:

(a) The tree structure implies that relationships between entities have *direction*. The concept of father and son enforces this.
(b) 'Things' of the real world are classified as entities or attributes. There would appear to be no rational for this distinction. Consider the colour of a plant. The colour is of much interest to an artist as the plant is to the gardener.

The asymmetry of the view leads to asymmetric models and, in the context of database work, to asymmetric implementation of access paths through data models. In general, hierarchical trees are represented by hierarchical data structures. Random access to elements in such structures is efficient only if it involves traversal down through the tree, and traversal from entities to their attributes.

APPLICABILITY OF THE HIERARCHICAL VIEW

The main advantage of the hierarchical view is that those parts of the universe which can be modelled using this view can be easily represented by hierarchical data structures. For example, entities can be mapped to files, records or fields in records and attributes can be mapped to fields within records (the word 'record' is used here with its traditional meaning). An example of a hierarchical data structure is shown in fig. 4.8.

Note, however, that problems may still occur with such a data structure even though it models a truly hierarchical situation:

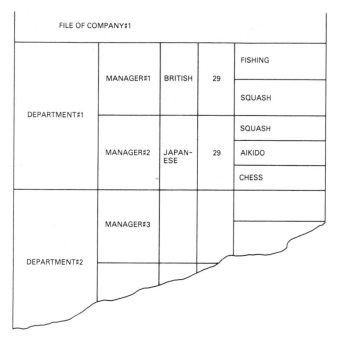

Fig. 4.8 A hierarchical data structure.

(a) If a record is deleted, then it is possible that some information might be inadvertently lost from the system. For example, if two departments were to be amalgamated, then care would need to be taken to ensure that all managers in these two departments were assigned to the new department before the old department records were erased.

(b) As mentioned, some access paths are implemented more efficiently than others. For example in fig. 4.8, the retrieval of data about a given manager is quite straightforward if the department and company in which he works are known (i.e. if there is sufficient information to select a 'tree' and traverse it from root to branch required). On the other hand, if a list of the probably few managers who practice the martial art of Aikido is required, then a search would have to be made through all of the files, examining all of the records.

In conclusion, therefore, the hierarchical view should only be used: (i) when the situation to be modelled is truly hierarchical and (ii) when the required access to, and manipulation of, the resulting data model is also hierarchical in the sense that access to data is only required to be to and down trees and from entities to attributes, and insertion and deletion of data is only required to be 'branch at a time'. If this is the case, then the hierarchical view will lead to simple data structures and simple data manipulation algorithms.

In practice, many 'hierarchical' DBMSs do not require the user to perceive the universe according to the hierarchical view as described above. In general, the views are not so constraining. For example, situations such as that shown in fig. 4.9 can be accommodated by some systems and perceived as shown in fig. 4.3(c). However, this requires some entities to be regarded as existing in more than one place. The data model must then contain redundant representations of entities (in addition to the redundant representation of attributes which is the case in most data structures) or the use of pointers. Most hierarchical DBMSs can easily accommodate models of truly hierarchical situations, but their accommodation of non-hierarchical situations is possible only at the expense and danger of duplication of data, and/or the creation of secondary indexes, or the use of pointers.

THE NETWORK VIEW

In the *network view* the same distinction is made between entities and attributes as is made in the hierarchical view. However, the 'allowed' structures linking entities are much less constrained. Entities may be related to any number of other entities. An example of a model which has been constructed using the network view is given in fig. 4.10.

The network view can be used to readily create models of most organisational structures that we are likely to want to represent by data. However, the actual storage of such data models is more complicated than is the storage of hierarchical models. One method of implementation is to map entities to records, attributes to record fields and to represent relationships between entities by pointers as illustrated in fig. 4.11(a). Alternatively, entities *and* attributes could

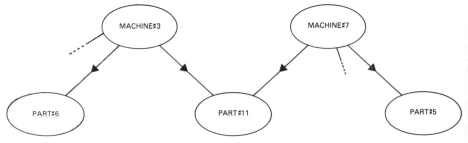

Fig. 4.9 A many to many situation which cannot be accommodated by the hierarchical view.

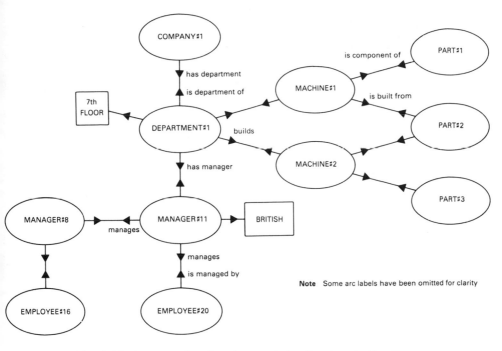

Fig. 4.10 An example of an (unconstrained) network situation.

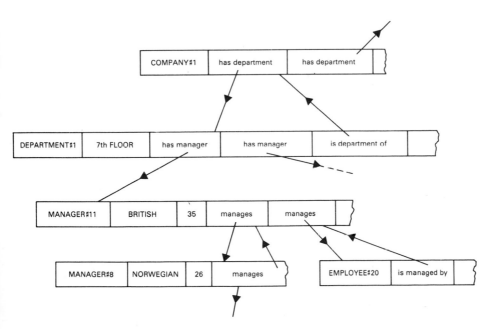

Fig. 4.11(a) An example of an (unconstrained) network data structure.

be mapped to 'records' and records could be linked by pointers as illustrated in fig. 4.11(b).

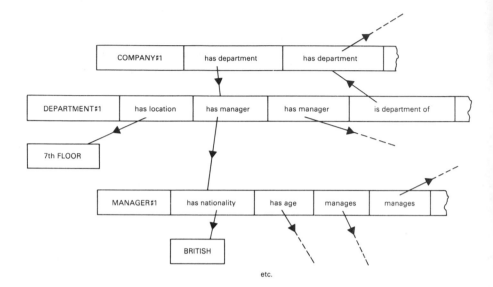

Fig. 4.11(b)   An alternative implementation of a network data model.

THE DBTG VIEW

In 1971, the Data Base Task Group (DBTG) of the CODASYL programming language committee published a report (DBTG, 1971) which contained definitions and guidelines for the construction of database and database management systems. Systems which are based on these recommendations are called CODASYL or DBTG sytems.

The DBTG report includes a description of a language for the specification of data models. The view of the universe which underlies this language may be regarded as a 'constrained' network view. The constraints are not as severe as those of the hierarchical view but are sufficient to ensure that all data models which can be built by use of the DBTG view can be readily accommodated by the 'set' data structure which is also defined by DBTG.

THE DBTG 'SET' DATA STRUCTURE
Because the DBTG view is closely related to the DBTG 'set' structure it is useful to consider this structure before considering the view. The

reason for some of the characteristics of the view will then be more apparent.

The data structure which is used in a DBTG system is called a DBTG *set*. A *set occurrence* is a collection of records one of which is the *owner* and the others are *members*. In hierarchical terms the owner is the 'father' and the members are the 'sons'. (Notice that a DBTG set has little in common with a mathematical set.) Fig. 4.12 illustrates three set occurrences of the same *set type*. Relationships which are represented in occurrences of a set type must be of the same type.

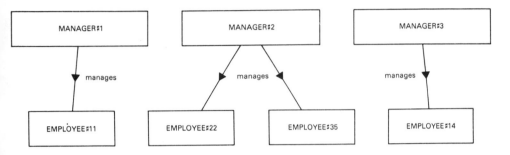

Fig. 4.12 Three set occurrences of the same type.

A set occurrence is like a hierarchical data structure consisting of two levels only.

The constraints which govern the presence of records in DBTG sets are as follows:

(a) All owner records of occurrences of the same set type must all be of the same record type. Notice that member records may be of different types as shown in fig. 4.13.

(b) The owner record type of a set type must be different from the types of the member records. For example, the structure illus-trated in fig. 4.14 is not allowed.

(c) A member record is only allowed to appear at most once in set occurrences of the same set type. This means that a record may only have one 'father' with respect to a particular relationship type. For example, the structure illustrated in fig. 4.15 is not allowed. Notice, however, that this does not preclude a record from having more than one father providing they are related to those fathers in different ways i.e. a record may be a member of more than one set occurrence providing that these are occur-rences of different set types.

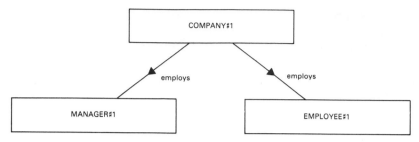

Fig. 4.13 Members of a DBTG set may be of different record type.

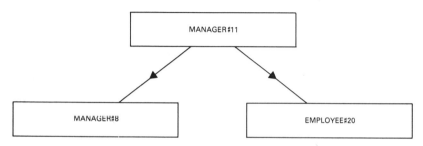

Fig. 4.14 An illegal set with owner type the same as one of the member types.

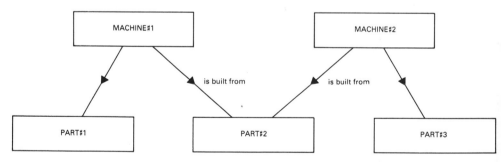

Fig. 4.15 An illegal DBTG set.

USE OF CONNECTION RECORDS IN DBTG SETS

The usefulness of DBTG sets can be extended by use of *connection records* as discussed below:

(a) Records of the same type may be indirectly related by the introduction of connection records as shown in fig. 4.16. Two set types are used both of which have the same connection records as members. Because these two types are different, a single connection record may occur once as a member in a set occurrence of both.

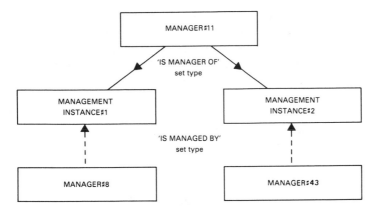

Fig. 4.16 Relationship between two records of the same type.

(b) 'Many to many' relations between two record types may be accommodated by the introduction of connection records as shown in fig. 4.17. Two set types are used in this example: *MC* and *PC*. Owner records of *MC* are of type machine and owner records of *PC* are of type part. *MC* and *PC* have the same connection records as members.

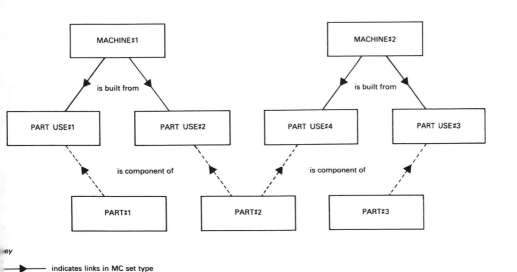

Fig. 4.17 Many to many relation using connection records.

(c) Relationships which involve more than two records may also be handled by the introduction of a connection record as shown in fig. 4.18. This record structure represents the fact that 'person #1 bought object #5 from person #6 at place #4'. This is how *n*-ary relationships between entities may be represented in the DBTG view.

Connection records may contain information as shown in fig. 4.19. This may be necessary to improve the efficiency of some of the access paths which may be required by the user.

For example, to find all of the parts used in the construction of machine #2 requires the system to:

- locate the set occurrence with machine #2 record as owner
- access all connection records which are members of this set occurrence
- look at the part field of each of these connection records to find the part number

If the connection records did not contain the part field or a pointer to part records then the system would have to look through all occurrences of the *PC* set type to find the part used.

THE DBTG VIEW

Now look at the view of the universe which underlies the DBTG recommendations. This view has never been formally defined and the discussion which follows does not attempt to do this, but simply to present an outline in order that the reader may gain an understanding of what is involved in using a DBTG system.

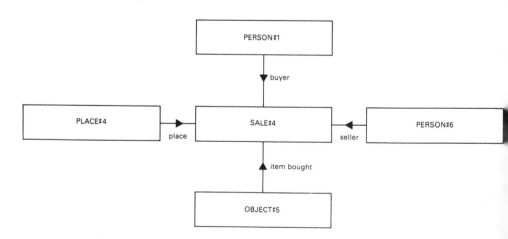

Fig. 4.18 A 'relationship' between four records.

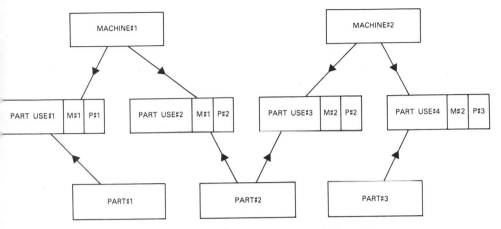

Fig. 4.19 Connection records may contain information.

Like the hierarchical view, the DBTG view regards the universe as consisting of entities and attributes. Entities are related to other entities and these relationships are classified as belonging to relations. Relationships are perceived as having a direction from what may be called the 'father' entity to the 'son' entity.

An entity may be the father of any number of sons. However, two entities of the same type may not be directly related (other than by the fact that they are of the same type). Also, an entity may only occur once as a son in a relationship of a given type (i.e. an entity may not have more than one father with respect to a given relation).

As an example of the use of the view, consider the situation shown in fig. 4.10 (this model was built by use of the unconstrained network view). This situation when perceived using the DBTG view may be modelled as shown in fig. 4.20. Notice that the arrows do not necessarily indicate the users access requirements. They indicate the DBTG set structure which must be used. Access in the direction of the arrow will therefore be provided. However, if access in the other direction is required, then either (a) additional sets must be provided or (b) member records will have to contain pointers to owners as discussed earlier.

APPLICABILITY OF THE DBTG VIEW

The DBTG view can be used to model most situations which can be modelled by the network view. However, this use is complicated by the need to introduce connection records. In addition, the DBTG set structure is asymmetric (access from owner to member is implemented in a different way to access in the other direction). This asymmetry is reflected in the DBTG view which complicates the construction of data models.

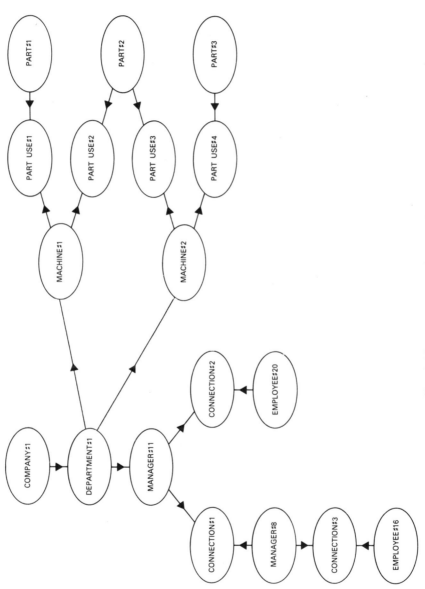

Fig. 4.20 An example of a DBTG model.

THE RELATIONAL VIEW

The *relational view* (Codd, 1970) regards the universe as consisting of *entities*, *entity sets* and *relations*. A relation is a set of *n*-tuples $(e1, e2, e3, \ldots\ldots\ldots, en)$ where entity $e1$ belongs to entity set $E1$, $e2$ belongs to entity set $E2$ and so on. A relation may be represented by a table as illustrated in fig. 4.21. This relation models a situation in which departments make machines, machines consist of parts and the quantity of each part used on each machine is known.

One difference between relational storage structures and files of records is that each entry in a relation is 'atomic'. Compare the relation in fig. 4.21 with the file of records shown in fig. 4.22. Relations are more symmetrical and this symmetry is enhanced by the fact that the order of the columns in a relation is not significant.

Dept.	Machine	Part	Quantity
D1	M1	P1	20
D1	M1	P2	40
D1	M2	P2	10
D1	M2	P3	20
D1	M2	P4	4

Fig. 4.21 An example of a relation.

departmental file

Machine	Part	Quantity
M1	P1	20
M1	P2	40
M2	P2	10
M2	P3	20
M2	P4	4

Fig. 4.22 A file of records.

Now consider a situation in which departments also employ people and are situated at known locations. In all, six entity sets are involved:

- departments
- locations

- employees
- machines
- parts
- quantities (of parts)

The 'unthinking' use of the relational view as described so far could result in one large relation as shown in fig. 4.23. This is (obviously) a 'poor' model of the situation for two reasons:

(a) There is a great deal of redundancy. For example, the fact that machine $M1$ is made in department $D1$ is modelled in four places.
(b) Different types of *relationships* between entities are modelled in the same way. For example, consider the first tuple in the relation. The relationship between $E1$ and 20 (quantity) is indirect, whereas the relationship between $E1$ and $D1$ is direct. Yet they are both modelled in the same way.

Location	Department	Employee	Age	Machine	Part	Quantity
London	D1	E1	29	M1	P1	20
London	D1	E1	29	M1	P2	40
London	D1	E2	33	M1	P1	20
London	D1	E2	33	M1	P2	40
London	D1	E1	29	M2	P2	10
London	D1	E1	29	M2	P3	20
London	D1	E1	29	M2	P4	4
London	D1	E2	33	M2	P2	10
London	D1	E2	33	M2	P3	20
London	D1	E2	33	M2	P4	4
...etc.						

Fig. 4.23 A 'poor' relational model.

These undesirable features can be removed as follows:

(a) The 'artificial' linking of machines with employees can be removed by replacing the large relation by two smaller ones. Essentially, a machine is only related to an employee by virtue of the fact that it is one of many machines which are made by a department with many employees. There is a *multi-valued dependency* between machines and employees. This dependency can be 'factored out' as shown in fig. 4.24.

(a) Department/employee relation

Location	Department	Employee
London	D1	E1
London	D1	E2

(b) Department/machine relation

Department	Machine	Part	Quantity
D1	M1	P1	20
D1	M1	P2	40
D1	M2	P2	10
D1	M2	P3	20
D1	M2	P4	4

Fig. 4.24 Relational model after the multivalued dependency between machines and employees has been factored out.

(b) Notice that there still exists some redundancy in the model. Each tuple in the department/machine relation contains information about the use of a particular part in a particular machine. The quantity value in a tuple refers to the part *and* the machine on which it is used. It would be meaningless to say that the quantity of *P2* used was 40 without saying which machine was involved. It is said that the quantity is *fully dependent* on the machine/part pair. This is not true for the department. Department is only dependent on the machine involved, therefore we can 'factor' this column out as shown in fig. 4.25.

(c) All redundancy has been removed from the model but there still exists an asymmetry in the department/employee relation. Employees are directly related to departments, but are only indirectly related to department location, yet these direct and indirect links are represented in the same way. This may be resolved by replacing the troublesome relation by two as shown in fig. 4.26.

There is now a better model consisting of relations which are said to be *fully normalised*. This was achieved by a rather unsystematic factoring process. In general, a fully normalised relational model can be built by the systematic application of well defined *normalisation rules*. These rules are described in more detail in chapter 7.

Location	Department	Employee
London	D1	E1
London	D1	E2

Machine	Part	Quantity
M1	P1	20
M1	P2	40
M2	P2	10
M2	P3	20
M2	P4	4

Department	Machine
D1	M1
D1	M2

Fig. 4.25 Relational model after the department/machine links have been factored out.

Department	Employee
D1	E1
D1	E2

Department	Location
D1	London

Machine	Part	Quantity
M1	P1	20
M1	P2	40
M2	P2	10
M2	P3	20
M2	P4	4

Department	Machine
D1	M1
D1	M2

Fig. 4.26 The final model.

Notice in fig. 4.26, that each tuple now refers to a single entity *or a single relationship* and that each tuple contains data representing some of the direct links which this entity *or relationship* has with other entities or relationships. For example:

(a) Tuple $(D1, E1)$ in the department/employee relation refers to entity $E1$ and represents the link which this entity has with department $D1$.

(b) Tuple (*M*1, *P*1, 20) in the machine/part relation refers to the *relationship* between machine *M*1 and part *P*1 and represents the link which this relationship has with quantity 20:

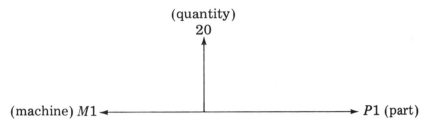

Therefore the relational view can be seen to be more flexible than the network view since relationships which involve more than two entities can be modelled in the same way as relationships between two entities.

For example, consider, the situation in which '*A* bought item *B*'. This can be modelled as:

Buyer	Item Bought
A	B

Now suppose we want to qualify this relationship by stating that '*A* bought *B* from *C*'. This 3 entity relationship can be modelled as:

Buyer	Item Bought	Seller
A	B	C

The extension to the model is relatively straightforward.

Now consider what would be involved if a network view were used. The initial model would be as shown in fig. 4.27. The appearance of *C* on the scene requires a 'new' entity to be introduced, as shown in fig. 4.28. A consequence of this is that the data structure in which the network model is stored could require extensive modification. In a DBTG system, new sets would have to be created with a new type of connection record as member. In a relational system, the model could be stored as a set of tables, one for each relation. The addition of columns to tables is less of a problem.

Fig. 4.27 Relationship involving two entities.

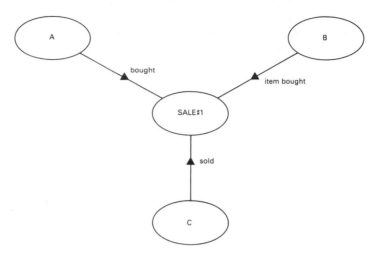

Fig. 4.28 A relationship involving three entities.

APPLICABILITY OF THE 'NORMALISED' RELATIONAL VIEW

Later it is seen that the normalisation process is quite complicated and consequently, the relational view requires a certain amount of expertise to be used correctly. However, a number of advantages derive from its use:

(a) It is powerful and can accomodate most situations where a model is required.
(b) The resulting model is reasonably symmetrical and does not reflect the (possibly short-lived) access requirements of users to any great extent. It is therefore a relatively stable model.
(c) The model can be mapped into storage with relative ease.

A main disadvantage of the relational view is that, at present, there are only a few DBMSs which are based on it.

EXAMPLES OF COMMERCIAL DBMSs

Commercially available DBMSs can be loosely classified according to the view on which they are based. The view has an influence on all aspects of the system. For example, relational DBMSs have tabular data structures, relational schema definition languages and data manipulation languages which are based on relational algebra or relational calculus. However, it should be recognised that such a classification is only a rough guide. Many 'hierarchical' systems, for example, also allow network structures to be modelled if the user is willing to fiddle with the system. The classification, therefore, only indicates which organisational structures can be *readily* modelled by the DBMS concerned.

It should also be mentioned that the facilities which are provided by the various DBMSs differ greatly and, consequently, the view on which a DBMS is based may not be a critical factor in its assessment for use. For example, a DBMS which is based on the unconstrained network view will have a powerful (and simple) modelling capacity but is of little use if it does not provide adequate security mechanisms.

The brief descriptions which follow are intended to provide the reader with a 'feel' for some of the DBMSs which are available. More detailed descriptions may be found in texts such as (Cardenas, 1979), (Date, 1977), (Deen, 1977), (Kroenke, 1977), (Robinson, 1981), (Tsichritzis, 1977) and (Online, 1983).

IDMS

The IDMS database management system is based on the CODASYL DBTG recommendations. It is marketed by the Cullinane Corporation and is available for the following computers: IBM 360, 370, Univac series 70, ICL 2900, and others.

The CODASYL DBTG recommendations refer to other aspects of DBMSs not just to the 'set' data structure as discussed earlier. Specifications of the architecture, schema definition language and data manipulation language are also given. IDMS adheres quite closely to these recommendations, and the following may be regarded as an introduction to many other CODASYL DBTG systems as well as IDMS.

The IDMS data model consists of *records* which are related in *sets*. A set consists of an owner record together with zero or more member records. The constraints on set membership are the same as those outlined for the DBTG model discussed earlier.

The whole data model is divided into *areas* which are themselves divided into *logical pages*. A logical page contains one or more records. Each record has a unique identifier assigned to it called a *database key*. The database key also uniquely identifies a location on a page and can therefore be used to identify the positions of records in the set of logical pages. A *file* in IDMS is a subdivision of the database into which areas are mapped. A file consists of an integral number of pages. Pages are mapped to physical blocks and are, therefore, the units of transfer between the physical database and main memory.

The database schema is defined by use of a data description language (DDL) which is somewhat like COBOL. An example of an IDMS schema is given in fig. 4.29. This schema is depicted graphically in fig. 4.30. Notice that a schema is simply a generalisation of a data

```
SCHEMA DESCRIPTION.
SCHEMA NAME IS SMACHINE.
FILE DESCRIPTION.
FILE NAME IS MACHINE-FILE ASSIGN TO MDB.
FILE NAME IS JOURNAL          ASSIGN TO JMDB.
AREA DESCRIPTION
AREA NAME  IS MC-AREA
    RANGE IS 1001 THRU 1050
    WITHIN FILE MACHINE-FILE FROM 1 THRU 50.
RECORD DESCRIPTION.
RECORD NAME IS MACHINE.
RECORD ID      IS 100.
LOCATION MODE IS CALC USING MACHINE-NUM.
WITHIN MC-AREA AREA.
    03 MACHINE-NUM   PIC 9(4).
RECORD NAME IS PART-USE.
RECORD ID      IS 200.
LOCATION MODE IS VIA USES-PART SET.
WITHIN MC-AREA AREA.
    03 USE-NUM        PIC 9(8).
    03 QUANTITY       PIC 9(6).

RECORD NAME IS PART.
RECORD ID      IS 300.
LOCATION MODE IS CALC USING PART-NAME
    DUPLICATES ARE NOT ALLOWED.
WITHIN MC-AREA AREA.
    03 PART-NUM    9(6).
    03 PART-NAME X(12).
SET DESCRIPTION.
SET NAME     IS USES-PART
    ORDER    IS FIRST.
    MODE     IS CHAIN.
    OWNER    IS MACHINE NEXT DBKEY POSITION IS 1.
    MEMBER IS PART-USE NEXT DBKEY POSITION IS 1.
    LINKED TO OWNER OWNER DBKEY POSITION IS 2.
    MANDATORY AUTOMATIC.
SET NAME     IS IS-USED-BY.
    ORDER    IS FIRST.
    MODE     IS CHAIN LINKED TO PRIOR.
    OWNER    IS PART NEXT DBKEY POSITION IS 1.
                PRIOR DBKEY POSITION IS 2.
    MEMBER IS PART-USE NEXT DBKEY POSITION IS 3.
                PRIOR DBKEY POSITION IS 4.
    LINKED TO OWNER OWNER DBKEY POSITION IS 5.
    MANDATORY AUTOMATIC.
```

Fig. 4.29 An IDMS database schema.

Fig. 4.30 A DBTG database schema.

model. The arrows in the example graphical schema indicate that there are two set types: one has machine type records as owner, the other has part type records as owner and both have part-use type records as member. An IDMS database schema typically consists of:

(a) A *file description* which assigns the database files to physical files whose names are known to the operating system. At least two files must be specified, one for the database and one for the journal.

(b) An *area description* which names the areas, indicates the number of logical pages in each area and specifies the name of the files in which areas are located.

(c) A set of *record descriptions*. A record description includes the record type name and an additional numeric identifier, the location mode, area and the format of the data-items which constitute the record. The *location mode* tells the computer how to store occurrences of that record type: (i) CALC location mode assigns a record to a location within an area by means of a hash function, (ii) VIA places record occurrences close to other record occurrences which are members of the same specified set type and (iii) DIRECT (of which no example is given) places record occurrences in specific pages of an area.

(d) A set of *set descriptions*. A set description includes a set name, set order, set mode, owner record type and member record type. The *set order* indicates the way in which members are to be placed in the set e.g. SORTED. The order FIRST means that new members are put at the beginning of the linked-list of members. IDMS only allows the CHAIN set mode, members being linked together in a list. Members may also contain pointers to PRIOR members and pointers to owner records if required. Because of these options, the user must specify the relative positions of pointers in records (this is necessary because a record may be a member of more than one set type). For example, records of type PART-USE in the example schema have five pointers as shown in fig. 4.31.

A record may be inserted into a DBTG set *automatically* or *manually*. In the former, if a schema specification of a set states that member record-type is AUTOMATIC then as soon as a record of this type is created in the database it is automatically made a member of the set

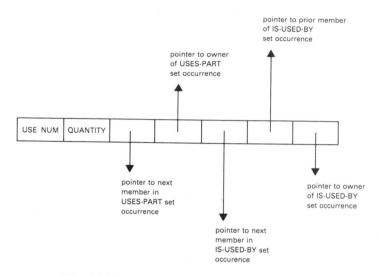

Fig. 4.31 The pointer structure of a part-use record.

concerned. If membership is declared to be MANUAL then the application program must explicitly make records members by use of the CONNECT command. The designer may also specify, in the schema, whether or not members can be readily removed from sets. If the membership is OPTIONAL then records can be removed. On the other hand, if the membership is MANDATORY, then records must remain members of a set type although they can be moved from one set occurrence to another of the same type.

IDMS also provides a *device media control language* (DMCL) which is used by the designer to specify some of the details of the mapping of the logical model onto the storage media. An example of a device media specification is given in fig. 4.32.

The designer is also required to specify a set of *sub-schemas*. A

DEVICE MEDIA DESCRIPTION. '
DEVICE MEDIA NAME IS DMACHINE OF SCHEMA NAME SMACHINE.

BUFFER SECTION.
    BUFFER NAME IS DM-BUFFER
    PAGE CONTAINS 512 CHARACTERS
    BUFFER CONTAINS 8 PAGES.

AREA SECTION.
    COPY MACHINE-AREA AREA.

Fig. 4.32 A device media specification.

sub-schema is a sub-set of the database schema which is of interest to a particular user or group of users. A sub-schema consists of a name, the name of the device media specification used, the name of the schema used and a description of the areas, records and sets which comprise that part of the database concerned. Privacy locks may be defined, names can be changed from those used in the schema and 'logical' records may be declared which are sub-sets of records declared in the database schema (fields may be omitted for example). An example of a sub-schema is given in fig. 4.33.

```
SUBSCHEMA IDENTIFICATION DIVISION.
SUBSCHEMA NAME IS SUB-1 OF SCHEMA NAME SMACHINE.
DEVICE MEDIA NAME IS DMACHINE.

SUBSCHEMA DATA DIVISION.

RENAMING SECTION.
    DATA-NAME PART-NUM IN SCHEMA IS CHANGED
                PART-ID.

AREA SECTION
    COPY MACHINE-AREA AREA
        PRIVACY LOCK FOR UPDATE IS 'NO'

RECORD SECTION
    01 PART.
        02 PART-ID.
    COPY MACHINE.
    COPY PART-USE.

SET SECTION.
    COPY USES-PART SET.
    COPY IS-USED-BY SET.
```

Fig. 4.33 Example of an IDMS sub-schema.

IDMS application programs typically consist of:

- commands to invoke a particular sub-schema e.g. INVOKE SUB-SCHEMA SUB-1 OF SMACHINE
- commands to open an area for the mode of operation required e.g. OPEN AREA MACHINE-AREA USAGE-MODE IS RETRIEVAL
- commands to manipulate records, e.g. FIND

Records may be found in various ways. If the record has been declared with location mode CALC then it can be found by supplying the hash field value, e.g.

```
MOVE 1234 TO MACHINE-NUM
FIND MACHINE RECORD
```

The machine record with machine number equal to 1234 would be found and then regarded as the *current* record of the record type MACHINE. Any subsequent reference to this record type or to sets which this type is an owner will refer, respectively, to record number 1234 and to the particular set occurrence of which this record is owner.

For example, to find the first part-use record which is related to machine 1234 one could write:

FIND FIRST RECORD OF USES-PART SET

This locates the first member record of the USES-PART set occurrence of which machine 1234 is owner. This part-use record is now the *current* member record of this set occurrence.

To find and retrieve the part record related to the current part-use record it is necessary to go from member to owner in the IS-USED-BY set. This is achieved by writing:

OBTAIN OWNER RECORD OF IS-USED-BY SET

To find the next part-use record (for machine 1234) one could write:

FIND NEXT RECORD OF USES-PART SET

INVOKE, OPEN AREA, FIND and OBTAIN are some of the IDMS procedures which may be called from within the *host* language being used. Resultant application programs are put through a pre-processor before being compiled. Processors for use with COBOL and PL/1 are available and these enable database manipulation operations to be included as direct procedural extensions to these two languages.

Creation of an IDMS database is, therefore, a four stage process:

- design, declaration and compilation of the database schema
- design and compilation of the device media control specification
- design, declaration and compilation of the sub-schemas
- design, coding and compilation of the application programs which include embedded data manipulation language (DML) commands such as INVOKE and FIND etc.

Only the device media control, sub-schema and application program object modules are required for processing the database. The database schema is not required. Its function is to assist in building the other components.

The manipulation of an IDMS database is fairly complex and this complexity is due to two factors: (i) the procedural nature of the application program host language combined with the 'record at a time' navigation through the database and (ii) the need for the programmer to be aware of the way in which access paths have been provided: e.g. as DIRECT, CALC or VIA and within sets by single or two-way pointers.

Other facilities provided by IDMS are as follows:

(a) Privacy locks may be specified at area, set and record level.
(b) Checkpoints and journal 'before' and 'after' images are recorded for forward or backward recovery. Areas are dumped regularly so that the database can be reconstructed in the event of a serious hardware or software failure.
(c) A report generator called CULPRIT is available.
(d) IDMS supports multi-users by its generalised communications interface (GCI) option which allows multiprocessing. GCI is not a communications processor but it can interface with processors such as CICS, INTERCOM and TASK MASTER.
(e) Errors due to concurrent update may be reduced since IDMS allows programmers to specify usage modes for areas opened by application programs. Areas may be opened for RETRIEVAL or UPDATE and the usage-mode for either may be EXCLUSIVE, PROTECTED or unspecified. If the EXCLUSIVE mode is used then no other run-unit can access that area in any way. If the PROTECTED mode is used then other run-units may retrieve data from the area but may not update. If no usage mode is specified, the other run-units may access the area in any way provided that none have EXCLUSIVE usage defined for them. Run-units which request a usage mode which is not allowed are put into the wait state until the conflicting activity terminates. This method of locking is in accordance with DBTG recommendations.

IMS
IMS (Information Mangement System) is a hierarchical system produced by IBM and is one of the most widely used DBMSs. It is available for the following computers: IBM 360/370, Models 40, 145 and others.

The storage structure consists of a collection of trees. Nodes in a tree may only have one parent, therefore networks may only be readily represented by the *duplication of nodes* as shown in fig. 4.34. However, IMS does provide a way to avoid such duplication by *virtual pairing* in which nodes are stored only once and their virtual presence in other trees is provided by means of pointers.

In IMS, what would be called the database schema consists of a specification of all of the types of trees which are stored in the database, including those which have virtual nodes. Database sub-schemas consist of specifications of sets of 'logical' tree-types each of which is

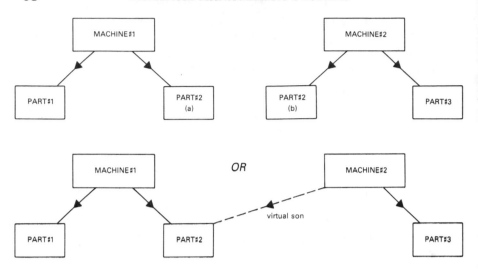

Fig. 4.34 Representations of a network situation in IMS.

a sub-set of one of the tree-types defined in the database schema. A logical tree-type is defined on a database tree-type and may omit one or more of the nodes (apart from the root node) together with all dependents of that node. Notice, however, that IMS terminology is quite different from that employed here. For example, records are called 'segments' and database sub-schemas are called 'program specification blocks'.

Three methods of access to data stored on disc are available:

(a) HISAM, the hierarchical indexed sequential access method allows roots to be accessed by an index and subordinate nodes to be accessed sequentially.

(b) HIDAM, the hierarchical indexed direct access method allows roots to be accessed by an index and subordinate nodes to be accessed directly by use of pointers.

(c) HDAM, the hierarchical direct access method allows roots to be accessed directly and subordinate nodes to be accessed directly by use of pointers.

IMS uses a host language approach in which database commands are used as procedure calls from within PL/1, COBOL or assembler programs. The set of procedure calls available constitutes a language called DL/1. Commands in this language include:

GET UNIQUE   GU
GET NEXT WITHIN PARENT GNP
GET NEXT   GN

REPLACE	REPL
INSERT	ISRT
DELETE	DLET

The unit of retrieval is a node and the meaning of 'next' is the next node to the right on the current level of the tree. DL/1 is a relatively easy language to master, but requires the user to navigate a path through the database.

IMS provides a data dictionary facility which is itself a hierarchically structured database system. Database privacy may be maintained in several ways including:

- the definition of sub-schemas to exclude those trees and branches of trees which are not allowed to be accessed by a given user or group of users
- encryption of data before storage
- use of passwords to restrict access to certain sub-schemas and application programs

IMS provides back-up and recovery by means of dump/restore and checkpoint/restart utility programs. All database modifications are recorded on a system log.

IMS software allows concurrent access to a database. When a run-unit updates a record, then that record is locked to prevent access by other run-units until the updating run-unit terminates. If the run-unit terminates abnormally then the IMS software 'rolls back' all updates made by that run-unit. If 'deadlock' occurs (i.e. two run-units lock data required by each other so neither can terminate) then IMS terminates one, rolls its updates back and lets the other carry on to successful termination. The run-unit which was rolled back is then allowed to start again.

IMS is a complex system and a more detailed account may be found in Walsh (1979).

TOTAL

TOTAL is a relatively simple DBTG-like system which is widely used. It is produced by Cincom Systems Limited. Packages are available for the following computers: Honeywell 2000, Borroughs 2500—4800, NCR Century 101, CDC 6000, IBM 360, 370 and System 3, PDP—11, Cyber 70—74, 170—175 and others.

The data storage structure used is similar to the set structure of DBTG. Two types of file are used: master files which contain master records (or owner records in DBTG terminology) and variable files which contain member records. Owners are related to members by means of linked lists as shown in fig. 4.35. The whole structure may therefore be thought of as a multi-list structure. Direct access from member to owner may be provided by hashing. The structure is similar to the DBTG structure except that variable files may not also be master files. Therefore, hierarchies of depth greater than two may only be accommodated by means of 'connection' records as shown in fig. 4.36.

The records of master and variable files are records in the conventional sense consisting of data items and groups of items called elements. Application programs can access elements of records and can construct 'logical' records made up of elements from several physical records, thereby demonstrating a degree of data-independence.

TOTAL provides no mechanism for checking the format of data input. However, it does provide a privacy sub-system and constraints may be expressed at data item level if required.

Two supporting software packages are available: SOCRATES, a report program generator, and ENVIRON/1, a real-time general tele-processing monitor which supports the concept of logical terminals and re-entrant application programs.

ADABAS

ADABAS is a network oriented DBMS although it does have some relational features. It is produced by Software AG of the Federal German Republic and is available for the following computers: IBM 360, 370, Univac 9000 series, Siemens 4004 and ICL System 4.

The logical data model of ADABAS is network structured in that entities may be represented by records and these records may be linked to a number of other records (up to a maximum which is dictated by implementation considerations). The physical storage structure consists of files of records together with inverted indexes

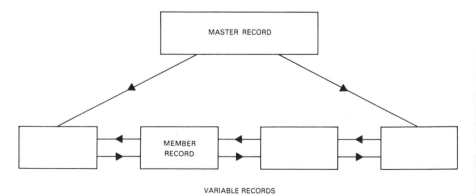

Fig. 4.35 The total data structure.

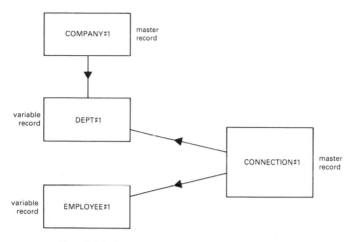

Fig. 4.36 Hierarchy representation in total.

held in the 'ASSOCIATOR'. Records are linked by means of common field values as illustrated in fig. 4.37.

To facilitate access, the system can be told to create inverted indexes which correspond to the linking of records by common field value. To do this, the user tells the system to 'couple' the two files involved 'on' the relevant field. The inverted list index is then generated as shown in fig. 4.38. Two files may only be coupled if the records in one of them contain field values matching field values of records in the other. Each record has a unique internal sequence number (ISN) assigned to it and it is these ISNs which are used in the inverted indexes.

Data compression techniques are used to reduce the size of files. Phonetic searching facilities are available and an encoding/decoding mechanism is provided to improve privacy. Fields may be added to records dynamically thereby demonstrating a degree of data-independence.

(a) Machine file

(b) Parts file

ISN	Machine	Part
259	M#1	P#1, P#2
682	M#2	P#2, P#3, P#4

ISN	Part	Supplier
56	P#1	SMITH
841	P#2	SMITH
291	P#3	JONES
106	P#4	JONES

Fig. 4.37 Examples of ADABAS files.

(a) Machine/Part index

| 259 | 56, 841 |
| 682 | 841, 291, 106 |

(b) Part/Machine index

56	259
841	259, 682
291	682
106	682

Fig. 4.38 Inverted indexes created by coupling machine and part files on part field.

For batch processing, ADABAS may be interfaced with COBOL, FORTRAN, PL/1 and assembler. For on-line processing it can be interfaced with TSO, CICS, INTERCOMM, TASKMASTER and ENVIRON/1. Database commands are implemented as procedure calls to a procedure called ADABAS which takes several parameters, one of which specifies which database command is to be invoked. A query language called ADASCRIPT is available.

INGRES

INGRES is a relational DBMS which was developed at the University of California, Berkeley. It is available on PDP and VAX computers and runs under the Unix operating system. Relations may be manipulated by use of the QUEL language which is based on relational calculus:

(a) Languages based on *relational calculus* are non-procedural languages which allow the user to state the data manipulation requirements without having to state the procedural steps to be carried out to obtain the required results.
(b) Languages based on *relational algebra* are procedural languages which allow programmers to manipulate relations, using relational algebraic operators, to obtain the results they want.

As an example, consider the relational database in fig. 4.39. To retrieve 'the managers of departments, which make machines, which use part *P2*', one could write the following QUEL statements:

```
RANGE OF DX IS D
RANGE OF MX IS M
RANGE OF PX IS P
RETRIEVE INTO RESULT (DX. MANAGER)
     WHERE DX. DEPT      = MX. DEPT
     AND MX. MACHINE     = PX. MACHINE
     AND PX. PART        = 'P2'
```

In a language based on relational algebra, one would have to issue commands equivalent to:

D	
Dept.	Manager
D1	MAN 1
D2	MAN 2

M	
Dept.	Machine
D1	M1
D1	M2
D2	M3

P	
Machine	Part
M1	P1
M1	P2
M2	P2
M2	P3
M2	P4

Fig. 4.39 Example relational database.

Restrict P to PART = '$P2$'
Join the results with M over MACHINE
Join the result with D over DEPT
Project the result over MANAGER

The relational algebraic operation 'join' takes two relations that have a common domain (column) D and joins them to form a new relation. Tuples of the new relation consist of tuples of the first relation concatenated with each tuple from the second relation which has the same domain D value. The relational algebraic operator 'project' takes a single relation and a set of specified domains and produces a new relation with only the specified domains and with no duplicate tuples. Fig. 4.40 illustrates the operations specified in the query above.

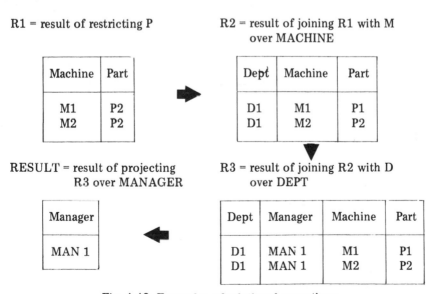

R1 = result of restricting P

R2 = result of joining R1 with M over MACHINE

RESULT = result of projecting R3 over MANAGER

R3 = result of joining R2 with D over DEPT

Fig. 4.40 Examples of relational operations

Integrity and privacy constraints may also be expressed in QUEL. INGRES is described further in chapter 11.

MAGNUM

MAGNUM is a relational DBMS which is supported by Tymeshare, a timesharing vendor in Cupertino, California. MAGNUM is a complete programming language and application programs are written in it rather than in some host language in which database management facilities are accessed via procedure calls. It is currently implemented on a PDP—10.

A relation in MAGNUM is stored as an indexed-sequential file, therefore, efficient access is only possible on a primary key column (a primary key is a combination of tuple fields whose value uniquely identifies that tuple). For this reason, the relational structure chosen by the designer must reflect the access requirements of the users.

The data manipulation language of MAGNUM is based on relational algebra. Tuples of a relation are selected by use of FOR EACH and SELECT constructs. The FOR EACH construct is used to select every tuple in a relation which has a given set of field (attribute) values. The SELECT construct is used to determine whether or not a tuple exists which has a given set of field values. Other constructs available include INSERT, DELETE and ALTER.

Privacy is maintained by use of passwords and back-up and recovery facilities include a BACKUP command which saves a named relation on file and RESTORE which can be used to copy a named relation back. No journal file is maintained, therefore there is no provision for forward or backward recovery.

OTHER COMMERCIAL DBMSs

A brief outline has been given of some of the more widely used DBMSs, others are listed in fig. 4.41. More information on currently available DBMSs can be found in (Online, 1983).

In the last year or two, small scale DBMSs have become available for microcomputer based systems, for example, dBASE II and MDBS. MDBS is described in chapter 6.

A DBMS can cost from less than US$2000 (£1000) for a micro-based system to over US$120 000 (£60 000) for a mainframe system.

DATA DICTIONARY SYSTEMS

Some commercial DBMSs come equipped with data dictionary facilities. If this is not the case, it is well worth investing in one of the packages which are available for use as stand-alone systems or as extensions to DBMSs. Fig. 4.42 describes some of the data dictionary systems which are commercially available. More information can be found in Van Duyn (1982) and Lomax (1978).

Name	Type	Computer
TOTAL	DBTG-like	Honeywell 200, Burroughs 2500-4800, NCR Century 101, CDC 6000, IBM 360, 370 and System 3, PDP-11, Cyber 70-74, Univac 9000
IMS	hierarchical	IBM 360/370, models 40, 145 and others
ADABAS	network oriented	IBM 360, 370, Univac 9000, Siemens 4004 and ICL System 4
INGRES	relational	PDP 11, VAX
MAGNUM	relational	available on a time-shared basis, California
IDMS	DBTG	IBM 360, 370 Univac series 70, ICL 2900, DEC, Siemens and others
S2000	hierarchical inverted	IBM 360/370, Univac 1100, CDC 6000 and Cyber 70 series
IDS	constrained network	Honeywell H400, H60/6000
DMS 1100	DBTG	Univac 1100 series
MARK IV	hierarchical	IBM 360/25 and up, 370/125 and up, Univac 9400, 70, 90 and Siemens 4004
DMS-II	network	Burroughs B6700, B7700
PHOLAS	DBTG	Phillips P1000
DBMS/10	DBTG	PDP10
IMAGE	network	HP 3000, 2100
APPEL IV	hierarchical	IBM 360/370, Burroughs 500/700
CDMS 500	hierarchical	PDP 11
DATASAAB	network	SAAB D22/D23
DBMS 1900	hierarchical (limited)	ICL 1903
FORDATA	network	CDC Cyber 76
HOPS	hierarchical	Burroughs 1726
ISAM 70	hierarchical	any FORTRAN system
RAPPORT	relational	PDP, VAX, Univac, Burroughs, DGC, SEL
FOCUS	network	IBM

Fig. 4.41 Some commercially available DBMSs.

DATABASE COMPUTERS (DBCs)

One criticism of the DBMSs discussed so far is concerned with their implementation. Because they are all based on conventional computer hardware, they suffer in performance. Conventional hardware locates data by position, whereas the main requirement in database applications is to locate data by content. That is, the 'logical' specification of required data is given in terms of values e.g. 'RETRIEVE RECORD WITH NAME = SMITH' and the DBMS must convert this 'logical' specification to a physical address on backing store in order to retrieve the required data. Relatively new techniques have been developed to speed up this conversion or to eliminate it altogether in some cases by the use of content addressing schemes. Special purpose

	Vendor	Computer(s)	Operating system	DBMS
BRITISH RAIL DD	British Rail	ICL 1900 IBM 360/370 Honeywell 2000	any batch system	stand alone
CINCOM DD	Cincom Systems, Inc.	IBM 360/370	OS or DOS	built for use with TOTAL
DATA CATALOGUE 2	Synergetics Corporation	IBM 360/370 Univac 1100	OS or DS/VS DOS or DOS/VS EXEC-8	Interfaces to S2000 and IDMS. Supports ADABAS, IMS, TOTAL, DMS and MARK IV.
DATA MANAGER	Management Systems and Programming Inc.	IBM 360/370 Amdahl 470 V-6	OS or DOS	Interfaces to ADABAS, IMS, TOTAL, IDMS, 52000 and MARK IV
DICTIONARY/3000	Imacs Systems Corporation	HP 3000	MPE/OS	requires IMAGE
IBM DD	IBM	IBM 370	OS/VS or DOS/VS	requires IMS/VS
ICL 2900 DD	ICL	ICL 2900 series	VME/B	uses an IDMS database but user need not purchase IDMS to use DD
UCC TEN DD	University Computing Company	IBM 360/370	OS or OS/VS	requires IMS.

processors and computers have been developed which use these new techniques.

Database computers based on content addressing schemes in which the whole database is scanned include CASSM (Content Addressable Segment Sequential Memory) system (Su and Lipovski, 1975), RAPS (Ozkarahan *et al.*, 1975), STARAN (Batcher, 1977), CAFS (ICL, 1977) and DBC (Banerjee *et al.*, 1979). These and other systems are described in Bray and Freeman (1979).

Other database computers speed up database management tasks by means of micro-coded database instructions. One such system is IBM's System/38. This system is described further in chapter 8.

At present, very few DBMSs are based on special purpose hardware. IBM's System/38 is perhaps the only commercial system which is widely used. However, it is likely that many similar systems will become commercially available in the mid 1980s.

AN ALTERNATIVE VIEW OF THE UNIVERSE AS A BASIS FOR DBMS ARCHITECTURE

Many of the problems of existing DBMSs derive from the views of the universe on which they are based. Hierarchical and network systems require the designer to distinguish between entities and attributes at an early stage in the design process. This distinction is really an implementation consideration: entities map to records and attributes to fields within records. Conceptually, there is no difference. Something which is regarded as an attribute by one person may be thought of as an entity by another. As far as the database system designer is concerned, it is recommended that he or she should look at access requirements to make the decision. If there is no need to know anything about a 'thing' X, then X may be regarded as an attribute and may be mapped into a field of a record. In most hierarchical and network DBMSs it is very inefficient to access records by giving values of fields unless those fields constitute the record key, i.e. unless the fields identify the entity which the record represents. Examples of things which are frequently regarded as attributes include: height, address, age, year-of-manufacture and so on. Such things are often represented by non-key fields. It is then quite difficult to access, for example, all employees of 'age 30'. In general, all employee records would have to be scanned. If this and other similar access paths were required to be used on a regular basis, then it would be better to treat 'age 30' as an entity and link employees to it using whatever entity—entity linking mechanism was available in the DBMS being used: e.g. father—son links in IMS or owner—member links in IDMS.

The problem is that once a thing has been regarded as an attribute and mapped to a non-key field, it generally requires extensive re-organisation of the database system to subsequently regard this thing as an entity.

Another difficulty which derives from existing views concerns the complications which are caused by their asymmetry. In all of the views considered so far, relationships between 'things' are asymmetric. In the hierarchical view the relationship is 'directed' from father to son and in the network view the direction is from owner to member. In both of these views, direction is also from entity to attribute. In the relational view, relationships are regarded as being of two types: relationships between elements of a tuple and relationships between tuples, e.g.

| tuple #1 | SMITH | 30 | 10 ORCHARD LANE |
| tuple #2 | DEPARTMENT #7 | | SMITH |

In effect, 'things' are represented by fields within tuples (e.g. 'age 30' and '10 ORCHARD LANE') or by the tuple itself (e.g. the 30 year-old person called SMITH who lives at 10 ORCHARD LANE is represented by tuple #1).

The problem is that this asymmetry (which really reflects the storage structure) complicates data manipulation. End-users and application programmers must learn how to use different types of access path, e.g. from owner to member and member to owner, from tuple to field within a tuple, and tuple to tuple. In addition, these asymmetrically specified relationships are typically implemented in asymmetrical storage structures.

The specification and enforcement of integrity and privacy constraints also suffer from the asymmetry of the conceptual and database schemas which derive from the asymmetric views.

Ideally, no distinction should be made between entities and attributes and all relationships between 'things' of the real world should be perceived and represented in a consistent way. All relationships which are of interest should be represented by access paths with equal efficiency.

A view of the universe which demonstrates these features has been developed at The University of Strathclyde and is called the simplified binary-relational (SBR) view. (Frost, March 1983). The SBR view may be informally defined as follows:

- the universe is regarded as consisting of entities with binary-relationships between them
- a binary-relationship can link an entity to at most one other entity or to itself

- entity sets such as 'EMPLOYEES' are treated like any other entity
- ϵ, the set-membership relation is treated like any other binary-relation

As an example of the use of the view, consider the following SBR model:

MANAGER #1. ϵ. MANAGERS
MANAGER #1. NATIONALITY. BRITISH
MANAGER #1. HOBBY. FISHING
MANAGER #1. HOBBY. SQUASH
MANAGER #1. WORKS IN. DEPARTMENT #1
DEPARTMENT #1. MAKES. MACHINE #1
etc.

The only asymmetry in this model concerns the names of the relationship types, e.g. the last triple is equivalent to:

MACHINE #1. MADE IN. DEPARTMENT #1

In all other respects, the view is symmetrical.

Frost (August and May 1983) has evaluated the SBR view as a basis for the design of a new type of DBMS and has shown that:

(a) Very flexible data storage structures can be built for an SBR DBMS. Such structures hold data as a set of triples, e.g.

a.	b.	c
x.	y.	z

etc.

such that retrieval is possible using any field or combination of fields as key. This gives eight modes of retrieval:

(? . ? . ?)	a database dump
(a . ? . ?)	retrieves all triples with 'a' in first field
(? . b . ?)	retrieves all triples with 'b' in second field
(? . ? . c)	.
(a . b . ?)	.
(? . b . c)	etc
(a . ? . c)	.
(a . b . c)	true or false depending on presence of triple in the database.

There are two main advantages of such a structure:

(i) New types of data may be added by simply adding extra triples, i.e the system is very data-independent.

(ii) Application programs and queries are easy to formulate. For example, using a query language developed at the University of Strathclyde, the 'total SALARY of all 30 year old EMPLOYEES who work in DEPARTMENT #1' can be obtained as follows:

    [(?E . works in . DEPARTMENT #1)
        AND
    (?E . ϵ . EMPLOYEES)
        AND
    (?E . aged . 30)] ;
    (E. has salary. ?S);
    print "total salary is", sum(S).

The first expression finds the 'bag' E, of all 30-year-old employees who work in DEPARTMENT #1. The second statement retrieves the bag, S, of all salaries of all members of the bag E. The final statement displays the sum of the members of S. The word 'bag' is used deliberately to distinguish the collection from a set. S, for example, could contain duplicate entries.

(b) Conceptual and database schema specification is straightforward and in addition, integrity constraints which arc expressed using a language called SCHEMAL (which is based on the SBR view) can be *automatically* enforced if an SBR storage structure is used. The designer has simply to specify the integrity constraints and the system will then automatically vet all input to the database against these constraints. For example, consider the following SCHEMAL statement:

$[(X.\epsilon.\text{managers}) \wedge [(Y.\epsilon.\text{employees}) V (Y.\epsilon.\text{managers})]] \Leftarrow (X.\text{manages}.Y)$

This means that something X is only allowed to manage something Y if X is known to be a manager and Y is known to be a manager or an employee. An attempt to input the triple (J SMITH. manages. P BROWN) will cause the system to automatically check to see if J SMITH is a manager and P BROWN is an employee or a manager.

It is predicted that it will also be possible, using the SBR view, to develop mechanisms for the automatic inference of data from inference rules and data which is stored explicitly in the database.

A DBMS based on the SBR view is being developed at The University of Strathclyde and a prototype system should be available by late 1984. Other similar systems are being developed both in industry and in universities. Particular attention is being paid to the extension of non-procedural languages such as

PROLOG. The use of 'semantic networks' by researchers in artificial intelligence has much in common with the use of the SBR view.

USING A COMMERCIAL DBMS

DBMS SOFTWARE

When a commercial DBMS is purchased it is delivered with one or more of three types of software:

(a) Software which is used to extend the capability of the existing operating system. For example, to manage concurrent access to the database.

(b) Software routines which can be CALLed from a host language such as COBOL, FORTRAN, PL/1 etc. These routines may be regarded as additions to the 'standard functions' or 'library routines' of the host language. Application programs may then be written in the host language and the database routines CALLed as required. Such calls may be issued, for example, when the programmer wants to FIND, DELETE or INSERT units of data in the database.

(c) Utility programs which may be executed as normal jobs in the conventional (or extended) operating system. These utility programs may be used, for example, to create, save or restore the database. Some DBMSs provide report program generators, query systems and data dictionary systems as sets of utility programs.

There will also be manuals and possibly short training courses to help in the use of the software.

USING THE DBMS

The construction of a database system using a commercial DBMS typically involves the following tasks.

Analysis of the user requirements

The DBMS package may contain advice on how to do this but it is unlikely. Cougar, Colter and Knapp's book on 'Advanced System Development/Feasibility Techniques' is useful reading material (Cougar *et al.*, 1982).

Creation of the conceptual schema

The conceptual schema is constructed according to the view of the universe which underlies the DBMS being used. Ideally, the conceptual schema would be constructed according to some powerful, universally accepted view (possibly a variation of the unconstrained network view). However, this would only be worthwhile if the DBMS available were based on this view. If this were not the case it is possible that you might create a model which could not be accommodated by the DBMS available. Therefore, it is very important that the view of the universe which underlies the DBMS being used is employed in the construction of the conceptual schema. Examples of conceptual models were presented when the four views were discussed. Conceptual schemas are simply generalisations of such models. Figs 4.43, 4.44, 4.45 and 4.46 show four conceptual schemas all describing the same part of the universe (note: labels have been omitted where the meaning of an arc is obvious). Currently available commercial DBMSs do not provide conceptual schema definition languages. However, some do give examples of the type of diagrams which designers should construct at this stage of the development process.

Construction of conceptual sub-schemas
A sub-schema is a subset of the conceptual schema which is of interest to a particular end-user or group of end-users. Ideally, the sub-schema would be specified according to a view of the universe which was most appropriate for the particular user (or group of

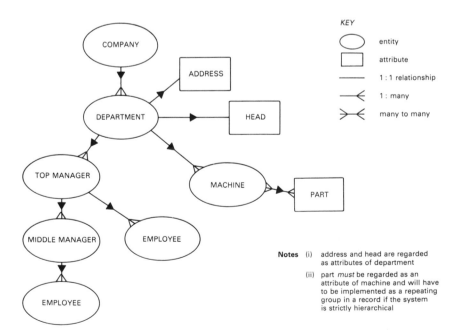

Fig. 4.43 A hierarchical conceptual schema.

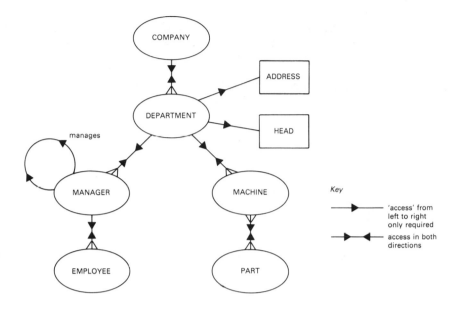

Fig. 4.44 An unconstrained network conceptual schema.

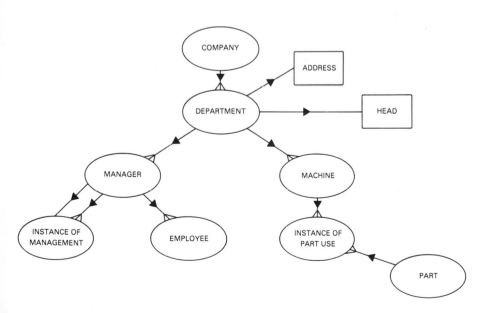

Fig. 4.45 A DBTG conceptual schema.

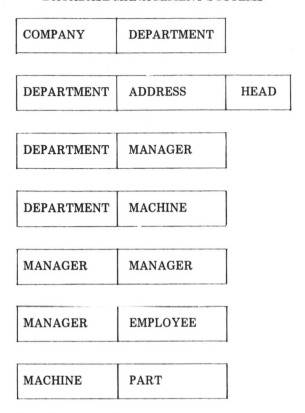

COMPANY	DEPARTMENT

DEPARTMENT	ADDRESS	HEAD

DEPARTMENT	MANAGER

DEPARTMENT	MACHINE

MANAGER	MANAGER

MANAGER	EMPLOYEE

MACHINE	PART

Fig. 4.46 A normalised relational conceptual schema.

users) concerned. In practice this is rarely done and when it is, it is done on an informal basis. It is good practice to draw diagrams representing sub-schemas and to use these diagrams during discussion with end-users and during the design of the privacy strategy. Currently available commercial DBMSs do not provide conceptual sub-schema definition languages.

Data analysis and creation of the data dictionary
At this stage, there should be a clear definition (the conceptual schema) of what parts of the universe are to be represented by data, i.e. what entity, attribute and relationship types are of interest to the end-users. You now have to formalise the definition of these 'things' and specify clearly how they are to be represented by data. This process is called *data analysis* and the results are put into the *data dictionary*. The DBMS may provide utility programs to help you do this, if not you should invest in a data dictionary system to complement your DBMS.

Construction of the database (logical) schema

Most commercial DBMSs provide some mechanism for the formal specification of the database schema. In some systems, this mechanism takes the shape of a special purpose *data description language* (DDL). In general, the DDL uses terminology which is based on physical data storage structures. For example, in IDMS, the database schema is defined in terms of files, areas and records. In many cases the designer must also supply some implementation information, for example such information might include: (i) identification of record-types which should be provided with hashed access in DBTG systems, (ii) identification of fields which should be used in the creation of indexes in inverted systems and (iii) identification of the access method which should be used in IMS like systems.

Essentially, the construction of the database schema requires the designer to map the conceptual schema into the abstract data structures provided by the DBMS being used. For example: (i) with IMS, the designer maps the hierarchical structures of the conceptual schema into trees and decides on the ordering of records on levels etc., (ii) with DBTG systems, the designer maps the constrained network structures of the conceptual schema into the DBTG 'set' structures and decides how members should access owners and (iii) with relational systems, the designer maps the relations of the conceptual schema into the tables of the system concerned and decides, for example, on the order of columns.

Compilation of the database schema

The database schema is then compiled by the DBMS and the physical storage structure is automatically configured. The system may require the designer to input blocking factors, type of data compression scheme required and the like, but in general such detailed implementation considerations are handled by the DBMS.

Database sub-schema specification

Many DBMSs also require designers to specify a set of sub-schemas at this stage. A database sub-schema (or simply sub-schema as it is generally called) is a sub-set of the database schema which is of interest to a particular user or group of users. Sub-schemas are normally specified in a language which is similar or the same as the DDL used for database schema definition. A sub-schema, typically, provides a level of privacy control by specifically excluding parts of the database from users who are allowed to use that sub-schema. Often sub-schemas also introduce an additional element of data-independence. For example, records which are defined in the sub-schema may be made up from parts taken from several records in the database schema. These composite records are often called *logical records*. A logical record may be thought of as being similar to the logical *input/output package* as discussed in earlier chapters of the book where the ideal database system architecture was considered.

Compilation of the sub-schemas

In many cases, the sub-schemas are compiled by the DBMS and the resultant object modules contain all of the necessary information to directly map the 'logical' structures of the sub-schema into the structures of the physical database. That is, the compiled sub-schemas are stand-alone object modules which can be linked to various application programs. This is the case in IDMS, for example. In other systems, the compiled sub-schema modules do not contain the mapping information which is necessary to locate data in the physical storage structure, this information is held in the database schema object module. The sub-schema modules only contain that information which is necessary to map 'logical' sub-schema structures into the structures of the database schema. In this case, only when an application program is executed does the linked sub-schema object code refer to some repository of mapping information in order to obtain the information necessary to locate data in physical storage.

Essentially, the physical storage mapping information is introduced at three different stages:

(a) When no DBMS is available, the programmer must introduce the mapping information into the application programs directly, for example, by refering to physical files by name and records by relative address on disc. Such information is then compiled into the application program object module.

(b) With some DBMSs, the sub-schema object modules contain the mapping information and these modules may be incorporated into application object modules by link editing, for example. In this case, the application programmer refers to a 'logical' data structure and the sub-schema module converts this logical description to physical locations.

(c) In other DBMSs, the mapping information is not made available until the application program is executed. In this case, the programmer refers to 'logical' records and these are mapped into database schema structures by the information in the sub-schema module. Only when the application program is executed are the database schema structures mapped into physical locations. The mapping information necessary to do this is held in a *logical to physical mapping module* (which might be part of the database schema itself). The mapping module is therefore part of the operational database system and is not just referred to in the compilation of sub-schemas.

In case (a) the system is said to be early-bound, in case (c) the system is late-bound. The idea of *binding* is very important. Late-bound systems are more data-independent than early-bound systems. In a late-bound system, a change in the organisation of the physical storage structure only requires the mapping module to be changed. Application programs and sub-schemas are left unchanged and do not need to be re-compiled. Note that (b) above is more data-independent than (a). In (b), a change in the organisation of the physical storage structure only requires those sub-schemas which are affected to be changed. Application programs may have to be re-compiled or their object modules link-edited to the new sub-schema object modules, but the application program source code remains unchanged. In (a), application programs which are affected will have to be re-written and re-compiled.

Creation of the back-up and recovery programs
Commercially available DBMSs vary greatly in the way in which they handle back-up and recovery. Some provide utility programs which can be used directly to SAVE and RESTORE, ROLL-BACK or ROLL-FORWARD a database. Others require designers to build programs for these tasks.

Loading of the database
Special purpose utility programs are typcially provided for the initial loading of the large quantities of data which constitute the database. This task could be carried out by writing and running application programs which insert data piecemeal, but this is likely to be too time-consuming.

Creation of application programs
Once the database has been loaded, it may be manipulated by application programs which are typically written in some host language. Such programs normally start by declaring the sub-schema which is to be used. That part of the database may then be manipulated by means of CALLS to DBMS procedures as required.

A general, yet detailed, account of the database system design process using commercially available DBMSs may be found in Cardenas (1979).

Seven case studies are now presented which are intended to help the reader acquire a 'feel' for what it is like to be involved in the use of a DBMS.

REFERENCES

Banerjee, J., Hsiao, D.K. and Kannan, K. (1979) 'DBC — a database computer for very large databases', *IEEE Transactions on Computers C—28*, (6), 414—429.

Batcher, K.E. (1977) 'STARAN Series E', *Proceedings of the 1977 International Conference on Parallel Processing*, pp. 140—143.

Bray, Olin H. and Freeman, H.A. (1979) *Data Base Computers*, Toronto: Lexington Books.

Cardenas, A.F. (1979) *Data Base Management Systems*, Allyn and Bacon.

Codd, E.F. (1970) 'A relational model of data for large shared data banks', *CACM*, 13(6).

Cougar, J.D., Colter, M.A. and Knapp, R.W. (1982) *Advanced System Development/Feasibility Techniques*, John Wiley and Sons.

Date, C.J. (1977) *An Introduction to Database Systems* (2nd Edition), Addison-Wesley Publishing Company.

DBTG (1971) CODASYL Data Base Task Group (DBTG). Report. ACM.

Deen, S.M. (1977) *Fundamentals of Data Base Systems*, Great Britain: Unwin Brothers Ltd.

Frost, R.A. (1982) 'Binary-relational storage structures', *The Computer Journal*, 25(3)

Frost, R.A. (August 1983) 'SCHEMAL: Yet another conceptual schema definition language', *The Computer Journal* 26(3).

Frost, R.A. and Whittaker, S. (May, 1983) 'A step towards the automatic maintenance of the semantic integrity of databases', *The Computer Journal* 26(2).

ICL (1977) 'ICL first with DB processor' *Computer Weekly*, No. 573, p. 1.

Kroenke, D. (1977) *Database Processing*, USA: Science Research Associates Inc.

Lomax, J.D. (1978) *Data Dictionary Systems*, England: NCC Publications.

Online (1983) *Database Techniques: Software Selection and Systems Development*, UK: Online Publications Limited.

Ozkarahan, E.A., Schuster, S.A. and Smith, K.C. (1975) 'RAP — an associative processor for data base management', *AFIPS Conference Proceedings 44* pp. 379—388.

Robinson, H. (1981) *Database Analysis and Design*, England: Chartwell-Bratt.

Su, S.Y.W. and Lipovski, G.J. (1975) 'CASSM: A cellular system for very large data bases', *Proceedings of the International Conference on Very Large Data Bases*.

Tsichritzis, D.S. and Lochovsky, F.H. (1977) *Data Base Management Systems*, Academic Press.

Van Duyn, J.V. (1982) *Developing a Data Dictionary System*, Englewood Cliffs, NJ: Prentice-Hall Inc.

Walsh, M.E. (1979) *Information Management Systems/Virtual Storage*, Reston, Virginia: Reston Publishing Company Inc.

PART 2
Case Studies

In this part several case studies based on real applications are presented, written by people involved in database system design and the use of DBMSs. Each case study is particularly concerned with one aspect of database management and discusses that aspect with respect to a specific application. Topics which are covered include:

- choosing the DBMS
- estimation of resource requirements
- data analysis and schema specification
- system integration
- design of end-user interfaces
- data integrity and database recovery
- data manipulation

CHAPTER 5

Choosing a DBMS

By S. Dunnachie (BRITOIL)

INTRODUCTION

When given responsibility for the first time for choosing (or what is more likely, leading the project to choose) a DBMS, you can be excused for initial feelings of worry, then after you have had time to think about it, terror! (Definition of 'confidence': the feeling you have when you don't really know what is going on!)

There can be many technical, strategic and political issues involved, and this chapter is intended to help those who need guidance in professionally organising and carrying out the demanding and challenging task of choosing a Database Management System for their organisation.

This chapter describes how to:

- handle the different circumstances and constraints which may exist
- plan the evaluation and selection processes
- compile the list of contenders
- draw up the short list
- make the evaluation and selection of the DBMS

There are many different situations and no one set of rules is applicable everywhere, but an attempt has been made here to describe an approach which should be generally applicable. The writer has had experience in the DBMS selection process at what might be seen as both ends of the spectrum — once with an established engineering company where the choice was limited, and also with a young oil company (BNOC) where the choice was wide. Some reference is made to these situations in the text which follows.

THE CIRCUMSTANCES AND CONSTRAINTS

The task of choosing a DBMS could be thought of as a fairly academic exercise involving the matching of technical requirements against available features. It is not that simple, however, and in the real world, the particular circumstances and constraints of each situation are a key factor in the whole process.

The situation where no DBMS software currently exists and a wide choice is available would seem ideal (although this has its own drawbacks such as learning factors still to be incurred and sometimes unreasonably high expectations) but more often than not there are constraints in existence. For example:

- the boss or some influential colleagues may have strong views on the ideal solution. They may have similarly strong views on DBMSs to avoid like the plague, or they might think the whole exercise is unnecessary and a waste of the company's time and money
- specific, high priority applications or certain users may be driving the project, and their DBMS requirements may not be consistent with broader aspects of the company's longer term DBMS needs
- there may be a need to link any new DBMS software to existing DBMSs or other software
- the choice may not be as wide as it would first seem

Recognition of the circumstances and real constraints is fundamental and it is vital to clarify and document the objectives and scope early on.

CLARIFYING OBJECTIVES AND SCOPE
When one is participating in (and particularly leading) a DBMS requirements study it is essential that there is a clear understanding of

(a) What the objectives are:
    - to assess the need for a DBMS?
    - to recommend the most suitable DBMS?
(b) What tasks are involved:
    - visits to vendors and other DBMS users
    - arranging presentations, benchmarks
    - involving other DP staff in the study
(c) The scope which exists for the choice of database:
    - must it be a proprietory system?
    - must it be currently in use?
    - can it be supplied by a third party?
(d) The timescales and resources allowed:
    - is there a critical target date linked to certain system developments?
    - can external consultancy be used?
    - is time allowed to go on courses or visit other users?
    - what are the capital cost constraints?

These objectives and scope should be documented in the *Terms of Reference* for the study.

POSSIBLE CONSTRAINTS

The database selection exercise may be a stand alone project, or it may be part of a wider selection or review of hardware and software. Being part of a wider exercise can impose an overriding broader-based decision which can affect the DBMS software selection. For example, from a choice of hardware *A* and *B*, *A* may have the best DBMS software, but *B*'s offering may have to be accepted because it is the 'best' choice from viewpoints such as vendor support, track record, general performance etc. Even if the DBMS software selection is a stand-alone project however, it is essential that account is taken of hardware and software plans and policies. It may be found that in bigger organisations where a variety of hardware and software is installed, there is a policy (declared or otherwise) towards phasing out certain hardware/software and promoting others — this is clearly vital input to any DBMS selection study.

Another area where policy must be known is systems development. Are there any trends or policies in relation to such issues as transaction processing, end-user facilities, systems centralisation/decentralisation, management information systems, data dictionary facilities, etc? This aspect of systems development strategy is another necessary input to the DBMS selection study.

PLANNING THE EVALUATION AND SELECTION

There are many tasks to be carried out and a documented plan for the evaluation and selection study is vital.

Terms of Reference form the basis from which a list of tasks should be drawn up. Where others are involved it is important to identify early on what information they require e.g., DP project leaders and managers may be asked for their database requirements in questionnaire forms, and/or individual or group discussions may be held. A consensus of agreement may be needed on such things before DBMS vendors can be contacted.

Consideration should be given to how the list of contenders will be arrived at — what sources of information will be used? (DATAPRO, AUERBACH, etc) if these are not available, how will access to them be arranged?

These are other questions:

- what will be the procedures for selection and how long will it take?
- how will the list be selected?

- if others are to be involved will they be available at the required time and do they know what their remit will be?
- what preparation is needed to arrange meaningful benchmarks?

WHO SHOULD BE INVOLVED?
Some text books say that the 'ideal' team comprises a systems analyst, programmer, operations person, system programmer, business analyst, etc. It works sometimes, but such committee-type approaches often fail — the most important thing is to ensure that all relevant functions are properly informed and involved. A better approach might be to have a couple of experienced people driving the project and reporting to a project management committee at agreed checkpoints. This reporting is best done in the form of presentations/meetings where questions can be asked and discussions held, rather than formal reports which are more time-consuming and restrict communication to one direction.

SCHEDULING THE STUDY
The main activities should include:

- propose and agree terms of reference
- identify the requirements
- compile the initial list of contenders and draw up the short list
- evaluate the short list and select.

PROPOSE AND AGREE TERMS OF REFERENCE
This is the first step in the whole exercise and it is essential to have the right framework agreed at this stage before any time is spent on subsequent activities. The time spent sorting out any misunderstanding or disagreements is nothing compared to the time lost later if this is not done. The content of the terms of reference were discussed in the last chapter, and can be summarised as being about aims, activities to achieve the aims, names of nominated contacts, resources, constraints, timescales and reporting mechanisms. Ensure enough time is allowed for agreement on these issues — it is the foundation for the rest of the project.

IDENTIFY THE REQUIREMENTS
If you are fortunate or someone has planned in advance, the data requirements have already been identified. More than likely they have not, and depending on the organisation and on how far computers have been used, this process could take a considerable amount of time.
    The information needed, at a high level, is:

- what areas of the company need databases (e.g. finance, engineering)?
- the use to which these databases will be put (e.g. information systems, production systems)?
- what is the nature of the databases (e.g. on-line, batch, distributed)?
- will end users use the database directly?
- are any other data management facilities needed (e.g. data dictionary, testing facilities, prototyping tools, etc)?

This is another area where agreement is needed from other parties. Make sure you now have a good idea of how much groundwork has already been done before proposing how long this process will take.

COMPILE THE INITIAL LIST OF CONTENDERS AND DRAW UP THE SHORT LIST

This involves matching requirements and constraints against the systems on the market. The list could be much longer than might be thought for an IBM installation and a free choice of DBMS software, but it could be shorter than imagined if the hardware is not IBM. In the latter case the initial list of contenders may be the same list as the short list! In the former, make sure enough time is allowed to satisfy yourself and others on what the key factors should be for entry to the short list. It can be dangerous to draw up the short list by simply ticking off requirements against a set of DBMS facilities. Try to obtain a description of each vendor's system from an independent source, with a summary of each facility. Make sure enough time is allowed to gather these sources of information and to study them.

EVALUATE THE SHORT LIST AND SELECT

This is the climax of the exercise, and the grouping of a number of activities. These include:

- informing the selected vendors that they are on the short list and will be invited to present their products
- organising vendor presentations and benchmarks
- holding internal meetings to discuss the various systems
- following up queries and obtaining further information from vendors
- recommending the DBMS to be installed to the project management committee
- getting a decision and informing all those involved

A large element of the work at this stage involves other people from within and outside the company. It is sometimes extremely difficult to arrange presentations and meetings at times to suit everyone. Plan to keep momentum going by getting views on vendors presentations out to those attending quickly after the presentations and ask for an early response.

When planning the schedule, check the availability of key people well in advance. Plan to advise people of presentations and meetings well in advance and put reminders of this into your schedule. Have your draft schedule agreed by the project management committee and make sure other key people involved are aware of it. The final report will come to fruition during this stage although it should be developing throughout the process — make sure you allow time for typing, distribution and feedback.

ESTABLISHING THE REQUIRED FACILITIES

The initiative for looking into DBMS requirements can come from a number of areas, such as:

- computer technicians (who may see database as a means of improved data-independence, recovery, back-up and other technical facilities)
- company management (who may see database as the answer to system integration and the management information requirement)
- DP managers (who may see database as the way to help in implementing on-line multi-user systems with a need for shared data, but should also be aware of the broader implications and opportunities)

Depending on where the interest originated (and who may since have become involved) it is important to ensure a balanced approach and ensure that the facilities which should be considered are given sufficient attention. For example, it may be that a technician's choice of system, which has superb back-up and recovery capabilities, is unsuitable because the product is not being complemented with accompanying dictionary and system building tools needed to make the use of database systems an attractive and economic proposition.

FAMILIES OF DATA MANAGEMENT PRODUCTS

The current trend nowadays is to look at a database handler not just as stand-alone pieces of software (which can make file handling more dependable and efficient), but as part of a set of data management tools. This toolkit could include, as well as a database handler:

- a transaction processing monitor
- a data dictionary
- a generalised query language

- a program (or system!) generation aid
- a graphics module

It is important to look at both future trends in technology and the company system development programme. This may result in certain requirements being given higher or lower levels of importance than they would have. For example is it worth considering an RPG facility which, although excellent for what it does, is now being superceded by non-procedural language software?

DIFFERENT TYPES OF DBMS REQUIREMENTS

Various types of facilities may be required from a DBMS and it is important not to confuse them with each other — it may be that no one product satisfies all the needs at the end of the day.

At BNOC, a need was identified for:

- a powerful DBMS capable of handling complex data structures and many on-line users
- a quick development tool
- a facility to handle unstructured text

After an extensive study lasting about nine months, it was decided to go for Cullinanes IDMS, Information Builders FOCUS and the UKAERE's STATUS as a set of products. Since then, these products have been used independently and in combination in successfully implementing a wide range of subject and application databases.

COMPILING THE LIST OF CONTENDERS

The list of contenders may be much larger than imagined if the hardware is IBM and freedom of choice exists. On many other machines there are often only one or two systems available. However, quite a number of systems which can be compiled on most mainframes and minis are now available (e.g. RAPPORT, MIMER) which is beginning to provide a better choice for some of the non-IBM systems than they have had in the past.

An example of some of the systems available is shown in fig. 4.41. This is not meant to be either an exhaustive or suggested list, but only to indicate the choice which may be available. New database management systems come onto the market at a very high rate, and it is therefore best to ensure that whatever source of data is used to compile a first draft should be up-to-date and reliable. There are companies who provide a service in information on database and data management products, e.g. DATAPRO and AUERBACH, and other sources like the CUYB in the UK. Such facilities can be used as a starting point. Other possible sources are:

- the computer manufacturer (although if they have a DBMS of their own they may not be the best people to ask about competitive products on their machine!)
- other users of the same hardware (a list of users should be available from the manufacturer or its user group — the user group may even have a database sub-user group of its own)

Certain rules should be drawn up to ensure as little time as possible is wasted on considering non-runners. Key considerations are:

- is the DBMS available on the required hardware? (If not, forget it unless there is a written commitment to make it available by a certain date.)
- what is the quality and quantity of support, and where is it situated? (A one or two-man support team in another continent is fraught with danger — even if the DBMS looks good.)
- what size and where is the user base? (A reasonable number of other accessible users with whom common problems and solutions can be shared is re-assuring when there are problems, and gives more strength in making representations to the vendor.)
- what are the cost constraints? (Is there a budget for the DBMS purchase?)
- is the DBMS compatible with other key software? (There may already be a transaction processor, data dictionary or file management system with which the DBMS *must* interlink.)

DRAWING UP THE SHORT LIST

The usual approach to compiling the short list is to evaluate each vendor offering against a list of requirements in a table. (See example in Fig. 5.1.) If every required facility was of equal importance, value and relevance the choice would automatically result from this process, but it is never that simple.

There are different techniques which can be used to compile the list such that it is more relevant to one's own situation, for example:

- rather than entering 'yes' or 'no' under a heading, insert 'good', 'average' or 'poor' as a judgement of each vendors facility
- form groups of facilities, categorised as 'necessary', 'desirable' or 'useful', which will show that in some cases even when a facility is 'good', its relevance to the requirements may only rank 'useful', thereby putting its rating in perspective
- weightings can be applied to features such that marks for quality of features are multiplied by a rating to arrive at its 'true' value.

Type of feature	Importance Factor	Product A	Product B	Product C
Multi user Support	1	P	P	G
Capability for handling large complex data structures	1	P	P	G
Communications Capability	1	A	A	G
Hierarchical Data Structuring	1	G	P	G
Multiple Indexing	1	Y	Y	Y
Restructuring Facilities	1	A	A	G
Recovery Facilities	1	A	P	G
Bridge to future	1	A	A	G
Privacy Control	1	A	A	G
Vendor System Support Large Number (>50) users world wide	2	Y	Y	Y
Large Number (>20) users UK	2	Y	Y	Y
Efficiency, Support & Performance	2	P	A	A
Network Data Structuring (directly)	2	G	P	G
Integrity Checking	2	N	N	A
Data Independence	2	G	G	G
Sequential Access	2	Y	Y	Y
FORTRAN Interface	2	Y	Y	Y
Vendor Training	2	A	G	A
Vendor Documentation	2	A	G	G
Codasyl System	2	N	N	Y
Performance Tools	2	A	P	A
Usability	2	G	A	G
Testing Aids	3	A	N	A
Cost Category	—	M	M	H

Cost Category	Feature Ratings	Feature Importance
L — Low (<£30K)	Y — Yes G — Good	1 Necessary
M — Med (£30K — £60K)	N — No A — Average	2 Desirable
H — High (>£60K)	P — Poor	3 Useful

Fig. 5.1 List of DBMS features.

This is an extension of the categorisation technique, and although it can be useful, it can become complicated and artificial as almost any system can look the best if the weightings are adjusted accordingly.

These tables are probably best seen as a good input to the process, but the decision on the short list should also take strong account of the dialogue which has been established with the vendors, how knowledgeable, communicative and helpful the staff are, and if you can manage to visit them, what established customers think of their vendor.

The procedure can be made much simpler if you can decide on a relatively small number of factors which are important to you, and concentrate on these. The factors might include

The Vendor:
- are they viable and forward-looking?
- what is their track record on meeting target dates?
- what length is their 'known bug' list?
- do they have good people?
- is support going to be adequate in your geographical area?

Data Structuring Capability:
- can all forms of data structures be represented?
- are the physical structuring methods natural or artificial?
- is the software architecture suitable for developing new types of structures?

Bridge to Future:
- is there cushioning from new versions of manufacturers hardware and software?
- is the product going to be supported through new generations of hardware and software?

Data Independence:
- is this an integral part of the software architecture?

Data Dictionary:
- is the dictionary genuinely treated as the one and only data description repository in the system?

Security, Integrity and Recovery:
- how easy are they to use?

Links to Other Products:
- are there other products (not necessarily the vendors own) which interlink with the DBMS? (For example, query languages, TP monitors.)

Development and Tuning:
- what is the future plan for maintaining and developing the software?
- what facilities exist for its measurement and tuning?

Cost:
- known (purchase, rental and support costs)
- hidden (the cost of delivery delays, poor support, numerous bugs etc.)

Any vendors who fail on more than one or two of your key criteria are candidates for a rejection.

EVALUATION AND SELECTION

The short list should comprise two or at most three vendors to examine in detail. Now you should consider what presentations, demonstrations and benchmark tests need to be organised and who will be involved. Also to be considered is which vendors and users to visit, and deciding on the key components of the final selection.

PRESENTATIONS AND DEMONSTRATIONS

This is an appropriate time to involve others who have some influence on the decision although they may not have been involved so far. This means a cross-section of people with different levels and types of knowledge will be participating and this must be borne in mind when organising presentations and demonstrations. Remember you are the potential customer and therefore call the tune, so there is no reason why you should not tell each vendor what ground you want him to cover at a presentation, the required level of detail, and how long is to be given to make a case. There is always a danger at this stage that as senior management may be present, presentations or demos will become sales-orientated, and this must always be avoided.

Vendors usually want to demonstrate their own pet system, but it may be more useful to ask them to demonstrate their software working to one of your systems specifications — as well as providing proof of technical capabilities, this tests out any claims being made about productivity of their system! If you do ask a vendor to do this, the scope of the test system needs to be kept in perspective, and it is best to provide a specification to all contenders at the same time. Vendors may have a genuine resource problem in getting someone to do the job, but if you can arrange to have one of your own people available to work with him and keep the total activity to less than seven or eight man days, most vendors who have nothing to hide will oblige. It will cost some time and money to do this, but there are some attractive pay-offs:

- a mini-system will have existed as a common denominator for all to be judged against

- a working-level dialogue will have taken place and there will be a better awareness of quality of vendor staff
- various technical answers to the same conceptual problem will be available for judgement
- a possible vehicle for benchmark testing will exist

It is essential to follow up presentations and demonstrations immediately afterwards by obtaining a view from your own colleagues. Try to hold a review a day or two later while thoughts are still fresh in everyone's mind, and it may get things moving by summarising the presentation and suggesting some conclusions from it. In addition to this, ask for written comments — a questionnaire approach can be a useful prompt for certain kinds of information and opinions.

BENCHMARKS

Benchmarks are concerned with relative performance figures for the same processing with different hardware and software. Simple benchmarks may not reveal a lot, but complicated benchmarks are time-consuming, complicated and the results are often subjective at the end of the day.

What is possibly more practical and useful in database system benchmarking is to find out what performance figures are available from the vendor. Verify these with simple benchmarks and then establish what rules or facilities exist for estimating or modelling more complex applications, which could then be simulated. It is necessary for fair comparisons between vendors to ensure that statistics are available in the same format, although some flexibility may be needed to allow explanations of certain results.

VISITS TO VENDORS AND USERS

If the vendor's offices have not already been visited, make a point of it at this stage.

By being on the vendor premises, meeting the staff, and seeing the environment in which they work, useful impressions will be formed. It is particularly useful to visit the development centre, and not just a sales office, but this is not always practical.

A visit to user sites can be even more enlightening, however, and this is essential when seriously considering a vendor. Rather than accept a name given by the vendor, ask for a complete list of users with an indication of the type of work for which they use the DBMS. It may not be proper to contact a user directly, but after deciding who you would like to see, ask the vendor to arrange for you to contact them directly. Users may not always be able to spare enough time to see you, but if this is the case do not rule out a telephone conversation if it is felt that there is a lot in common. When visiting users make sure you are well prepared and get as much as possible out of the visit, which can be helped by having a check list of questions and topics to discuss.

THE SELECTION

By this time you should have as much information as you need and can handle. It is possible to go on looking at new pieces of software, talking to users, and evaluating facilities for years — it has been done! Better to know your objectives, set your timescales and keep to them, unless there are really exceptional reasons for delaying.

The final considerations should be based on:

(a) *The vendor and their support.* You now know them fairly well and might even have worked briefly with them. Are they the kind of organisation to whom you are happy to entrust your company's data management future? Remember their employees attitudes and abilities are just as important as their product.

(b) *The product and its future.* Is the product stable, but yet modern and developing? It is dangerous to go for an unproven product, but this extreme must be balanced against settling for one which has run its course. There should be a happy medium where you are not pioneering the unknown, but using a proven product with good facilities and exciting development potential.

(c) *The role of database within your organisation.* The role of database, and the relationship of both the software and the staff to other software and staff is fundamental to the selection process. If this is not thought to be important you are likely to identify a good stand-alone DBMS. If it *is* thought to be important, you are likely to identify a good DBMS which is also part of a set of data management and software products — a much better recipe for success.

CONCLUSIONS

The writer's experience at BNOC, where IDMS, FOCUS and STATUS are now used, is that simple check lists of requirements against features are of extremely limited value.

A thorough and proper DBMS evaluation and selection process requires:

- clear objectives
- management involvement and commitment
- adequate project team manpower resources in quantity and quality
- an awareness of the company's systems and data planning strategies

Given this, you have a good chance of success.

CHAPTER 6

Estimation of Resource Requirements for a Micro-based DBMS

By S.C. Tannahill (University of Strathclyde)

INTRODUCTION

Three types of resources are required in order to set up a database system — hardware, software, and manpower. The construction of a database system on an 8-bit microcomputer can pose severe difficulties because of the 64K byte maximal capacity of the random access memory (RAM). These difficulties stem from the very considerable storage requirements of the operating system, the database schema, the data manipulation system, the host language and the applications programs used to interface with the database, which all reside in RAM. The software requirements are for a database management system (DBMS) which facilitates the implementation of the database system on the microcomputer. The software should provide the means of storing, up-dating, manipulating and retrieving data efficiently. The third resource, manpower, is required in a number of different forms. The first form is that of the designer who identifies the data entities, their interrelations and applications, and who develops the schema. The second is that of the computer programmer who writes programs for the basic input/output functions and the major applications of the data. The third is that of the database administrator who considers the requirements of the end-users and decides on changes to be made to the database. In the initial stages, the designer has a dialogue with all end-users so that the system which is eventually implemented is that perceived as being required. If the information system is used for management decision making, the designer requires a model-building capability such as that supplied by management science or operational research.

The investigation, which is described in the following chapters, began in October 1980 with a survey of database management systems and available host languages. Preliminary work on the design of the school information system indicated that a network (Codasyl) database and a structured language such as PASCAL would be most appropriate. The factors on which the selection of a DBMS was based were as follows:

- support of Codasyl-type databases whose structure is the same as that of the conceptual model created
- provision of very good data integrity, data security and data independence
- execution in many different microcomputers using different operating systems
- provision of many host language interfaces to the database such as FORTRAN, COBOL, PASCAL, PL/1 and BASIC
- provision of useful sub-systems with which to restructure the database, to recover the database if it should be corrupted, and to generate reports without the need to write application programs

The widely-used CP/M (Control Program/Monitor) operating system was chosen which provides support for many useful facilities such as word processing.

PASCAL/M was chosen as the host language since it has a better structure than FORTRAN, COBOL and BASIC, it supports overlay programming and direct or random access files not then available in PASCAL/Z, and it is easier to learn than PL/1.

Three main factors were considered when choosing a microcomputer which was specific to our needs:

- does it have sufficient on-line storage?
- does it have sufficient RAM?
- is it fast enough?

An analysis of the database schema estimated the size of the database at over 3M bytes for a school of 1500 pupils. This amount of storage could only be provided by a hard disk which, in turn, required a magnetic tape unit for back-up purposes.

When using the PASCAL/M interface to the database the RAM is split into 8 parts as shown in fig. 6.1.

The 10 Kbytes of RAM available for the database schema together with the database page buffer and the 15 Kbytes of RAM available for the PASCAL library together with the PASCAL/M P-code program and run-time stack were identified as possible areas for concern. However, it was not possible to achieve a better memory mapping in an 8-bit microcomputer and so the possible limitation in available RAM was accepted.

In any highly interactive system such as a database system, it is important that information, once retrieved, is transmitted to the visual display unit (VDU) without a delay which is perceptible to the

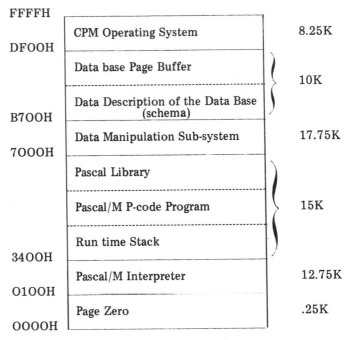

Fig. 6.1 RAM allocation.

operator. This was an immediate consideration in choosing the microcomputer.

The microcomputer system chosen comprised a Z—80A 8-bit microprocessor operating at a clock speed of 4 MHz with 64 Kbytes RAM, a 10 Mbyte hard disk unit, a 13.5 Mbyte magnetic tape unit, a 0.5 Mbyte floppy disk unit, a VDU and keyboard, and a dot matrix printer with an operating speed of 150 characters per second.

At the time of purchasing this system, the first 16-bit microcomputers were being announced. These were not considered to be suitable for this investigation on the grounds that:

- some, if not all, were using operating systems designed for 8-bit microprocessors thus cancelling the advantage of the higher clock speeds
- most were expensive
- all were untried
- most importantly, PASCAL/M and the DBMS were not yet available on the 16-bit systems

Some of the dificulties which might be met in estimating and meeting resource requirements have been referred to above. In respect of the software, the main difficulty is not knowing how the response time will degrade for input/output operations as the database fills up with data. The software designers recognise that there is a degradation and this can be ameliorated by having sufficient database buffer capacity. However, no benchmark tests exist because of the individuality of each database design. There is a concomitant lack of precision in estimating how much RAM is used for a given design and this leads to uncertainty in the availability of database buffer capacity.

One of the main difficulties in any application area which, like education, is continually evolving and developing is in anticipating change and allowing for it in the design. Thus a very strong input is required from the end-users who need to know, not just what one school requires but, what schools, in general, need.

THE APPLICATION: A SCHOOL INFORMATION SYSTEM

Since 1945, the demands upon the educational service in Britain have grown enormously and the service has become very expensive in its use of manpower. The number of administrative details undertaken in a school is consequently very large. Since the duration of this study was limited to two years in the first instance, it was decided to create an integrated data base to hold some of the basic information and serve some of the fundamental tasks in a school. A decision was made to include the structure of the school, the allocation of pupils, pupils' attendance and their assessment at the initial stage. The expansion of the database to cope with more administrative tasks and some potential usage of the database is also examined.

The approach is to identify and construct an information system which is capable of storing, retrieving and updating data which will reflect the organisational structure of the school, the hierarchy of responsibility and the information flows, and be capable of coping with the volume of information and its processing in a reasonable time. The structure of the database will enable the information pertaining to the goals to be achieved or, at least, be consistent with these goals. In particular, information necessary for curriculum development and pupil assessment is mandatory together with adequate security control with respect to access to the data. One essential feature should be the consistency and integrity of the data and a desirable aim is to enable the head teacher to respond more quickly to parental enquiry on an individual pupil or to enquiries on groups of pupils from the educational authority.

Any information system should be comprehensive within the school, should be flexible to enable widespread implementation, and be able to respond to the dynamic nature of school organisation and administration within the educational process.

The most important information in a school is pupil-based and concerns the pupil response to teaching. Such information is of immediate import to the class teacher who is concerned with monitoring the effectiveness of his teaching as a function of the response of the pupils. It is also of consequence to the departmental head responsible for the teaching of the subjects of that department and, ultimately, to the headteacher who is responsible for the school. However, a computer-based information system requires all information which is related to the teaching of pupils to be processed and available for certain purposes. Thus, information on teaching departments, their composition, the subjects taught and at what level, as well as which subjects each teacher is qualified to teach are clearly essential.

The information generated in a school is used for administrative and managerial purposes. Pupil-based information is generated in the register class where attendance is recorded (a legal requirement) twice daily, in the teaching section where assessment of response to teaching is carried out, and in the supervised aspects of the curriculum where social activities are monitored. Pupil report cards are sent, usually once a term, to parents giving an informative synopsis of each pupil's academic achievements. Aggregate information on pupils is sent as required to the local education authority who are responsible for all aspects of the provision of education and to the Scottish Education Department who are responsible for the planning of education and the inspection of schools nationally.

A series of forms, eighteen in all, were designed to capture the data required to maintain the school database. The forms are used for the input, modification, or deletion of data on the record types of the database. Each form identifies the user, the computer program which processes the data, and the fields of the record together with their length, type and, where applicable, range of values. The pupil record, for example, consists of the data items shown in fig. 6.2. The pupil record form, to be completed by the assistant headteacher (AHT) or the principal teacher of guidance (PTG) responsible for the house, if any, to which the pupil belongs is as shown in fig. 6.3.

Additional computer programs are required to retrieve information from the database according to the application involved, e.g. aggregate information for external statutory agencies.

The requirement for a computer within the school is the capability of running the software which will support an integrated database containing information on the school, teachers, pupils, departments, subject and their levels, pupil sections, pupil assessments, marks processing, report cards, and the organisational structures to which these entities belong.

PUPIL RECORD (without Personal Particulars)

Item no.	Name	Type	Description
1.	PUPILN	Numeric	Pupil's identification number which is unique for each pupil. Values range from 1 to 32767.
2.	PSNAME	Alpha(16)	Pupil's surname. Not more than 16 characters.
3.	PFNAME	Alpha(16)	Pupil's forename(s). Not more than 16 characters.
4.	DOB	Alpha(8)	Pupil's Date-of-Birth. Format is YY/MM/DD.
5.	SEX	Alpha(1)	Sex. (F/M). F for Female, M for Male.
6.	PHOUSE	Alpha(14)	The name of the House to which the pupil belongs. Not more than 14 characters.
7.	PCLASS	Alpha(6)	The name of the Register Class to which the pupil belongs. Not more than 6 characters.

Fig. 6.2 The pupil record.

A computer which meets these requirements could, quite clearly, be used for the education of pupils in computers and computing. However, one factor militates against this use. It is not possible to know in advance when the school database will be in use thereby making it difficult to timetable classes. For example, at the present time it may take several days to obtain information required to deal with a parental enquiry. With the computer database, such enquiries could be dealt with in less than an hour and an appointment made for a parent to meet the appropriate member of staff on the same day. Also, the falling cost of microcomputers makes it likely that schools will be able to afford at least one other system which would be used solely for teaching purposes.

The most important aspect of the expansion of the use of the microcomputer within schools lies in the areas of curriculum reform and continuous assessment.

Two reports (Munn, 1977) and (Dunning, 1977) on secondary education in Scotland provide ample evidence of a keen professional interest in assessing pupil progress, in matching the curricular experience of pupils to their needs, and in providing a basis of evaluation of proposed reforms in teaching methods and the curriculum. If these proposals are implemented, it would result in an

Input/Modify/Delete   Program PUPILR
                                                To be filled in by AHT/PTG

PUPIL RECORD   YEAR: _ _ _ _ _

PUPILN	PSNAME	PFNAME	DOB	SEX	PHOUSE	PCLASS
	POSFAM	LASTSCH				
	ADDRESS			ENTRYDT	DOCPHONE	
	LGSNAME	LGFNAME	LGPHONE	RELATION	LGOCCUP	
	LGEMP			EMPPHONE	MUMEMP	
	REPSTAGE	TAKENSCE	DTOFLV	PARISH	BUSSERV	BUSCONTR

Fig. 6.3 The pupil record form.

increased staffing requirement of 3.4%. In particular, the implementation of the Dunning Committee's proposals to extend the nature, purpose and scope of assessment procedures would have important repercussions on the administrative structure of secondary schools. The work involved in the tabulation, accumulation and combination of marks would be considerable and computer facilities will be necessary. Assessment undoubtedly requires additional staff time but there is considerable potential for containing this by the use of computers (SED, 1979).

Many schools have been using computers to assist in a variety of single-task administrative uses such as marks processing, choice of option blocks, and so on. However the investigation of an integrated approach to process all inter-related administrative tasks has not been examined. Clearly, the amount of information in a school is finite, and many administrative tasks are closely related often using the same basic data. If these tasks are dealt with separately with the aid of computers, many files would have to be created to hold the relevant information. Such an approach will end up with a huge number of files, each of them being used for a specific task. Inevitably, some information will exist in a number of files, and to maintain the consistency of these files would be a very time-consuming and tedious task.

The above considerations made it quite clear that the database system should be designed not just for the present school management system but for the system which would encompass the variety of curricula envisaged by Munn and the continuity of assessment proposed by Dunning.

A main application of the database system would be that of continuous assessment, and the allocation of sufficient storage to implement such assessment together with the processing of raw marks for the variety of subject levels would be a first priority. However, such an application requires data to be stored and retrieved and operations such as these also require application programs.

Several objectives were set when writing the application programs in PASCAL/M.

(a) Programs should be user-friendly. The programs are to be used by users such as teachers, operators etc., who do not have much knowledge about the computer. Hence they must be as easy to use as possible. Menu driven functions could be used to ease the operations.

(b) Programs should be well-structured and be easy to amend. Many programs will be written to perform functions like input new record occurrences, modify existing record occurrences and delete exising record occurrences. If the programs are written such that they are all based on a similar programming structure, then a user will find it very easy to amend any of them once he has fully understood the programming structure.

(c) Programs should make full use of available RAM. One of the main disadvantages of using the micro-computer is the limitation of RAM available to the programmer. Previously it was stated that the amount of RAM which could be used for the PASCAL P-code is about 15K. In order to produce a more user-friendly environment, each application program should have as many prompts as possible. In other words, a bigger program with more P-code. The potential problem can be reduced since PASCAL/M supports a program overlay feature by using Segment procedures. Such procedures are only loaded into RAM when they are called, and the portion of RAM used is free for other usage after exiting from these procedures. However, up to 10 segment procedures only are allowed, hence these must be used wisely.

Fifteen application programs have been written, and their functions are listed below. Each application program is used for only a few types of Records. The following are all the application programs, and the Record Types with which each one deals are given in fig. 6.4. Apart from programs PUPILAT and LPUPREP, the programs are used for four operations on each type of Record. These operations are:

- input new record occurrences
- list all record occurrences
- modify existing record occurrences
- delete existing record occurrences

Program Name	Record types	users		
		PTD	RGT	SUBT
TEACHER R	TEACHER RECORD.			
SCHR	SCHOOL RECORD.			
SCHOOL	YEAR RECORD, HOUSE RECORD, and REGISTER CLASS RECORD			
PUPILR	PUPIL RECORD	X		X
PUPILAT	PUPIL ATTENDANCE RECORD			X
DEPTR	DEPARTMENT RECORD and SUBJECT RECORD.		X	
LOSR	SUBJECT LEVEL RECORD		X	
CATR	SUBJECT CATEGORY RECORD		X	
SECTR	SECTION RECORD		X	
PSR	PUPIL SECTION RECORD		X	
ASSR	ASSESSMENT RECORD		X	
PASSR	PUPIL ASSESSMENT RECORD		X	
MP	MARKS PROCESSING RECORD		X	
REPORT	REPORT CARD RECORD		X	X
LPUPREP	LIST PUPIL REPORT CARD		X	X

X : Denotes users in a particular group who are not allowed to use the program, eg. for program PUPILR, users in PTD and SUBT groups are not allowed to use this program. All other users are allowed to use any programs listed above.

Fig. 6.4 The application programs used.

The forms mentioned earlier were designed to help the school to create its database. Every data item in each form is fully described, and if there is any constraint applied to the values of an item, this is stated in the description. The top right hand corner of each form identifies the person who is expected to complete it, and the name of the application program to be used in conjunction with it. Items which are to be verified by the computer are embedded by square brackets. The operator does not have to type in such items, but has to ensure that they are consistent with the values displayed by the computer. These forms can also be used to modify or delete items or records in the database by deleting the non-appropriate operation mode(s) in the top left hand corner of the form. When the modification mode is selected, it is recommended that three lines should be used for modifying one record. The first line indicates the record to be modified, the second line indicates the modified entries, and the third line is left blank for legibility.

When a form is completed, it is passed to the operator who runs the appropriate application program and performs the required operation. After which, the operator may produce a listing of the resulting records in the database for verification by the person concerned.

When the database is initialised, it contains only the description of each data item, record type and set type. Apart from this, there is no information about the school, pupil, or teacher, etc. in the database. Hence the very first application program to be run is SCHR, which can be used to input information about the school. After this information is inserted into the database, program TEACHERR can be run to input teachers' records and personal particulars. The third program SCHOOL enables information about Houses, Register Classes, and Years to be inserted. After which, the operator can either run application program DEPTR or PUPILR to input information about subject departments and the subjects which they offer in the school, or the pupil's records and their personal particulars, respectively. Once program DEPTR has been run, programs LOSR, CATR, SECTR can be run consecutively to input information about the level of each subject, their categories of class and the teaching sections in each category. After this information is stored the program PSR can be run to input information about pupils and the teaching sections to which they are allocated. After the program PSR is run, the basic information to be stored in the school database is complete.

The program PUPILAT is run at the end of each week to input information about pupils' attendances. If any assessment test has been given to the pupils, program ASSR, MP is run to store information about the assessment and program PASSR run to input the pupils' performance. By the end of a term, program REPORT is run to set up the content of the pupils' report cards and program LPUPREP run to produce a report card for each pupil.

The procedure governing the input of data into the database is illustrated by the network diagram illustrated in fig. 6.5.

THE ENVIRONMENT

There are three aspects of the environment which impinge on the school database design — that of microcomputer systems, of school staff, and that of secondary schools in general.

From the beginning of a preliminary investigation in 1979, progress in microcomputer technology has been rapid and many computer systems were rapidly becoming out-of-date. The school had purchased an 8-bit microcomputer in 1978 which, at that time, was in the forefront of microcomputer systems designed for educational purposes. However, this system was found to have severe limitations from the database point of view due to certain design features. The microcomputer possessed a systems program which served the dual purpose of controlling both the cassette operating system and disk operating system configurations. This was expensive in random-access storage and together with the CP/M operating system reduced the nominal 64 Kbyte RAM to 50 Kbytes. The development and growth of the school database design made the replacement of this system inevitable.

The second aspect of the environment concerns staff. Schools in Britain employ no trained computer staff. Computing is mostly taught within mathematics departments and it is from the mathematical sciences that excursions into the realms of computer administration tend to begin. Such forays have limited aims although they might be of general use. A vital requirement of the database system is that it should be able to be used by an operator with no more than basic typewriting skills. This would certainly make it possible for teachers, especially senior members of the management hierarchy, to use the system if required. Such a circumstance might arise if administrative staff, who are members of a clerical union were instructed not to use the microcomputer. This was a real fear during our experimental investigation and steps were taken to avoid dispute. Of course,

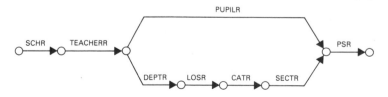

Fig. 6.5 Flow of data to set up the database.

implementation of the database system runs the risk of trade union dispute and this is a problem which the headteacher may yet have to face.

The difficulty that the non-specialist user faces is the problem of understanding the schema as a whole in all its complexity. While the DBMS chosen supports both database and physical schemas, it does not support sub-schemas. Thus it was decided to create a menu-type man—machine interface which would list the options open to a user within one of the defined user groups. On running a program which interfaces with the database, the user is asked for his user group and his password. If these are valid, the database is opened and a menu of all record types which are subject to this application program is listed on the visual display unit. After a record type is selected, the user is offered a further menu containing those options appropriate to the user's group. Thus the menu:

PUPIL RECORD
1. FINISH
2. LIST ALL RECORD OCCURRENCES
3. INPUT NEW PUPIL RECORD
4. MODIFY PUPIL RECORD
5. DELETE PUPIL RECORD

would be available to the RECTOR group which is the highest group, whereas all other user groups would have the curtailed menu consisting of items 1 and 2.

From this stage onwards, the user is guided by the program through the operations to be performed. Instructions are given on what data should be input so that the system can be used without reference to an instruction manual.

One of the nurses in the school was trained to use the computer system. After one hour of training and a few hours of practice, she had gained confidence in using the system and was able to input, delete, modify or list records when required, by answering the questions prompted by the computer. She was also trained to perform the backup operation on the database by dumping the database file onto magnetic tape at the end of the day. The nurse was quite amused to learn that she had simply to put the cartridge into the magnetic tape unit and type 'TAPE BACKUP' and the microcomputer would automatically do the backup.

The third aspect of the environment which impinges the school database design is that of the structure of secondary schools, in general. Although the design of the schema is based on one school, Garrion Academy, it is believed that the design is suffcently general to apply to most schools in Britain, at least. While many of the entities in the schema are common to most schools, the factors which do vary from school to school are:

- the maximum number of subjects that can be offered to each pupil
- the total number of pupils in each year group
- the total number of assessments performed in each subject at a given level

These factors are parameters of the design and later a sensitivity analysis of the size of the database with respect to these parameters is given.

THE DBMS USED

Preliminary investigations had shown that a file management system would be inadequate for our purposes and that an integrated database system would be required to facilitate data independence and minimise data redundancy. Our experience in writing a file management system indicated that we would have insufficient time to write an integrated Database Management System (DBMS) and to develop the school database schema. A survey was made of commercially-available DBMSs and one of these, from the U.S. company Micro Data Base Systems Inc. (MDBS), was chosen on the following grounds:

- it supports CODASYL-type databases
- it provides good data integrity, data security and data-independence
- it can be executed in many different microcomputers under different operating systems
- it provides many host language interfaces to the database, e.g. COBOL, FORTRAN, PASCAL/M, PASCAL/Z, PL/1 and BASIC
- it provides three useful subsystems, one to restructure the database, one to recover the database when it becomes corrupted, and a powerful report-writer subsystem which allows users to interrogate the database without writing application programs

The database management system MDBS Version 1 was purchased at a cost of US$1900 (£950) in January 1981.

The microcomputer operating system was chosen to be the widely-used Control Program/Monitor (CP/M) Operating System. CP/M supports the programming language PASCAL/M and provides many useful packages, e.g. a word processor, for other purposes.

A computer language is required for writing programs which perform the basic operations of data entry, up-dating, retrieval and in addition, the many applications in which the data items are put to use, e.g. pupil report cards. One advantage sought from the computer language was the facility for supporting random access files. This was only available in the language PASCAL/M of the host languages which were available with MDBS 1. This language, which has a better structure than COBOL, FORTRAN and BASIC and is easier to learn than PL/1, also had the advantage of program overlay structures which make more efficient use of RAM. Thus PASCAL/M was adopted. At the present date, many languages have random access file support, including improved versions of PASCAL, and this is no longer a constraint on the development of the database systems.

Micro Data Base Systems (MDBS) is a CODASYL type of database management system which consists of two main pieces of software:

- Data Description Language (DDL)
- Data Manipulation Language (DMS)

The DDL has three integrated modes of operation:

- text entry/command mode, where data descriptions are entered
- line editing mode, where text lines are altered
- DDL analyser mode, where a database description is analysed and a database initialised

The DML system contains all the facilities required to manipulate the information in the database using application programs. The types of facilities can be classified into eleven classes:

Type	Description	Command Name
CREATE	create record occurrences	
	value unset	CR
	create and store value	CRS
ASSIGN	assign value of	
	an item in a record occurrence	SFX
	all items in a record occurrence	PUTX
GET	get value of	
	an item in a record occurrence	GFX
	all items in a record occurrence	GETX
DELETE	delete record occurrence physically	
	and logically	DRX
REMOVE	disconnect, logically, a member	
	from a set	RMS
	all members of an owner	RSM
ADD	add current run of unit to set	ACS
	add member to set	AMS

Type	Description	Command Name
SEARCH	search for a member/owner based on a given item value of the member/owner required	FINDM/O
	a given sort key value of the member/owner required	FMSK/FOSK
	find first member/owner in a set	FFM/O
	find last member/owner in a set	FLM/O
	find next member/owner in a set	FNM/O
	find previous member/owner in a set	FPM/O
SET	set currency indicators set current of run unit based on member/owner/record type	SCM/O/R
	set member based on current unit/member/owner/record	SMX
	set owner based on current unit/member/owner/record	SOX
	set record based on current unit/member/owner	SRC/M/O
OPEN	to open the database	OPEN
CLOSE	to close the database	CLOSE
MISC.	other DML routines which are not used in the application programs. (See MDBS user's manual for details.)	

where X can be C/M/O/R for current unit/member/owner/record type.

The order in which the database specification is presented to the DDL analyser is as follows:

```
FILE (optional)
        DRIVE
PASSWORDS
RECORD
        ITEM (optional)
SET
        OWNER
        MEMBER
END
```

Each line of text must be preceded by a four digit line number and a blank space so that column 1 would refer to the sixth character entered.

The FILE line defines the filename of the database, the number of disk drives involved, and the page size of the database.

The DRIVE line specifies the number of database pages that reside on a particular drive. The drives are numbered 1, 2, 3, ... according to the operating system. The maximal number of pages is 8191.

The PASSWORDS line defines the users who are allowed to access the database and specifies their passwords and access levels.

The RECORD line defines the start of a record description with the record name as a parameter.

The ITEM line defines a data item within the most recently-defined record type. Parameters include the item name, type, size and the number of applications of repeated items.

The SET line consists of two lines. The first line includes the set name, mode, type, and the second includes the owner order and sort key, and the member order and sort key.

The OWNER line specifies the owner record type of a set type.

The MEMBER line specifies the member record type of a set type.

The END line signifies the end of the database description.

CALLING DML ROUTINES FROM APPLICATION PROGRAMS

When calling DML routines from Pascal/M programs, external procedures have to be declared. For example:

```
TYPE CMDSTR: PACKED ARRAY [1:30] OF CHAR;
VAR  ER,TEANO   : INTEGER;
FUNCTION DMS(A:CMDSTR)      : INTEGER; EXTERNAL 1;
FUNCTION DMSINT (A:CMDSTR; B: INTEGER): INTEGER;
EXTERNAL 2;
```

To open the database a statement

```
ER: =DMS ('OPEN');
```

is inserted into the program.

The result of the external function call return by the DML is stored in variable ER. If the value is not zero, this indicates that some error has been encountered while calling the DML routine.

To find the teacher record occurrence with teacher number (TEANO) equal to 34, the statement

```
ER: =DMSINT ('FMSK, S5', TEANO);
```

is inserted into the program, where $S5$ is the set type which connects the teacher record type, as member, to the system record type, as owner.

Notice that MDBS is of an extended DBTG architecture in that *sets* can represent many to many relations between entities. The designer does not have to create 'connection' entities (or records) to overcome the restriction in DBTG sets that a record may only be a member in at most one occurrence of a given set type. Strictly speaking then, the DBMS used by the writer was an unconstrained network system.

AN INTEGRATED DATABASE APPROACH TO SCHOOL ADMINISTRATION

In terms of school organisation, Garrion Academy Secondary School is regarded as being representative of secondary schools within Strathclyde Region, which encompasses approximately half the Scottish population of school age.

In the school, teaching staff are classified into seven categories:

(a) The Rector. The head of the whole school and decisions of any consequence in the school are made or approved by him.

(b) The Depute Rector. When the Rector is not available, the Depute Rector stands in for him, and makes the decisions the Rector would have made. He is also responsible for the general day-to-day running of the school.

(c) Assistant Head Teachers:

  (i) Assistant Head Teacher of Guidance (AHTG). The AHTG is in charge of all guidance teachers in the school. The function of guidance is to promote and monitor the personal, social, academic and vocational development of each pupil, this being done through close contact, formal and informal, being made and nurtured in the 'house'.

  (ii) Assistant Head Teacher of Schools (AHT). There are three assistant head teachers in Garrion Academy, one for each of the upper, middle and lower schools. The AHT of upper school is responsible for the supervision of the curriculum and careers guidance and parent liaison in the fifth and sixth years, providing information on universities and colleges, and writing references for pupils going on to higher education. The AHT of middle school has responsibility for parent liaison and the curriculum in the third and fourth years, with particular reference to developing suitable curricula for those who will leave school at the statutory leaving age. The AHT of lower school is in charge of liaison with primary schools, arranging visits for the new intake and meetings for their parents, allocating pupils to courses and houses, and has responsibility for supervising the curriculum in the first and second years. The AHTs of schools are responsible for discipline in their respective year groupings.

(d) Principal/Assistant Principal Teacher of Guidance. There is a Principal Teacher of Guidance (PTG) in charge of each of the

Houses in the School. The PTGs are responsible for the welfare of the pupils allocated to their houses. In Garrion Academy, there are altogether five houses, namely, Fleming, Livingstone, Scott, Watt and Hunter. Pupils in the first, second, third and fourth years are allocated randomly to the first four of these houses, and pupils in Hunter comprise the entire fifth and sixth years. For every house, there is at least one assistant principal teacher of guidance (APTG) to share the workload with the PTG of that house. These guidance teachers are responsible to the AHTG for the welfare and pastoral care of their house.

(e) Principal/Assistant Principal Teachers of Department. The principal teacher of department (PTD) is in charge of the teaching in his/her subject, and is responsible for the progress of the pupils taking this subject. If it is a large department, one or two assistant principal teachers of department (APTD) will be appointed to assist the PTD of that department.

(f) Register Class Teachers. Pupils are allocated to register classes, and each register class teacher (REGT) is responsible to the AHT of the year and to the PTG of the house for attendance and some aspects of pastoral care.

(g) Subject Teachers. Pupils are grouped into different sections for teaching purposes either according to their ability or mixture of abilities depending on the nature of the subject. The subject teachers (SUBT) in a department who are qualified to teach a particular subject(s) are assigned to teach certain sections. They are responsible to the PTD of the department for the progress of the pupils in their sections.

The organisation chart of Garrion Academy can be illustrated as shown in fig. 6.6. It can be seen that the teaching staff are organised into a hierarchy, with teachers lower down the hierarchy reporting to those higher up. The Rector has over-all responsibility for all activities in the school, the PTDs are responsible to him for the teaching in their departments, and the subject teachers are responsible to their PTDs for the teaching of their sections.

There are three categories of information concerning pupils which are very important:

- personal particulars and family background
- attendance
- assessment of performance

The information flow from one category of teacher to another is best illustrated by the information flow chart given in fig. 6.7.

The SUBT and PTD are grouped together and this is shown as a

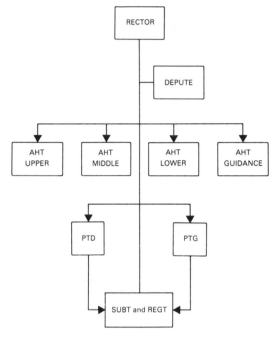

Fig. **6.6** An organisation chart.

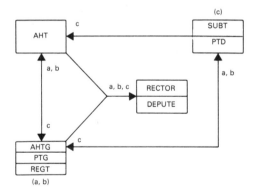

Fig. **6.7** An information-flow chart.

rectangular box in the diagram. This shows explicitly that information is exchanged between SUBT and PTD. While this exchange is
two-way, clearly information on performance from SUBT to PTD
is mandatory whereas information in the opposite direction is at the
discretion of the PTD. Similarly, AHTG, PTG, and REGT are also
grouped together since their major functions are in the same
classification. Letters a, b and c are used to indicate information

about pupil's particulars and family background, attendance and assessment of performance respectively. When they are embedded in parentheses, it means that such information is available from the categories of teachers in the adjacent rectangular box. Unembedded letters indicate transmitted information which is obtained from another category of teachers. The head of an arrow shows the direction of the information flow. Note that the RECTOR and his DEPUTE can obtain the attendance of pupils either from the AHT or from the AHTG/PTG/REGT in charge of the pupils.

There are many kinds of relationship between one teacher and another. For example, a REGT may be responsible to PTG for the welfare and behaviour of a class. He may also be a teacher in chemistry department responsible to the PTD of chemistry for the teaching and progress of his sections in chemistry. One of the reasons why a teacher may be involved in so many relationships is because of increased specialisation in schools. In small schools in the past (and even today in some areas) the Rector alone was responsible for the welfare and behaviour, attendance and academic progress of his pupils and perhaps also for some of the everyday teaching in school. In large schools with many teachers, no one person can retain all the information pertaining to all pupils so that communication is of the utmost importance. There is exchange of information between teachers within the same subject, within related subjects, e.g. the science subjects, and within some organisationally-related subjects, e.g. the social studies subjects. It is essential that lines of communication are clear-cut with respect to responsibility. However, it is acknowledged that there does exist informal communication through the medium of staff room discussion.

As far as pupil organisation is concerned, pupils enter the school after primary education to 12 years of age and, generally speaking, progress through the school at yearly intervals. Pupils are allocated to a registration class where the attendances are marked; they are organised into teaching sections according to ability, mixed ability, or possibly sex. The registration classes may be composed of pupils from the same house if the school has a house system and register classes based upon it, or they may be mixed. Schools also differ in the choice of curriculum given to the pupils. Some schools decide between pupils on the basis that some are academic pupils and will, therefore, take an academic course, non-academic pupils take a non-academic course. Others decide on the basis of the pupils' ability in a particular subject what level of teaching is offered in that subject.

At the moment, the time required to obtain information on the performance of pupils is quite considerable. When a parent enquires about his child's performance, either the AHT or AHTG in charge of the pupils has to gather the pupil's performance in all the subjects taken. This means that all the relevant PTDs are involved and eventually the individual subject teachers. The AHT or AHTG also has to consult the REGT of the pupil to obtain his attendance. The number of teachers involved in such an enqiry means that there may be a delay of as much as three days to collect the required information. This manual system and the time delay could easily influence the quality of the information and have adverse effects on the decisions made either by the Rector or by the parents.

Local Authorities and the Scottish Education Department, from time to time, require survey information about pupils in specified categories. To obtain the list of pupils in these categories can take several weeks of intensive effort. On the other hand, the Depute Rector is also responsible for certain annual statistical returns to the Local Authorities. In order to produce such returns, the Depute Rector has to collect information from AHT, PTG, PTD, SUBT or REGT, and thus most teachers are involved. Once the Depute Rector has obtained the information, he may have to carry out some analyses, or provide certain summaries of the information from the teachers. Again, considerable time delays are inevitable and information collected by central authorities may be out-of-date by the time decisions based on the information are made.

No matter how the school is organised, the information flows within the school, especially information on the pupils, are of fundamental importance. The volume of information, and the speed of processing or obtaining the information are important considera tions and, even at the most mundane levels, are beyond the capabilities of a significant number of extra teachers. Ideally, the information obtained in the school should provide evidence of the school's achievement of its goals.

DATA ANALYSIS AND DATABASE SCHEMA DESIGN
Having considered the problem of information within the school, the next step is to perform a data analysis study. The main objective of data analysis is to investigate the 'natural structure' of the information to be stored, (this means deciding exactly what are the relationships between individual items of data). The purpose of database schema design is to produce a representation of the data which can be manipulated by the particular DBMS being used.

The information stored within the database is a model of the real world. It is desirable that the structure for the information stored in the database should be close to the natural structure of the data in the 'real world' situation. If the two are similar, the database structure should be capable of easily representing all the real world situations that are likely to occur. It is important to stress that data analysis is not yet a science, hence the database schemas derived by a different people exhibit minor differences.

A few important terms used for our data analysis study may be described as follows. These terms relate to the particular DBMS which is used:

A *record type* is a concept of fundamental importance. For example, PUPIL or REGISTER CLASS. A record type defines many *record occurrences*. For example, pupil A. Smith can be represented as a PUPIL occurrence, and pupil J. Brown as another occurrence. The diagrammatic representation of a record type is a rectangular box containing the record name.

A *data item type* is a descriptive characteristic of a record. For example, teacher-name, or register-class-teacher.

A *set type* is used to define a relationship between two or more record types. For example, in reality, a register class comprises a number of pupils. Thus the record type REGISTER CLASS owns the record type PUPIL through the set type PUPIL-IN-CLASS. Diagrammatically, the set type is represented by an arrow labelled PUPIL-IN-CLASS directed from the owner record type REGISTER CLASS to the member PUPIL. Since a pupil belongs to only one register class then this set type is a one-to-many $(1 : N)$ relation.

The other relation types used are one-to-one $(1 : 1)$ as in the case of PUPIL to PUPIL-PARTICULARS (PUPPART), and many-to-many $(N : M)$ as in the case of PUPIL to SECTION where one SECTION record occurrence comprises the many pupils taught together for a specified subject while each PUPIL record occurrence can be related to many sections organised for the teaching of different subjects taken by the pupil. A *null set* is a set occurrence in which there is no member record occurrence connected to owner record occurrences.

Every set type has a *currency indicator* which indicates the current owner or member record occurrence of the set type. When a new record is stored in the database or connected into a set, its position in the set is determined by the currency indicator according to the specified set order.

The *set order* defines the logical order of member record occurrences within each occurrence of the set and is independent of the physical placement of the records. The set order options in our DBMS are First-In-First-Out (FIFO), Last-In-Last-Out (LIFO), SORTED, Immaterial (IMMAT), PRIOR and NEXT. FIFO and LIFO place a new member record occurrence last and first, respectively, in the set. Sorted member record occurrences are placed in either ascending order of sort key value, i.e. the smallest is first, or in descending order with the largest sort key value first. Ascending order is assumed for SORTED unless otherwise specified. In PRIOR and NEXT set orders, a new member occurrence is logically placed immediately before and immediately after, respectively, the record occurrence which is indicated by the currency indicator. If the currency indicator for the current member of the set type is null, the FIFO order is used for PRIOR and the LIFO is used for NEXT.

Finally, a storage class must be declared for each member in a set type, either automatic or manual. When a new record occurrence is created it is connected either automatically to one set occurrence of the set type or an instruction must be given manually to make the connection. Thus a full description of the set type PUPIL-IN-CLASS is a $1 : N$ relation, automatic storage class, with sorted key pupil-number (ascending).

The data analysis and database schema design was approached in a top-down manner and can be identified with the following steps:

(a) Identify all the basic record types first.
(b) Establish the relationships between these record types.
(c) Identify the secondary record types which are closely related to the basic record type and, at the same time, establish the relationships between them. Where there is an option in the design for connecting a record type to any other existing record type, then the speed of accessing for each case will be considered, and the most efficient one selected.
(e) Identify data items in each basic and secondary record types.
(f) Identify the set types and determine the nature of the set type, i.e. whether it is sorted or it is a $1 : N$ relationship and so on.
(g) Assemble the network.

The seven fundamental entities in schools are SCHOOL, YEAR, HOUSE, REGISTER CLASS, PUPIL, TEACHER and DEPART-MENT, and a record type for each of these entities was created in the database.

The record types and their contents are as follows:

SCHOOL :   has an occurrence which holds information about the school, e.g. name, address, etc.

YEAR :   has an occurrence for each year in the school and holds information such as the year tutor's name, etc.

HOUSE :   has an occurrence for each house in the school and holds information such as the house master's name.

REG. CLASS :   has an occurrence for each register class in the school and holds information such as the class room used and the class teacher's name.

DEPARTMENT :   has an occurrence for each department in the school and holds information such as the name of the principal teacher of the department.

TEACHER :   has an occurrence for each teacher in the school and holds information such as the teacher's name, identification number, and password to use the computer system.

PUPIL :   has an occurrence for each pupil in the school and holds information such as the name, date-of-birth, pupil identification number, etc. of the pupil.

At this stage of the analysis, although the identity of many data items for each record type is known, their formal identification is left until later in order to keep the analysis simple.

In a school, each pupil is allocated to a house, a register class, and a year. The criterion for allocating the pupils varies from school to school. Some schools do not have a house structure simply because their rolls are quite small or due to organisational preferences. Hence the design of the school database should be flexible enough to cope with these situations. Three set types are introduced at this stage to show the relationships between pupil and house, pupil and year, and pupil and register class.

The initial database schema is shown in fig. 6.8. Based on this design, no matter how pupils are allocated, the model is able to cope with it. If there is no house structure in a school, that record type can be ignored. At this stage, the set types are not determined, although the idea of sorting them by pupil's name, date-of-birth, or pupil's identification number does exist.

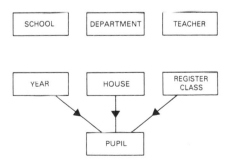

Fig. 6.8 The initial database schema.

In each school, a subject department offers a number of subjects. For example, a science department might offer physics, chemistry, biology, etc., a classics department might offer Latin and Greek. Each subject is offered at different levels to different year groups, for example, English for S1, English for S2 and so on. Each level of subject is offered to different categories of classes of pupils, for example, certificate level, non-certificate level, or mixed levels. Based on these facts, three more record types, SUBJECT, LEVEL OF SUBJECT, and CATEGORY are introduced, and three more set types have also been introduced to show the hierarchical relationships of DEPARTMENT, SUBJECT, LEVEL OF SUBJECT and CATEGORY, as illustrated in fig. 6.9.

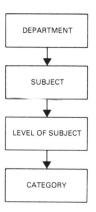

Fig. 6.9 An extension to the schema.

For each category of class, there are a number of sections, each taught by a teacher. Assessments are made of each pupil's progress in each subject taken according to the category of class of the section in which the pupil is taught. For example, in mathematics at a given level, one assessment test is given to 'certificate' classes, and a different assessment test (a comparatively simpler one) to 'non-certificate' classes. At this stage, two more record types and four more set types have been introduced as shown in fig. 6.10.

One of the most important items of information in schools is the result of the pupil's assessment. It is also the most difficult one to create in the database. It could be attached to each subject. For example, all the marks of the pupils taking physics are recorded in that subject and attached to record type SUBJECT. It could be attached to each assessment. For example, all the marks of certificate level pupils in assessment number 1 in physics are recorded in assessment 1 under category 'certificate level' in physics. It could also be

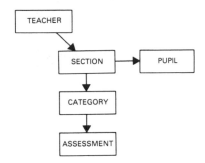

Fig. 6.10 Another extension to the schema.

attached to the pupils' records. For example, each pupil's assessments for 'certificate level' in physics are attached to the pupil. Hence there are at least three ways to organise the marks of any pupil in each assessment.

The first way does not give a good response if the marks of a particular pupil are wanted for all the assessments in all the subjects taken. Demands like this occur very often in schools, hence the first method is ruled out.

The second way gives a better response than the first, if the marks of the pupils are wanted in certain assessments of each subject studied. However it is still not a very good way to organise the marks of the pupils.

The last way is to attach the results of all assessments for each pupil to the PUPIL record type. The response in getting the marks of a pupil for all assessments is much better than the first two cases. However, to obtain information on the performance of pupils in a particular assessment, the response is not as good as that in the second case. Hence, some compromise is needed. It is assumed that, most of the time, teachers are concerned with a pupil's marks in all assessments and comparatively less interested in the performance of a class of pupils as a whole. However, it does not mean that this should be totally ignored. Thus, a decision was made to attach the marks of the pupils to the PUPIL record type and, at the same time, an index was introduced between the assessment and each pupil's performance in that assessment. Hence, the schema becomes that shown in fig. 6.11. The dotted line indicates that some sort of indexing or hashing method should be used so that the marks of all pupils in an assessment can be retrieved more efficiently.

In order to make the model flexible so that it is able to cope with different ways of assessing pupils, it was decided that in the record type GRADES AND MARKS, a maximum of ninety spaces would be allocated to hold the pupils' assessments. For each assessment, three

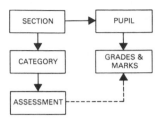

Fig. 6.11 Revised schema.

spaces are used for the assessment index number, the overall result, and the effort put in by the pupil. A maximum of six spaces are allocated to hold the results of the pupils performance in six different subject contents in the assessment. Therefore, for example, if it was decided that six subject contents should be assessed in each assessment for a particular subject at a particular level and category, then the total number of assessments that can be stored is $90/(6 + 3) = 10$. If it was decided that only three subject contents should be assessed in each assessment, then the maximum number of assessments that can be stored is $90/(3 + 3) = 15$. It is important to stress that different subjects have different ways of assessing the pupil performance. The suggested ways of organising the assessment results of the pupils makes it very flexible, and storage can be utilised to the best effect.

This flexibility is extremely important because of the wide variation in the frequency and, by implication, the content of each assessment across subjects and across schools. This organisation should make it possible to achieve the increased assessment called for by the proposals of Dunning in all schools. It is unlikely that any school will wish to record 80 items of data on pupil response to teaching in each subject which is, after all, equivalent to two data items per week.

When producing the pupils' report cards only certain assessments in each subject are recorded in the report cards. Hence a record type REPORT has been introduced to hold the information on which are the assessments to be included in the report card. It should be attached to the YEAR record type since it is closely related to each year group. The database schema is now that illustrated in fig. 6.12.

At this stage, the data items in each record type can be defined, and the key data items underlined. As an example, let us consider the teacher record. As an element of the database, the teacher record type has two functions. The first is to supply information relating to each teacher which is essential for the operation of the database and its applications. The second is to hold the personal and professional information of each teacher which is required periodically by the Rector. In the first category there is the teacher's identification

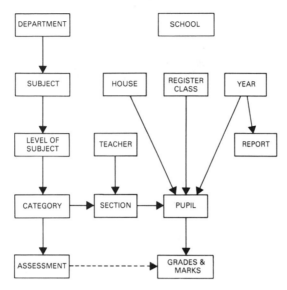

Fig. 6.12 Towards the final schema.

number which is the key data item, the teacher's name, and the teacher's personal password which allows access to the database system, in the second category, all other information relating to the teacher which is of legitimate interest to the Rector.

It is necessary, therefore, to split the teacher record into two records, one named 'teacher' and the other 'teacher particulars'. Clearly, there is a one-to-one correspondence between these two record types. These two record types are as follows.

Teacher record

Item name	Description
TEANO	Teacher's identification number which is an unique value for each teacher in the range 100 to 998.
TNAME	Teacher's name. Not more than 32 characters including space.
TPASS	Teacher's personal password. Not more than 12 characters.

Teacher particulars record (TEAPART)

Item name	Description
DOB	Teacher's Date-of-Birth. Format is YY/MM/DD. e.g. September 20th, 1936 is 36/09/20.

TEAPART (continued)

Item name	Description
FTEX100	Full time equivalent weight. Values range from 0 to 100 where 100(%) is used for a full time teacher.
TENTRYDT	The date of entry to the school. Format is YY/MM/DD as in item DOB.
FAPPT	The teacher's first appointment. Not more than 10 characters.
SUPNO	The teacher's superannuation number. Not more than 8 characters.
EMPNO	The teacher's employee number. Not more than 6 characters.
ADDRESS	Teacher's address. Not more than 50 characters.
PHONE	Teacher's telephone number. Not more than 14 characters.
UNIVCOLL	Teacher's university or college attended. Not more than 14 characters.
PROFHIST	Teacher's previous schools and dates. Not more than 30 characters.
PROFQUAL	Teacher's professional qualifications. Not more than 14 characters.
TRCOLL	Teacher's training college. Not more than 14 characters.
NOOFSUB	Number of subjects that the teacher is qualified to teach. Not more than 3 subjects.
SUBJECT	The subjects that the teacher is qualified to teach. Not more than 14 characters for each of them.

The other record types are similarly fully defined and any special features incorporated as required. For example, the record type ASSESSMT for Assessment contains a field IDXTOGM. This is an index which points to the location of the GRADMARK record, for Grades and Marks, that is used to store the performance of the pupil in this assessment as discussed earlier.

After the data items have been identified, we may formally identify the set relationships between the record types and hence the set types. Each set type has a name, an owner record type, a member record type, a storage class (either automatic or manual), a relationship, a set order, and a key data item. Thus the set types for the database schema of the school database are as follows:

Set name	Owner Auto/Manu	Relation	Member Set Order	Key item
S6	YEAR RECORD		PUPIL	
	Auto	1 : N	SORTED	PUPILN
HP	HOUSE		PUPIL	
	Auto	1 : N	SORTED	PUPILN
RP	REGISTER CLASS		PUPIL	
	Auto	1 : N	SORTED	PUPILN
TP	TEACHER		TEACHER PARTICULARS	
	Auto	1 : 1	IMMAT	
PP	PUPIL		PUPIL PARTICULARS	
	Auto	1 : 1	IMMAT	
DHASSUB	DEPT		SUBJECT	
	Auto	1 : N	SORTED	SUBNO
SLOS	SUBJECT		LEVEL OF SUBJECT	
	Auto	1 : N	SORTED	LOSNO
CAT	LEVEL OF SUBJECT		CATEGORY	
	Auto	1 : N	FIFO	
CS	CATEGORY		SECTION	
	Auto	1 : N	SORTED	SECTNO
TEACH	TEACHER		SECTION	
	Auto	1 : N	SORTED	SECTNO
CA	CATEGORY		ASSESSMENT	
	Auto	1 : N	SORTED	ASSESSN
PUPSECT	SECTION		PUPIL	
	Auto	N : M	SORTED	SECTNO for owner
			SORTED	PUPILN for member
PMCURR	PUPIL		GRADMARK	
	Auto	1 : N	SORTED	LOSNO
YY	YEAR RECORD		REPORT	
	Auto	1 : N	SORTED	REPORTN

In addition to the above sets, a few more sets have to be created to link all the record types, which are not a member of any set above, to the SYSTEM record type.

Set name	Owner Auto/Manu	Relation	Member Set order	Key item
SCH	SYSTEM		SCHOOL	
	Auto	1 : 1	IMMAT	
S1	SYSTEM		YEAR RECORD	
	Auto	1 : N	SORTED	YEARN
S2	SYSTEM		HOUSE	
	Auto	1: N	SORTED	HOUSEN
S3	SYSTEM		REGISTER CLASS	
	Auto	1 : N	SORTED	REGCLN

continued

Set name	Owner Auto/Manu	Relation	Member Set order	Key item
S4	SYSTEM		DEPT	
	Auto	1 : *N*	SORTED	DEPTNME
S5	SYSTEM		TEACHER	
	Auto	1 : *N*	SORTED	TEANO
S7	SYSTEM		LEVEL OF SUBJECT	
	Auto	1 : *N*	SORTED	LOSNO

The following sets are also required to retrieve the record occurrences in different orders:

Set name	Owner Auto/Manu	Relation	Member Set order	Key item
S51	SYSTEM		TEACHER	
	Auto	1 : *N*	SORTED	TNAME
S61	YEAR RECORD		PUPIL	
	Auto	1 : *N*	SORTED	PNAME
S62	YEAR RECORD		PUPIL	
	Auto	1 : *N*	SORTED	DOB
HP1	HOUSE		PUPIL	
	Auto	1 : *N*	SORTED	PNAME
RP1	REGISTER CLASS		PUPIL	
	Auto	1 : *N*	SORTED	PNAME

This completes the design of the database schema of the school database (Tannahill, 1983). The record types and the set types listed above define the complete schema illustrated in fig. 6.13.

ESTIMATING THE SIZE OF THE SYSTEM

Having selected the DBMS and having constructed the schema, the size of the database can now be calculated. According to the DBMS suppliers, the amount of storage required to hold a record type is $NRO * (5 + IS + 8 * NS)$ bytes.

Where NRO is the expected number of record occurrences of the record type.

IS is the number of bytes required for all the data items in the record type.

NS is the number of set types that are connected to the record type.

Hence the size of the school database can be calculated from this formula, and the result is shown in fig. 6.14.

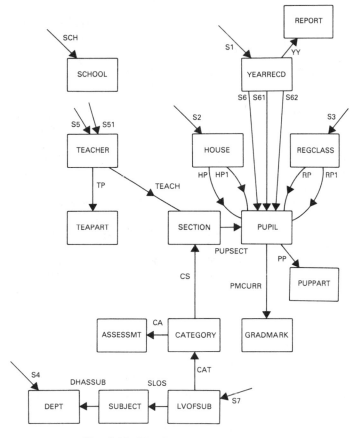

Fig. 6.13 The final database schema.

where Y is the number of year groups in the database.

         P is the number of pupils' records in the database.

         A is the expected number of assessments for a level of subject category of class.

        PS is the total number of record occurrences for record type GRADMARK. For example, if there are 300 pupils and each of them is allowed to study seven subjects, then the total number of record occurrences for record type GRADMARK is 300 * 7 = 2100.

     $PS/25$ the average sze of a teaching section is about 25 pupils, hence if 300 pupils, each studies seven subjects, then the expected number of teaching sections will be 300 * 7/25 = 84.

Record type	NRO	IS	NS	Storage required (bytes)
SYSTEM	1	0	8	69
YEARRECD	Y	20	5	65Y
REPORT	3Y	206	1	657Y
TEACHER	120	46	4	9960
TEAPART	120	240	1	30360
HOUSE	5	22	3	255
REGCLASS	12Y	16	3	540Y
PUPIL	P	56	10	141P
PUPPART	P	248	1	261P
GRADMARK	PS	4+18A	1	(17+18A)PS
DEPT	25	20	2	1025
SUBJECT	40	20	2	1640
LVOFSUB	40Y	10	3	1560Y
CATEGORY	40*3Y	8	3	4440Y
SECTION	PS/25	6	3	1.4PS
ASSESSMENT	40*3AY	108	1	14520AY
SCHOOL	1	106	1	119

Fig. 6.14 Database storage requirement.

Hence the size of the database (T) is estimated to be

$$T = 43427 + 7262Y + 402P + (17 + 18A)PS + 1.4PS + 14520AY$$

If the number of pupils and the number of subjects they are allowed to take is as shown in fig. 6.15 and it is expected that there will be ten assessments for each level of subject in each category, then the size of the database will be about 3.4 Megabytes.

YEAR no i	No. of pupils in year i (P_i)	No of subjects taken in year i (S_i)	$P_i * S_i$
1	250	10	2500
2	250	10	2500
3	250	8	2000
4	250	8	2000
5	180	5	900
6	80	3	240

Total P = 1260   Total PS = 10140

Fig. 6.15 Number of pupils and subjects.

The above formula, however, does not take into account the amount of RAM available for holding the database schema and the database input/output buffer. Now, it was noted in the introduction that these are allocated a total of about 10 Kbytes of RAM and are, therefore, interactive. According to the DBMS suppliers, the size of the table region of the database schema (D) in bytes is given roughly by:

D = 42
+ 25 * No. of record types
+ 21 * No. of items
+ 42 * No. of set types
+ 3 * No. of owners
+ 3 * No. of members
+ 30 * No. of passwords
+ 2 * No. of pages allocated to store the entire database
+ 44 * No. of disc drives

This yields

$$D = 42 + 25 * R + 21 * I + 42 * S + 3 * Ow + 3 * M + 30 * Pw + 2 * Pa + 44 * Dk$$

and since, for our database,

$R = 16$; $I = 92$; $S = 26$; $Ow = 26$; $M = 26$; $Pw = 6$ and $Dk = 2$,

hence $D = 3911 + 2 * Pa$

where Pa denotes the number of pages allocated to store the entire database. The number of pages available to the database page buffer (N) can be calculated from the given formula

$$N = \frac{10 \text{ Kbytes} - D}{Page \ size + 3}$$

where $Page\ size$ is the size of a page (in bytes) in the database as defined in the Data Description Language

Hence $N = \dfrac{1024 * 10 - 3911 - 2Pa}{Page \ size + 3} = \dfrac{6329 - 2Pa}{Page \ size + 3}$

or $Pa = 3164.5 - (Page \ size + 3)*N/2$

Thus, the size of the database is constrained to be

$(3164.5 - (Page \ size + 3) * N/2) * Page \ size/1024$ Kbytes.

The variation of the size of the database against N and $Page\ size$ is shown in fig. 6.16. Underlined figures indicate the maximum value of database size in each row. Thus, if $N = 2$, there are two pages of page buffer in the RAM, and selecting the page size to be 1536 bytes gives the maximum size of the database to be about 2.4 Megabytes.

In order to accommodate the school database which is 3.4 Mbytes, we have to choose $N = 1$, one page for the page buffer, with at least 1536 bytes as the page size. (Note that choosing a page size of 3072 bytes will give 4.8 Mbytes of database, and that the size of the database will decrease if page size is greater than 3072 bytes.)

Size of Data Base (Kbytes)

N	Page size	512	1024	1536	2048	2560	3072	3584
1		1453.5	2651.0	3592.5	4278.0	4707.5	4881.0	4798.5
2		1324.0	2137.5	2438.3	2227.0	1503.8	268.5	–ve
3		1196.0	1624.0	1284.0	176.0	–ve	–ve	–ve
4		1067.0	1110.5	129.8	–ve	–ve	–ve	–ve
5		938.5	597.0	–ve	–ve	–ve	–ve	–ve
6		809.8	83.5	–ve	–ve	–ve	–ve	–ve
7		681.0	–ve	–ve	–ve	–ve	–ve	–ve
8		553.0	–ve	–ve	–ve	–ve	–ve	–ve

Fig. 6.16 Available space for the database.

SENSITIVITY ANALYSIS

Although the design of the schema as described earlier is based on the structure of Garrion Academy, it is believed that it will also apply to most other schools. Almost all of the entities in the conceptual model such as house, register class, year, department, subject etc. etc. are commonly found in most schools. However, there are a few factors that will vary from school to school. These factors are:

(a) The maximum number of subjects that can be offered to each pupil in the school. Some schools have a bigger roll than others and correspondingly have more teachers in more subjects. This may allow pupils in years S3 and S4 in such schools to take up to 11 subjects, whereas in smaller schools this number might only be eight. This factor is very dpendent on the resources available.

(b) The total number of pupils in each year which depends directly on the size of the first year entry.

(c) The total number of assessments in each subject at a particular level. This is expected to vary from subject to subject as well as from school to school. Some subjects might prefer to have more frequent assessments in a few subject contents whereas others might prefer a few assessments in a larger number of subject contents. However, if Dunning's proposals are implemented, it is expected that more internal assessments will be required.

All these factors affect the size of the database, which in turn is proportional to the total number of pages assigned to the database. As noted earlier, every page of the database requires two bytes in the DDL tables situated in the RAM for identification. Hence, a bigger database, with more pages being assigned, occupies more space in the RAM, which in turn reduces the amount of RAM available for allocation to the database page buffer. If the amount of RAM available for the database page buffer is not sufficient to fit into one page of the database, no communication with the database is possible. In order to assess at what stage this happens, a sensitivity analysis was performed and the size of the database computed for a range of variation of the above three factors.

The analysis assumes that the minimal numbers of subjects offered to each pupil, according to year, are:

Year:	S1	S2	S3	S4	S5	S6
Number of subjects:	8	8	6	6	3	1

These numbers are allowed to vary from +1 to +4 simultaneously so that the maximal numbers of subjects are 12, 12, 10, 10, 7 and 5 in years 1 to 6 respectively. Thus the numbers of subjects given in fig. 6.15 correspond to columns headed + 2 in fig. 6.17. The values in each table are calculated using the formula for T above for the assumed number of assessments A in each subject and the given number of pupils P.

On the assumption that $A = 10$, the column headed + 2 gives the previously-assessed distribution of subjects over years confirming that the size of the database for Garrion Academy (1400 pupils) is about 3.4 Mbytes. The same table shows that if the total number of pupils is increased to 1860, then the size of the database increases to 4.48 Mbytes, which is still well below the 4.88 Mbytes available. However, if the total number of pupils is increased to 2160, a single database for the six year groups of pupils is not possible, since the size of the database increases to about 5.0 Mbytes. The critical value 4.88 Mbytes divides each column into two portions such that values above the dividing line are feasible databases having one database buffer page while those below the line are infeasible having none. However, if the number of assessments A is reduced to five, then a single integrated database for all six year groups is valid even though the total number of pupils increases to 2760, and the basic number of subjects offered for each year is increased by four since the size of the database will only be 4.416 Mbytes. Also, in the case of Garrion Academy, there are two database buffer pages available. On the other

Number of assessments A = 5

P	no. of subject offered ⟶					
	+ 0	+ 1	+ 2	+ 3	+ 4	
1260	1811	1945	2078	2211	2345	2
1560	2098	2263	2429	2594	2759	
1860	2385	2582	2779	2976	3173	
2160	2673	2901	3130	3359	3587	
2460	2960	3220	3481	3741	4001	
2760	3247	3539	3831	4123	4416	

Number of assessments A = 10

P	no. of subject offered ⟶					
	+ 0	+ 1	+ 2	+ 3	+ 4	
1260	2906	3150	3395	3639	3883	
1560	3334	3636	3939	4241	4543	1
1860	3762	4122	4483	4843	5203	
2160	4190	4608	5027	5445	5864	imp.
2460	4617	5094	5571	6047	6524	
2760	5045	5580	6115	6649	7184	

* imp: impossible

Number of assessments A = 15

P	no. of subject offered ⟶					
	+ 0	+ 1	+ 2	+ 3	+ 4	
						1
1260	4001	4356	4711	5066	5421	
1560	4570	5009	5448	5888	6327	
1860	5138	5662	6186	6710	7234	imp.
2160	5707	6315	6923	7532	8140	
2460	6275	6968	7661	8353	9046	
2760	6843	7621	8398	9175	9953	

Fig. 6.17 Storage space in Kbytes.

hand, if the number of assessments A is increased to 15, the size of the database (for the basic number of subjects + 2) becomes 4.71 Mbytes, and accommodates little more than 1260 pupils.

Nevertheless, the analysis shows that if an integrated database of six year groups, with 10 assessments (one every four weeks) and six subject contents in each assessment, for each level of subject in each category of class is constructed, the system is valid for the following combinations of number of pupils and number of subjects offered:

- maximum number of 1560 pupils, and number of subjects offered to S1, S2, S3, S4, S5 and S6 are 12, 12, 10, 10, 7 and 5 respectively
- maximum number of 1860 pupils, and number of subjects offered to S1, S2, S3, S4, S5 and S6 are 11, 11, 9, 9, 6 and 4 respectively
- Maximum number of 2160 pupils, and number of subjects offered to S1, S2, S3, S4, S5 and S6 are 8, 8, 6, 6, 3 and 1 respectively

These figures show that the system is valid for most cases, with exceptions where:

- schools have a very large roll (> 2500 say)
- schools which assess pupils more frequently than once every four weeks
- schools which offer more than 10, 10, 8, 8, 5 and 3 subjects to S1, S2, S3, S4, S5 and S6 respectively

PRIVACY

Passwords are the most common technique for protecting databases. A user who desires access to protected data must supply a password before access is allowed. A password may be used for the entire database or for any portion of the database down to the item level. For example, there can be a database password, database record password, and database item password. There can be several passwords for the same record or item.

In MDBS data protection is available down to the item level. Each user has a read and write access level which are numbers between 0 to 255. Every set type, record type, item type is also assigned to a read and a write access level. If the read access level of a user is greater than a read access level of a set type, a record type or an item type, then the user is allowed to read such set, record or item type. Similarly for the write access level. Thus, a user is allowed to read all the occurrences in a record type if his read access level is greater than the record read access level.

For example, the Rector is allowed to read/write all occurrences of the TEACHER record type and the TEACHER PARTICULARS record type, but any teacher is only allowed to read the TEACHER record type and not the TEACHER PARTICULARS record type. In this case, the read/write access level of the Rector must be greater than the read/write access level of the TEACHER and TEACHER PARTICULARS record types, and the read/write access level of the teacher must be greater than TEACHER record type but less than TEACHER PARTICULARS record type.

A different type of data protection is required in the case of pupils. Pupils are taught in different sections and it is natural that a teacher is only allowed to access information about the assessments of the pupils who are in sections taught by him. This is referred to as layer protection, distinguishing it from the level protection of the earlier example. Most DBMSs have level protection but do not have layer protection. To provide layer protection every teacher is given a personal password to be used to determine what information about which group of pupils can be assessed by the teacher.

There are altogether six user groups:

(a) REC: The Rector group which includes the Rector, his depute, and the operators.
(b) AHT: The year tutors group. The official status of a year tutor is Assistant Head Teacher.
(c) PTG: The Principal Teacher of Guidance group.
(d) PTD: The Departmental Principal Teacher group.
(e) REG: The Register Class Teacher group.
(f) SUBT: The Subject Teachers group which includes all teachers who teach at least one section of pupils.

Each user needs two passwords to gain entry to the computer system:

- the password of a user group
- a personal password

PASSWORD OF A USER GROUP
The assumption is made that any teacher can be classified in not more than one of the groups REC, AHT, PTG and PTD and that most teachers are classified in groups REGT and SUBT. It is important to stress that it is membership of a particular user group which allows a user to access the portion of the database relevant to that group. The actual data made available to a user is further controlled by the user's personal password, where this is required.

Teachers in groups SUBT and REGT share the same password since most subject teachers are also register teachers and it could cause confusion to have separate passwords. This password is four characters long. Teachers in groups REC, AHT, PTG and PTD have a different password for each group. Their passwords must be at least four characters long, and must not be more than 12 characters. The first four characters of these passwords must be identical to the password of groups REGT and SUBT.

For example,

User group	Group password
SUBT, REGT	OVER
REC	OVERBEAR
AHT	OVERVIEW

PTG   OVERSEER
PTD   OVERMANN

PERSONAL PASSWORD

Every teacher has a personal password which must not exceed 12 characters in length. Every teacher also has an identification number whose value lies between 100 and 998. The first three characters of a personal password must be the teacher's identification number.

If the teacher is an assistant year tutor, assistant principal teacher of guidance, or assistant departmental principal teacher, the 4th to 7th characters of his personal passwords must be identical to that of the year tutor, principal teacher of guidance, or departmental principal teacher respectively. These four characters are used as the code of the respective year group, house, or department.

For example

Teacher			Personal
No.	Name	Appointment	Password
105	Mr X	Teacher	105QWERTY
203	Miss Y	Teacher	203CODE
104	Mrs Z	Year Tutor of S1	104YRS1XYZ
133	Miss B	Asst. Year Tutor of S1	133YRS1CCC
111	Mr P	Principal Teacher of Guidance of Lister House	111ASEPMRP
136	Mr L	Asst. P.T.G. of Lister House	136ASEPPET
320	Mr T	Asst. P.T.G. of Cochrane House	320BRIGHHH
145	Mr G	Asst. P.T.G. of Cochrane House	145BRIGGGG
202	Miss D	Science Department Principal Teacher	202BOHRLAW
233	Miss V	Asst. D.P.T. of Science	233BOHR

In order to run an application program, a user has to supply the name of the user group, the password of the relevant user group and, if necessary, his personal password. For example, the year tutor (Mrs Z) who is in charge of year S1 might teach physics to section number 14266 in year S2. In order to access the marks of the pupils in that section, it is sufficient for the year tutor to supply SUBT (the subject teacher group) as the appropriate user group, OVER-VIEW (her group password as an AHT) as the group password and also her personal password. If she uses the year tutor user group, she will not be allowed to access the marks of the pupils in the section specified, since the pupils involved are in S2, and she is not in charge of Year S2. Similarly, if she is also the register class teacher of class 3TIO, which happens to be a class of pupils in year S3, she will have to use REGT, OVERVIEW and her personal password in order to access the attendance of pupils in that class.

In summary:

Year tutor of S1:   Mrs Z
User group password: OVERVIEW
Personal password: 104YRS1XYZ

Access information about pupils in	User Name	Group Password	Personal Password
S1	AHT	OVERVIEW	104YRS1XYZ
Section 14266	SUBT	OVERVIEW	104YRS1XYZ
Reg. Class 3T10	REGT	OVERVIEW	104YRS1XYZ

Thus the year tutor can enter the database either as a year tutor (AHT) or as a class teacher (REGT or SUBT) using the user group password OVERKING but the portion of the database which is accessed is specified by the user group name.

EXPERIENCE

Information is needed in secondary schools according to vertical stratifications of pupils, such as that which occurs in subject teaching and house structure for pastoral purposes. Information is also required according to a horizontal stratification according to the year structure and the sub-school structures identified for the purposes of the curriculum and its development. This pupil-based information on response to teaching and social interaction is required according to a horizontal stratification according to the year structure and the sub-school structures identified for the purposes of the curriculum and its development. This pupil-based information on response to teaching and social interaction is required to be available in various forms to facilitate the work of teachers charged with the responsibilities governing their functions within the school management system.

Three categories of pupil information were identified:

• personal particulars and family background
• attendance
• assessment of performance

Thus, flows of information from these information categories between four main category-groups of teachers were identified:

• rector, depute-rector
• assistant head teacher (sub-school)

- assistant head teacher of guidance, principal teacher of guidance, and register teacher
- principal teacher department, subject teacher

Information flows, largely mandatory, also occur within category-groups containing more than one category of teacher, generally in the upward direction of responsibility. The informational needs of pupil organisation in terms of allocation to register classes, houses, teaching sections, the level of teaching offered, and selection of subject options at appropriate times during progress through the school were identified and incorporated into the database.

No matter how a school is organised, the information flows within the school, especially those involving pupil information, are of fundamental importance. Any increase in the volume of data and the speed of obtaining and processing information are important considerations. Even a relatively mundane improvement of manual performance in these areas presumes a capacity beyond a significant number of extra teachers, even if economic circumstances allowed this possibility for local authorities.

Educational and practical considerations dictated the somewhat pragmatic approach to assessment as follows. The frequency and the content of an assessment is a matter for the professional judgement of the principal teacher of each subject. The frequency varies between subjects and both frequency and content vary within the same subject between schools. In order to try and accommodate the variation in assessment, a maximum of ninety spaces was allocated to hold the complete assessment for each assessable subject in each pupil's curriculum. For each assessment, three spaces would be allocated, one to identify the assessment, one for the overall result and the other for some measure of the effort put into the subject by the pupil. In addition, a maximum of six spaces would be allocated for the 'marks' obtained in the different subject contents in any assessment. The ninety spaces can be used flexibly in that an assessment might contain fewer than six subject contents and the subject contents need not be the same for each assessment. Thus if all six subject contents were used each time there would be a maximum of $90 / (3 + 6)$ giving a potential of 10 such assessments in the year or a frequency of once per month. If, on the other hand, only one subject content was assessed each time, the mark for that subject content would be the overall result and there could be a maximum of $90 / (3 + 0) = 30$ assessments in the year or roughly once a week. It is anticipated that this potential quantity of assessment data arranged in such a flexible manner will accommodate the continuous assessment proposed by Dunning (1977).

The design approach was to identify and construct an information system which is capable of storing, retrieving and up-dating data which reflects the organisational structure of the school, the hierarchy of responsibility, and the information and its processing in a reasonable time. The provision of information required for pupil assessment and curriculum development was regarded as being mandatory together with adequate security control with respect to access to the data. An essential feature of the database was the consistency and integrity of the data and a desirable aim was to enable the Rector to respond more quickly to parental enquiries on an individual pupil, or to enquiries from the educational authority on groups of pupils. Finally, the information system should be comprehensive within the school, be flexible in order to achieve widespread implementation, and be able to respond to the dynamic nature of school organisation and management within the education process.

Preliminary work indicated that the database should have a general network structure in order that the data model should accommodate the school organisational and management structures described above. The approach used in the construction of the database schema was the following.

(a) Identify all basic record types.
(b) Establish the relationships between these record types.
(c) Identify the secondary record types which are closely-related to the basic ones and establish the relationships between them. Where there are options in the design for connecting a record type to other existing record types, the speed of accessing and data volume for each case of data retrieval was considered and the most efficient one was chosen.
(d) Identify all data items in each basic and secondary record type.
(e) Identify the relationship set types and determine their nature, e.g. sorted, $1 : N$ relation, and so on.
(f) Assemble the complete database schema.

The basic record types identified were school, year, house, register class, pupil, department, subject, teacher and section. The secondary record types identified were report (year), pupil particulars (pupil), grademark (pupil), level-of-subject (subject), category-of-class (section and subject), assessment (subject and section), and teacher's particulars (teacher).

The first limitation encountered was due to the design of the school's only microcomputer. This microcomputer possessed a systems program which served the dual purpose of controlling both the cassette operating system and the disk operating system configurations. This was expensive in storage and together with CP/M reduced the available RAM to 50K. The development and growth of the school database design made the replacement of this system inevitable. A new system, the Clenlo Conqueror based on Morrow Designs, was bought at a cost of US$20 000 (£10 000) and installed in Garrion Academy in November 1981. This system comprised 64 Kbytes RAM, and 10 Mbyte hard disk unit, a 13.5 Mbyte magnetic tape back-up unit, a 0.5 Mbyte floppy disk drive unit, a visual display unit and keyboard, and an ANACON 150 dot matrix printer with an operating speed of 150 characters per second.

Three main factors were considered when choosing a micro-computer which was specific to our needs.

- does it have sufficient on-line storage?
- does it have sufficient RAM?
- is it fast enough?

An analysis of the database schema estimated the size of the database as

$$43427 + 7262\,Y + 402P + (17 + 18A)R + 1.4R + 14520A\,Y$$

where Y is the number of year groups;
   P is the number of pupil records;
   A is the expected number of assessments for a level of subject in a category of class;
   R is the number of record occurrences of assessment.

For a school of 1560 pupils making maximal use of assessment, the amount of storage required is about 3.4 Mbytes. Thus, on-line storage was deemed to be sufficient.

The availability of only 10 Kbytes of RAM for the database schema together with the database page buffer and 15 Kbytes for the PASCAL library together with the PASCAL/M P-code program and run-time stack were identified as possible areas for concern. However, it was not possible to achieve a better memory mapping in the 8-bit microcomputer and the possible limitation of RAM available was accepted.

The new microcomputer was designed round a Z80A central processing unit (CPU) which operates at a clock speed of 4 MHz. Tests on the microcomputer showed that input/output operations were fast and it did not suffer from the slow input/output functions of the previous machine which had to call the cassette operating system to perform these functions.

At the time of our survey, the first 16-bit microcomputers were being announced. They were not considered suitable for this investigation on the grounds that:

- some were using operating systems designed for 8-bit micro-computers thus cancelling the advantage of the higher clock speeds

- they were expensive
- and, most importantly MDBS and PASCAL/M were not yet available on the 16-bit systems

One advantage sought from the computer host language was the facility for supporting random access files. This was only available in the language PASCAL/M of the host languages which were available with MDBS I. This language, which has a better structure than COBOL, FORTRAN and BASIC and is easier to learn than PL/1, also had the advantage of program overlay structures which make more efficient use of RAM. Thus PASCAL/M was adopted. At the present date, many languages have random access file support, including improved versions of PASCAL, and this is no longer a constraint on the development of database systems.

The second and most important limitation encountered was due to the availability of only 10 Kbytes of RAM to the combination of the database schema and the database page buffer, mentioned above. Formulae supplied by MDBS for the size of the table region of the database schema reduced to the relation:

Size of database + (3164.6 − (*page size* + 3) * $N/2$) * *page size* / 1024 Kbytes,

where N is the number of pages available to the database buffer. Thus, size of database is quadratic in page size.

Fig. 6.16 shows the variation of the size of the database against N and *Page size*. The underlined figures indicate the maximal value in each row. In order to accommodate a school database of 3.4 Mbytes we can only achieve $N = 1$, one page for the page buffer, with at least 1536 bytes as the page size. The maximal size of database which can be constructed is 4.8 Mbytes using a page size of 3072 bytes.

The significance of the number of pages available to the database buffer lies in the reduction of the execution time as the number of pages available to the system increases. The primary cause of differences in execution speed is due to the number of disk accesses performed by the system. The more buffer pages resident in RAM, the greater is the chance that a given page will be resident in memory when it is required, thus saving a disk access. The actual CPU processing time is trivial compared to the amount of time spent on input/output operations.

The minimal number of buffer pages that must be available to the system is one. A significant decrease in speed was noted as the amount of data stored in the database increased although this levelled out and no further impairment of speed of data entry occurred. However, further tests need to be carried out in this area before any empirical relationship between size of database, volume of data, and speed of input/output operations can be derived.

Consideration was given to the splitting of the database into two or more smaller component databases in order to provide more buffer pages in RAM. For example, if the school database of 3.4 Mbytes is split into two equal-sized databases, both will be about 1.8 Mbytes and two pages can be allocated to the database buffer instead of one. However, the efficiency of increasing the number of buffer pages has yet to be measured.

One problem which will emerge if this approach is adopted is the introduction of data redundancy. Since year groups are natural divisions in the organisation of secondary schools in the United Kingdom it would be perfectly feasible to construct six databases, one for each year group. In such a case, the redundant information is contained in record types: school, teacher, teacher's particulars, department, subject, house and register class (if houses and register classes are organised across a number of year groups of pupils). The amount of redundant data is less than 46 Kbytes and is quite acceptable. None of the year group databases would exceed 0.8 Mbyte and each would have at least six buffer pages available. Some record types which are used only occasionally, e.g. teacher's particulars, could be removed from the database and stored in a file. This would avoid the danger that inconsistency is introduced if not all the year group databases are correctly up-dated. Thus, a combination of databases and files may be used when splitting the school database with some, not serious, loss of integration.

Although the design of the database schema is based on one school, Garrion Academy, it is believed that the design is sufficiently general to apply to many schools. While many of the entities are common to most schools, some factors do vary from school to school. Among these are:

- the maximum number of subjects that can be offered to each pupil
- the total number of pupils allocated to each year
- the total number of assessments performed in each subject at a particular level

All these factors will affect the size of the database which is expressed as a number of pages of the size selected. Since each page of the database requires two bytes for identification in the data description tables held in RAM, the more pages assigned to the database the fewer will be available for allocation to the database buffer. Clearly, if the amount of RAM available for the database buffer is not sufficient to fit into one page of the database of the size selected, no communication with the database is possible.

The database management system MDBS I had many advantages.

Both the DDL and the DML were an integral part of the DBMS. The DDL was fully adequate for defining the school database, analysing its description, and carrying out the initialisation. The DML system contains all the facilities required by the application programs to manipulate the information in the database. MDBS I facilitated the protection of data in the database against unauthorised disclosure, alteration, or destruction. The privacy of the database was achieved by using both horizontal and vertical divisions so that each user group could only access the data relevant to that user group. A severe disadvantage of MDBS I is the need to store the page hole index (2 bytes per page) in RAM thereby reducing the space available for the database page buffers. This defect is remedied in the very much more expensive MDBS III. The other disadvantage is one which is true of Codasyl-type databases and that is the extensive programming required for the many applications which the database supports.

The author of this chapter would like to acknowledge his grateful thanks to Mr W.L. Gold, rector of Garrion Academy, and to his research assistant, Dr T.H. Pang, without whom this study and the results achieved would not have been possible.

REFERENCES

Dunning, J (1977) *Assessment for all*, Scottish Education Department, Her Majesty's Stationary Office.

Munn, J. (1977) *The Structure of the Curriculum in the Third and Fourth Years of the Scottish Secondary School*, Scottish Education Department Consultative Committee on the Curriculum, Her Majesty's Stationary Office.

SED (1979) *Curriculum and Assessment in the Third and Fourth Years of Secondary Education in Scotland: A Feasibility Study*, Her Majesty's Stationary Office.

Tannahill, S.C., Pang, T.H. and Gold, W.L. (1983) *The Formulation of the School Management Information Problem*, available from the University of Strathclyde.

CHAPTER 7

Data Analysis

By D. Crabtree (independent computer consultant)

ANALYSING THE DATA FROM THE TOP

A few years ago the Kekule Chemical Company, a wholly owned subsidiary, decided that it would conduct a comprehensive, top-down study of its business information requirements. There are a number of well-established methodologies for studies of this kind. That year the one in fashion was IBM's 'Business Systems Planning' technique (IBM, 1975). A cornerstone of the overview was the identification of the essential processes carried out to operate the business and the general data categories needed to support these business processes. Some 125 business processes were identified in seven areas of activity, supported in all by 90 data categories, as shown in fig. 7.1.

The formal definition of a *data category* is a single representation of events, things, knowledge, requirements and computations relevant to the enterprise which are individually able to be expressed in unique and usually exact terms by descriptions, codes and numbers. The different concepts implicit in a particular data category are those judged to have an affinity from the view of their use in the enterprise. Formulation of the data categories was not a rigorous procedure.

Members of the study team, with a good knowledge of the Company sharpened by defining the business processes, tried as far as possible to put down data categories that were exclusive in meaning and between them covered the whole organisation. Each data category consisted of a one line name, a fuller definition of what was meant and a number of specific examples of low level data. The following was typical:

Name:	engineering materials movements data
Description:	data recording the movement of all engineering and building materials into Company stock from external companies and from Company workshops, the movement of stock within the Company (stocking points/sites of use), and the movement of stock to non-company sites

Marketing and business control
Sales product movements data —
    requirements
Sales product sales data — forecast
Sales product sales data — actual
Sales product movements data — actual
Sales product stock data
Transport data
Sundry materials data
Selling methods and regulations data
Customer description data
Customer support data
Economic data
Market description data — current
Market shares and performance data —
    current
Market description data — forecast
Market shares and performance data —
    forecast
Patent, tradename and copyright data
Competitor general description data
Competitor sales data
Competitor product description data
Competitor produce application data
Sales product techno/commercial data
Chemicals description data
Materials hazards data
Chemicals product research and development
    data
Publicity and promotion data
External authority data
Periodicals reference data

Manufacturing activities
Competitor manufacturing data
Chemical product manufacturing process
    data
Materials handling methods and regulations
    data
Services selling data
Plant and buildings performance data —
    actual
Production data — actual
Chemical (non sales product) movements
    data — actual
Chemical (non sales product) stock data
Plant and buildings performance data —
    planned
Production data — planned
Chemicals purchasing data — requirements
Chemical (non sales product) movements
    data — requirements
Plant and buildings performance data —
    requirements
Chemicals purchasing data — actual
Chemicals purchasing data — forecast
Chemical (non sales product) sales data

Supply
Competitor purchasing data
Supplier description data
Supplier relationships data
Services purchasing data
Engineering materials purchasing data

Business planning
Purchasing methods and regulations data
Engineering methods and regulations data
Financial methods and regulations data
Business performance data
Business objectives/targets data
Manpower data — target
Company organisation/structure data

Financial/accounting activities
Financial reference data
Non-chemical sales income data
Chemical sales income data
Purchased services costs data
Material costs data
Manpower costs data
Budgets data (inc. actuals)
Working capital data
Fixed capital data
Parent Company authority/instructions
    data

Engineering activities
Land data
Services description data
Engineering materials description data
Engineering equipment data
Plant and buildings construction data
Plant and buildings design data
Plant and buildings technical support data
Plant and buildings maintenance data
Engineering materials movements data
Engineering materials stock data
Plant and buildings description data
Operating methods and regulations data

Personnel
Personnel performance data
Personnel policy data
Terms and conditions data
Representation data
Procedures and employment regulations
    data
Job data
Training support data
Skills and experience data
Health and welfare data
Personnel description data
Manpower data — actual
Remuneration data
Work load data

Fig. 7.1 Data categories.

Data examples: name/code of material
                   quantity moved
                   quality, and other relevant data on material moved
                   date promised for shipment (v. date shipped)
                   mode of transport and carrier
                   data on delivery notes
                   date promised for delivery (v. date arrived)
                   sending location data
                   acceptance confirmation data by receiving location

Because the definition in each data category was so unstructured there was considerable difficulty in deciding which one to use in individual circumstances. The team relied on a thorough knowledge of all definitions of the categories and the data examples associated with them. It would have been impossible to cope with many more than 90 data categories.

The names of the data categories are shown in fig. 7.1 and give a good idea of the immense span of data dealt with by any commercial and manufacturing concern. The data categories are grouped under their seven headings, but of course the use of data in a category often spans several such headings. The groupings show where data is more likely to be used, and most likely to be raised or first introduced into the total information system.

It can be seen from the data categories that the choice of level of any data category is somewhat arbitrary. However, there is a limit to the depth, or fineness, of level of data. This limit is governed by two factors. First, there is a level that is most useful for information systems planning purposes. Clearly ten data categories to cover all the Company's data would be as worthless as 1000 categories would be unmanageable. Second, there is a level below which the theoretical relationships between data items becomes too confused. For example, consider the data items 'invoice number', 'customer code' and 'chemical order'. These are all valid free-standing items which also form a particular relationship when brought together called 'invoice'. At some point, as the level of data categories gets lower, the ability to deal with the increasing number of relationships that spring up becomes almost impossible. To go below that point requires special techniques that cannot be reconciled with the information systems planning aims of the Business Systems Planning methodology. In short, data analysis shows the sudden collapse from large, easily discussed concepts to the atomic particles of their constituents. The phenomenon is not confined to data. One of the most misleading diagrams used in data processing is shown in fig. 7.2, where the pyramid is supposed to divide top information systems from the middle control systems and the lower level data collection systems. In terms of imagery, numbers of systems, times to implement them and data volumes handled, the cake and candle in fig. 7.3 is a more accurate representation.

Fig. 7.2 Misleading view of data processing systems.

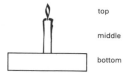

Fig. 7.3 A more accurate view of data processing systems.

Analysing data from the top is a worthwhile exercise if an overall view is required such as was sought from the Business System Planning exercise. There is no doubt that excellent business and general information system guidelines were produced and general data areas highlighted at the data category level. In an attempt to make the data categories useful at the lower levels several techniques were investigated. These included the librarian's faceted classification and decimal indexing methods (Vickery, 1960) and (Meadow, 1967). Unfortunately nothing could make the data categories useful as a starting point to more rigorous lower level data analysis. The categories could only remain general guidelines to the information systems they had been intended to serve in the first place.

DATA ANALYSIS

Despite the failure to make anything more of the data categories, the Kekule Chemical Company believed it was important to find some method of rigorously categorising data. For one thing the Business System Planning study had shown the advantages of analyses with long-term validity. For another, Kekule, with a heavy commitment to database methods, was aware of the theoretical need for a systematic means of representing data. This theory is simply explained. Earlier representations of database systems envisaged a physical schema (the physical database) and subschemas (individual views of the users) (CODASYL, 1971). But as old subschemas became obsolete or unimportant and new ones arrived, it would be necessary to change the old physical schema to a new form. It was feared that the new mappings from the new schema to the subschemas would then lead to inefficiencies or even breakdowns in the system — the very things database proponents said should not happen. Fig. 7.4 illustrates this. It is of course a representation of the facts of today's database situation. The fears expressed have become a reality only able to be mitigated by ingenuity and data duplication, at least in organisations with long experience of evolving database implementations such as the Kekule Company's. This fact is being vividly illustrated nowadays in off-the-shelf applications software based on a specific DBMS. It is little advantage to a database user to find an application package vendor employing the same DBMS. The user's and the vendor's files will not fit and cannot be brought together, except by an old-fashioned interface. So if an interface is needed, why not choose the best package, even if it has a 'foreign' DBMS? (Packages which come with multi-DBMS options get the worst of all worlds. The package code will not be written to get the best from a given DBMS option, and the user will still require an interface).

To overcome the deficiencies apparent in the representation in fig. 7.4 a new schema was proposed, to lie between the physical internal database and the outside user views (ANSI/X3/SPARC DBMS Study Group, 1975). New outside views would cause changes to the internal database, but only a single new mapping to the new schema would be involved. Fig. 7.5 is a representation.

The literature has quite a lot to say about this stable, database schema and how it might work. It was obvious, however, that such a

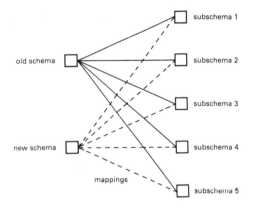

Fig. 7.4 Introduction of a new schema.

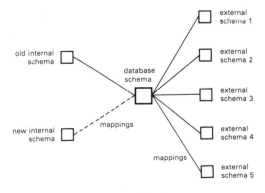

Fig. 7.5 Use of the database schema.

change would only come about from radical advances in database hardware and software technology. Meanwhile it seemed to the Kekule Chemical Company that nothing would be lost by starting the necessary data analysis. The resultant analyses could be stored on one of the emergent data dictionaries, would be somehow useful for the future, would rigorously categorise data for general systems reference and would enable the conceptual representations to be related to physical database data also held on the data dictionary.

More is said about data dictionaries later. At this point it is necessary to know that in effect two dictionaries were to be maintained, one termed the conceptual DD and the other the physical DD. It is also necessary to know that data dictionaries are used to store information about processes as well as data. For the physical DD these processes were the physical systems, programs and modules etc. For the conceptual DD they were of course the constant overview business processes and their subdivisions.

In summary then the objectives of the conceptual DD and the consequent objectives of conceptual data analysis were as follows:

(a) To provide a framework in which the relatively unchanging processes and meta data dealt with by the Company could be identified and stored. (Meta data means a description of data, not the data values themselves. 'Smith', 'Jones' and 'Robinson' are data, 'Name' is meta data).

(b) To provide an anchor point that was independent of particular physical system implementation but able to be related to them. The objective was always to follow the heavy line in the picture below in considering and designing systems:

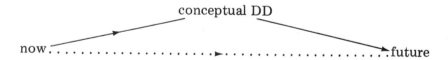

If the dotted line is followed the cycle of obsolescence is never broken since the future becomes the past.

(c) To maintain a relationship between the conceptual DD and the physical DD (and then to the physical database). This could be done in the following way:

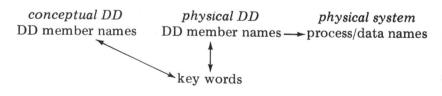

(d) To provide a means by which potential new areas for computer systems could be explored, because of the existence of a steady model of the company.

A number of methods were available to the company for performing the actual data analysis. The one selected (and slightly modified) was *entity/role analysis.* The method consists of analysing both general and particular data into one or more of the six classifications which follow, and then categorising the data by a unique combination of identified named classes (Bachman and Daya, 1977).

The class *entity* is defined as a person, place, thing or idea which exists free-standing in reality. Examples are 'product' (that is, a chemical, independent of how it is used), a 'site' (such as a factory, which only ceases to be relevant to the company when it is sold) or a 'person'. As it happens, because data is being analysed from the Kekule Company's point of view, it was more useful to distinguish a person who was a company employee and one who was not, even though conceptually they are the same.

A *role* on the other hand is a behaviour pattern which characterises an entity. Thus a 'sales product' is a product which plays the part of being a chemical offered by the Company to potential customers. Similarly a 'manufacturing cost centre' is a site categorised by accountants and manufacturing staff as fulfilling the role of manufacturing area.

Entities have a cross-relationship with roles. An example is shown in fig. 7.6, where the asterisks indicate valid entity/role pairs.

Role / Entity	Manufacturer	Component	Customer	Employee	Employer	Supplier	Asset
Company			*		*	*	
External Company			*			*	
Product	*	*					*
Person			*	*	*	*	
Plant	*						*

Fig. 7.6 Cross-relationship between entities and roles.

The next classification is *relationship*. A relationship is a role-to-role pairing which is used to characterise a relationship between two entities. Relationships are always one-to-one, with one role being the owner and the other the member. An example is 'employment' (that is, the role employer, from entity company, owning the role employee, from entity person). Again, 'market' (the role sales product, from entity product, owning customer, from entity customer). Or again, 'manufacture' (manufacturing site from site, owning process from plant).

A large group of analytical characterisations come under the meta meta data heading *attribute*. (The term meta meta data is used to mean this kind of theoretical data categorisation, as opposed to the general name — meta data — or data itself, the data value.) An attribute is the characterisation of a role of an entity, and is derived from a set of values drawn up to describe a role's existence for practical presentation and decision purposes. Examples are employee name (from employee), supplier address, product yield, and very many more.

The next group classification is very general and termed *space*. Space characteristics are further broad descriptions of attributes that state whether the data being analysed is, say, ordinal or cardinal, or whether it is to do with length or weight. Almost the full set of general space terms can be given:

cardinal
    dimension (e.g. length, weight)
      specific physical measure (kilos, litre)
    precision
      implicit
      explicit
    limits (validations)

ordinal
    unconstrained (e.g. free text)
    constrained
      internal (physical appearance)
      external
        list (e.g. Mr, Mrs, Miss, Ms)
        table (stored elsewhere)
        key (equivalence to the whole data being described).

The last classification is *time*. The correct treatment of time with respect to data seemed particularly important but also difficult. Its importance is clear to anyone used to data and who has had to ensure, say, that the correct weeks files have been matched. The difficulty of course is that even if the conceptual data dictionary was at one point in perfect synchronisation with the data it described, data has already started an ageing process the moment it is conveyed from its information source. And of course by the nature of observation the information source almost always lags at least somewhat behind the event. The analysis finally arrived at was:

absolute time
    time stamp (e.g. 11 a.m. GMT, 11/11/1918)
    general period (e.g. a cost period)
    fixed period (time x to y)
relative time
    future (always future)
    present (always present)
    past (always past, and the usual condition of data)

Data dictionaries are designed to allow reasonably complex relationships to be expressed, say as between a record and its fields or a field and a module. Thus there was no difficulty either expressing the relationships between the classifications in the conceptual DD, or expressing relationships between combinations of named classes and business processes. The data dictionary chosen by Kekule was DATAMANAGER which, like many others on the market, has a key word facility. Consequently there was again no difficulty in enabling individual links to be set up between the conceptual DD and the physical DD. The theory and the practical means to implement it were in place.

In the end, of course, the whole thing was a total failure, and for those tempted to tread the same path or a similar one the reasons for failure are now given.

The real world of the Kekule Chemical Company deals with far more complicated data and concepts than the items used to formulate or explain theory. Even the seemingly simpler data can be complex enough. For example, consider Kekule's definition of 'fixed assets': these comprise:

'Physical assets and intangible assets. The former consists of freehold and leasehold land and buildings, freehold and leasehold estate property, plant and machinery (including standby spares), explosives magazines, transport, rolling stock and other equipment, furniture, fittings and office equipment. The latter consists of patents, trademarks and processes, but it should be noted that good will, issue expenses and preliminary expenses are not included being instead written off against the holding Company's reserves.'

The time and intellectual effort needed to analyse such data was eventually seen to be so great that no justification could be made for it. In fact the Kekule Company eventually had grave doubts whether much could have been achieved anyway, even if they had persevered. The reason is that generally DP personnel do not make mistakes with obvious and clearly explainable data. Mistakes, which might persist for years, arise because of very fine nuances in the meaning of data. Take the Kekule Company's definition of 'sales' as follows:

> 'All sales of products and services to, less returns from, external and Parent Company customers, including sundry sales and sales of products purchased for resale but not royalty or know how receipts. The value is the amount invoiced to the customer exclusive of Value Added Tax and other sales taxes and excise duties; all other charges (e.g. inland carriage, freight and import duty) shown on the face of the invoice are included. Quality and other rebates, allowances and discounts, other than those charged in Variable Selling and and Distribution Expenses, are deducted.'

A sales analysis which mistakenly included VAT would quickly be spotted in the development phase. An analysis mistake which resulted in failure to deduct Kekule's % August Discount might never be discovered. The point at issue is whether conceptual data analysis could rigorously express the subtleties of the definition of 'sales'. If it could, perhaps the expression would be so complex that not only would the August Discount mistake still be made, but the analysis would also be incapable of fulfilling its other purposes.

Another reason for the failure of Kekule's conceptual analysis was the immense difficulty in obtaining reliable definitions of meta data. It is true that much of Kekule's accounting data was well defined because, as a subsidiary, it was important to the parent company to know it was adding apples and apples in consolidating its accounts. Other definitions, of which many thousands were required, were far less easy to obtain, e.g. 'returnable overseas container', 'notifiable chemical hazard', 'remuneration not liable for pension calculation'. The analyst cannot guess at these definitions. In each case the right mananger has to be found, and he must give his thought and time.

It might be argued that the Kekule Chemical Company was too impatient in its aims. Instead it might have only attempted conceptual data analysis on data which was already being investigated as a new system was being implemented. This does not avoid any of the analytical difficulties and fails to meet a major objective of constructing a company model.

A cause of failure is that the theory is capable of generality but the practice is not. It is like devising a schema for a database and expecting the implemented DBMS somehow to start processing data at a word of command. A second cause is the arrogance of belief that everything is capable of submission to the analyst's desire for overview. Superman might achieve it, but analysts would do better to pick discrete, manageable subsets. At the end of the day the Kekule Company constructed a list of about 150 key words describing entities and generalised attributes. From these an appropriate, unique subset was chosen to represent a physical data item. It is a long way from conceptual data analysis, but it is practical and useful. More is said about the method later when analysis and data dictionaries are dealt with.

DATA ANALYSIS TO THIRD NORMAL FORM

At about the time that conceptual data analysis was being studied, the Kekule Chemical Company was also paying close attention to *Third Normal Form* data analysis. Third Normal Form (TNF) analysis consists of analysing data and successively reducing it to sets of simple tables, each table with a unique data key. The ultimate set of tables was originally meant to be the basis of a potential new 'Relational Database' implementation (Codd, 1972). However, the simplicity of the method and the orderliness of the resultant data clearly makes Third Normal Form more widely attractive. The tables seem a good start for design using any DBMS, and the presentations appear also to be an appropriate and rigorous technique for use by systems analysts in data investigations. The method is explained by reference to typical Kekule Company data.

Fig. 7.7. shows a table with a key of 'product code' (keys are italicised). The table is known in TNF as a *relation*. Frequently,

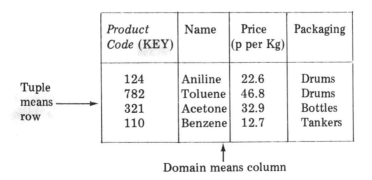

Product Code (KEY)	Name	Price (p per Kg)	Packaging
124	Aniline	22.6	Drums
782	Toluene	46.8	Drums
321	Acetone	32.9	Bottles
110	Benzene	12.7	Tankers

Tuple means → row

↑
Domain means column

Fig. 7.7 A product table.

also, the columns of the table are referred to as *domains*, and the rows referred to as *tuples* (pronounced 'tuppels').

The Product Table has the following properties:

- the key (product code) is the only possible key
- no two rows are the same
- every column has a different, unique, meaning
- the order of the rows is not significant
- the order of the columns is not significant

It is common for table keys to be compounds of two or more codes. In fig. 7.8 the key is the compound expression of both 'derived product code'/'product code': column 1 is the chemical product code which is derived from the chemical in column 2. Column 3 is the time in weeks needed to derive it.

Last, before showing how TNF analysis is done, the expression *foreign key* should be explained. If a data item type appears ordinarily within a table but also appears as a key of another table, the data item type is known as a foreign key within the first table. Fig. 7.9 illustrated this with the data item type *zone code* being a foreign key in the customer table (and so denoted by an asterisk).

Derived Product Code	Product Code	Lead time in weeks
632	624	4
632	782	8
474	321	13
474	310	2

compound keys

Fig. 7.8 Example of compound keys.

Customer Table   *Zone Table*

Customer Code	Zone Code
Customer Name	Zone Name
Customer Address	Zone Population
* Zone code	

Fig. 7.9 Example of a foreign key.

THIRD NORMAL FORM ANALYSIS STEPS

The analysis steps of Third Normal Form are simply the methodical finding of keys in the construction of tables. The starting data is of course all the data needing to be analysed. The five steps involved are as follows:

(a) Arrange the data into basic tables known as 'unnormalised' tables.
(b) Convert the unnormalised tables into First Normal Form (FNF).
(c) Convert FNF tables to Second Normal Form (SNF).
(d) Convert SNF tables to Third Normal Form (TNF).
(e) Optimise all TNF tables from this and other analyses.

Examples of these steps follow.

Step 1 Arrange the data into unnormalised tables

A sales analysis form identified during the systems analysis phase of a new sales system is shown in fig. 7.10. Two sales analysis forms set out as an unnormalised table are shown in fig. 7.11. Step 1 is now complete.

Product Code: 782				Product Type: Basic	
Product Name: Toluene					
Customer Code	Customer Name	Zone	Country	Date last Order	Quantity last order (t)
4161	Braun	Eur	Swit	10/11/81	20.9
2396	Tan	Asia	Thai	3/2/82	32.0
7717	Jones	Eur	UK	12/9/81	6.0
4267	Pinero	SA	Peru	3/3/82	13.0

Fig. 7.10 Analysis of product sales.

Product code	Product type	Product name	Customer code	Customer name	Zone	Country	Date last order	Quantity last order
782	Basic	Toluene	4161	Braun	Eur	Swit	10/11/81	20.9
			2396	Tan	Asia	Thai	3/2/82	32.0
			7717	Jones	Eur	UK	12/9/81	6.0
			4267	Pinero	SA	Peru	3/3/82	13.0
944	Fine	Thiazide	2279	Roberts	Eur	UK	4/2/82	1.2
			5152	Wagner	NA	USA	9/12/81	0.5
			3139	Nieuwland	Eur	NL	10/11/81	1.9

Fig. 7.11 An unnormalised table.

Step 2 Remove repeating groups
The data items that repeat are placed in a separate table as in fig. 7.12. The key of this table is then added to each table that contained the repeating groups. The result is placed in a new 'non-repeating' table, shown in fig. 7.13. Both tables are in FNF. Note that the table in fig. 7.13 has a compound key made up of Product Code/Customer Code.

Step 3 Test whether data depends on the whole key
To move from FNF to SNF each data item within the tables should be examined in turn and the question asked, 'Does the item depend on the whole FNF key?' Taking each data item in turn in our example:

- does Customer Name depend on the whole key? No, only on customer code
- does Zone depend on the whole key? No, only on Customer code
- does Country depend on the whole key? No, only on Customer code
- does Date-last-order depend on the whole key? Yes
- does Quantity-last-order depend on the whole key? Yes

The first three data items relate only to the Customer Code of the compound key. This 'partial key dependency' enables the affected

Product code	Product type	Product name
782 944	Basic Fine	Toluene Thiazide

Fig. 7.12 Separate table holding data items which repeat.

Product code	Customer code	Customer name	Zone	Country	Date last order	Quantity last order
782	4161	Braun	Eur	Swit	10/11/81	20.9
782	2396	Tan	Asia	Thai	3/2/82	32.0
782	7717	Jones	Eur	UK	12/9/81	6.0
782	4267	Pinero	SA	Peru	3/3/82	13.0
944	2279	Roberts	Eur	UK	4/2/82	1.2
944	5152	Wagner	NA	USA	9/12/81	0.5
944	3139	Nieuwland	Eur	NL	10/11/81	1.9

Fig. 7.13 A new non-repeating table.

data items to be removed to a separate table with their relevant key. The data items that were dependent on the whole key stay where they are. Fig. 7.14 and 7.15 show the new tables and keys.

Customer code	Customer Name	Zone	Country
4161	Braun	Eur	Swit
2396	Tan	Asia	Thai
7717	Jones	Eur	UK
4267	Pinero	SA	Peru
2279	Roberts	Eur	UK
5152	Wagner	NA	USA
3139	Nieuwland	Eur	NL

Fig. 7.14 New table after step 3.

Product code	Customer code	Date last order	Quantity last order
782	4161	10/11/81	20.9
782	2396	3/2/82	32.0
782	7717	12/9/81	6.0
782	4267	3/3/82	13.0
944	2279	4/2/82	1.2
944	5152	9/12/81	0.5
944	3139	10/11/81	1.9

Fig. 7.15 New table after step 3.

Step 4 Test whether data items depend on each other
In Step 4 SNF is moved finally to TNF. So far the concern has been the initial establishment of table keys, and finding whether or not data items depend on these established keys. In this step the concern is whether any items within tables depend on each other, and if so which. Strictly speaking, every data item within each table should be compared to every other item within that table. Then the question should be asked, 'If one data item is known, does it follow the other could be known?' In practice it will be apparent which data items ought to be considered.

In the above example knowledge of the data will cause Zone and Country to be related. Asking the question the right way round, 'If Country is known, is Zone known?' yields the answer Yes. Thus the table in fig. 7.14 can be split into two tables as shown in fig. 7.16.

Customer code	Customer name	*Country
4161	Braun	Swit
2396	Tan	Thai
7717	Jones	UK
4267	Pinero	Peru
2279	Roberts	UK
5152	Wagner	USA
3139	Nieuwland	NL

Country	Zone
Swit	Eur
NL	Eur
UK	Eur
Peru	SA
USA	NA
Thai	Asia

Fig. 7.16 Tables in third normal form.

The end of step 4 gives all the TNF tables for the data originally in the analysis. For the product sales data the tables are as shown in fig. 7.17.

Step 5 Combine other tables with identical keys
A result of analysis of other data related to product sales (say, from the study of other documents) will yield other tables also in TNF. If any of these have the same keys they must be combined. For example, other analysis may have yielded the table:

Product Code	Product Name	Product Unit Price

Clearly then this table can be combined with fig. 7.12 (one of those existing in fig. 7.17) to give the optimised table in fig. 7.18.

The Kekule Chemical Company used Third Normal Form data analysis just once, successfully if laboriously, for a small system being implemented about the time TNF lectures were at their most popular. It has not been used since then, and there are no plans to revive it.

It is true that there are a few minor criticisms of TNF itself. For example the table in fig. 7.18 could easily be amended to include the data item 'product health hazard'. It might then be argued that the blind following of rules had resulted in product financial data being mixed with medical data. More thinking analysis would have resulted in two tables.

The main reason, however, that TNF is not used at Kekule is more serious. Not only does TNF give few advantages over conventional methods of analysis, if anything it is inferior. The real weakness stems from what TNF theoreticians claim to be a strength. This is that the tables are totally free of the processing requirements of the

Product code	Product type	Product name
782	Basic	Toluene
944	Fine	Thiazide

Product code	Customer code	Date last order	Quantity last order
782	4161	10/11/81	20.9
782	2396	3/2/82	32.0
782	7717	12/9/81	6.0
782	4267	3/3/82	13.0
944	2279	4/2/82	1.2
944	5152	9/12/81	0.5
944	3139	10/11/81	1.9

Customer code	Customer name	* Country
4161	Baun	Swit
2396	Tan	Thai
7717	Jones	UK
4267	Pinero	Peru
2279	Roberts	UK
5152	Wagner	USA
3139	Nieuwland	NL

Country	Zone
Swit	Eur
NL	Eur
UK	Eur
Peru	SA
USA	NA
Thai	Asia

Fig. 7.17 New tables after step 4.

Product code
Product type
Product name
Product unit price

Fig. 7.18 An optimised table.

systems that will operate on the data. If the tables were to be mapped to a relational database system this would not matter; a relational system, which needs data in this form, would process the data with equally high efficiency whether there were 90 or 900 tables to deal with, each with 90 or 9 million entries. But relational systems do not yet exist, or at least the hardware does not exist to accommodate them efficiently. It is true some systems claim to be relational. Although their files need to be flat — i.e. no repeating groups are allowed — data access is often by certain declared keys, not freely among columns. If free access is allowed volumes need to be small. Even then updates will be expensive. The situation is comparable to a flat file under the management of the ADABAS DBMS, but with every field inverted. The volume of data that would then be in the associator, the inverted lists and the internal sequence numbers, would far exceed the original data. Processing time to update the lists would bring the system to a halt. So it is seen that TNF tables are only a tidy laying out of data that must then be scrambled into forms which satisfy all useful, identified processing access paths, and produce high performance along the principal routes.

It has been shown that TNF tables enable sets of rules to be formulated to convert the data into physical file designs according to the particular DBMS to be used and after the processing access paths have been identified. The Kekule Company's experience was that these rules produced designs that were not only inadequate, but barely acceptable as starting points. It is true that designs were valid for Kekule's DBMS, but they were far more inefficient than those produced by a database designer. This particular experience is at the heart of the broader truth. General processing software has its strengths and weaknesses, and particular processing software has its goals of performance. Experienced people have the flair to match these facts with data to produce the most acceptable designs. Technology and automated techniques cannot yet compete with people in this craft.

DATA DICTIONARIES AND DATA ANALYSIS

It had become apparent to the Kekule Chemical Company from quite an early point that a data dictionary (DD) should be acquired. The motivation was not primarily data analysis but database systems control — that is, DBMS data and processes. Formerly Kekule had developed and implemented self-contained systems with little data sharing except through well-defined interfaces. One beneficial result is that maintenance of these systems is comparatively safe. Boundaries are tight and knock-on effects are few. It is true that the quite different philosophy of database has not been a complete success. For performance reasons systems data is not as open as was first supposed, and data structures tend to be project driven not data driven. Even so there is enough data sharing to suggest that future database systems maintenance will be a perilous activity. Kekule believes that by the late 1980s control and maintenance will be exceedingly difficult and costly, and changes in one system will entail high risks to other unintended areas. The only way out the Company sees is firm control of the database systems by a DD.

Some reasons for a DD at least were for data analysis. For example, as discussed earlier it was expected that a DD would assist conceptual data analysis. It had also been suggested by proponents of structured design techniques that a DD should hold data being analysed into TNF (Gane and Sarson, 1977). As it happens Kekule later found this particular use to be worthless. In experiment the TNF analyses took far longer and were more liable to error when a DD was used, and storing the final tables seemed to gain nothing because of their transitory nature.

Choosing the DD software did not take long. DATAMANAGER had the advantages of flexibility, comprehensiveness and ease of use. It also seemed to be an advantage that it was 'free-standing' — that is, independent of particular DBMS packages but with interfaces to most. Finally in choosing it must be remembered that the current generation of dictionaries is virtually free of processing performance considerations. The dictionaries are passive things and do not take control of data management in the way future database schemas may. Their current capabilities slant their use heavily to centralised documentation, and the scope of them can be judged from typical member types: data items, files, modules, programs, jobs etc. Indeed, it has been suggested that these present-day packages would be better termed 'information resource dictionaries' (Canning, 1981).

No installation should begin to use a DBMS without the parallel use of a DD to record details of the database data and processes, and their interrelationships. Because Kekule had not followed this precept, the major tasks were loading and checking the DD, and setting up procedures to ensure the database systems and their DD description would not get out-of-line in future. Optionally of course the amount of information capable of being stored about a DD member is considerable. In practice for Kekule, starting after the event, available information was severely limited. Data definitions were non-rigorous one-line titles and data characteristics were extracted by programs from internal DBMS utility files. The important thing was that the data/process relationships were found. This involved some ingenious, painstaking detective work. It is unlikely it could have been achieved but for the company's first class naming standards.

The devising and maintenance of good data and process naming standards is an old-fashioned virtue. Few are as easy to adopt, or give the same high returns of systems control or, even, opportunities for analysis. At the Kekule Chemical Company naming standards are based on three principles:

(a) It must be possible to tell from the structure of a name exactly what kind of thing is being named. For example a job name must be distinguishable from a module name by characters or whatever, in some obvious, visible way.

(b) Where it is relevant and useful to associate a thing being named with another thing of a similar or broader type, the association must be obvious from the two names. For example KDFM 26 is a module in the Kekule demand forecasting system KDF.

(c) Things of the same type and association being named should be capable of differentiation in a logical way. For example KDFM26, KDFM27.

The principles of naming had been used by the Kekule installation for everything — tabulations, screens, transactions, job suites etc. Perhaps the only deviation was data items. Database data items, however, were distinguished by not beginning with K, and all data items from the same file began with the same two letters. Assistance in loading the DD came from two sources. First, there was the Kekule Company's normal Job Control Language (JCL) analyses. As the name implies the programs read the JCL for one or more suites and show in various required orders such information as which jobs use which procedures/programs, which DD names are used in which jobs, etc. (The analyses resemble in some way the output from normal DD reports.) Second, considerable use was made of scans of the disk-held source program libraries. Thus by one means and another the DD was loaded.

Keeping the dictionary up-to-date currently presents its own special problems. Information sheets have to be completed which contain the required subsets for each dictionary member type. In general, systems analysts submit those for data items and programming/design staff complete the details for most other components. A further difficulty lies in keeping up-to-date the relationships between DD members. Except in very limited ways, easy to circumvent, (such as automatic program inclusion of dictionary-generated file declarations) DDs do not drive data processing. Tight management control is necessary to ensure that programmers under the stress of implementation deadlines nevertheless notify correctly all relationships. It is an inherent weakness of this generation of dictionaries that the information contained in them can so easily be wrong. And a wrong piece of information acted on in an urgent maintenance task may sour the whole DD for all staff. Nevertheless staff themselves, knowing the importance of DD correctness, are encouraged to comply with extra willingness with directives aimed at good dictionary management. In addition of course regular reports are produced to assist maintenance work. At Kekule the most important of these is a list of processing modules showing for each module the associated files, screens, tabulations and further modules calling the module being described.

In the area of data and data analysis the DD produces database and database file reports fuller than those previously produced by DBMS utilities, although the difference is not enough itself to justify the DD. As new data is loaded to the database, however, much more information can be stored than before, and stored in a more structured and cohesive way. Each DD data member is in effect a documentation source and a discipline to documentation. In addition it helps to ensure that synonyms are recognised. A synonym is a data item of the same meaning as another but having a different spelling. Each data item is allocated a subset of entity and attribute terms from a list of key words. These are then entered into the dictionary member's key words list and checked for uniqueness. Without a good naming system homographs might also have become a problem. A homograph is a word of the same spelling as another but of different meaning, say, 'address' meaning both customer address and supplier address. Naturally the DD software prevents the second member being loaded to the dictionary, but the problem remains of what to do with it, especially since both names will be used throughout the database. It is possible that the key word method could be used for data analysis, such as by searching and listing all data classified under particular entity types. This has not, however, proved to be useful, in part because file organisation already tends to classify data in this way.

CONCLUSIONS

By now the reader's view of data analysis must be after Dr Samuel Johnson's opinion of a cucumber — 'It should be well sliced, and dressed with pepper and vinegar, and then thrown out as good for nothing'. Things are not really so bad. Data control and analysis is a large and complex affair. The future will clearly bring major advances in data management technology as practical implementations are made which represent the database and physical schemas. Organisations which have made a determined, systematic start to the job of putting their data in good order will gain in two ways. In the short term they will achieve more effective management and increasingly sure development of new database systems. In the long term the eventual demands of new technology will ensure that organisations which have prepared for these advances by effective, automated data categorisation and documentation will be better placed to make immediate and effective use of them.

REFERENCES

ANSI/X3/SPARC DBMS Study Group (1975) Interim Report, various sources.

Bachman, C.W. and Daya, M. (1977) 'The Role Concept in Data Models', *Honeywell Information Systems*, Billerica, MA.

Canning, R.G. (July 1981) 'A View of Data Dictionaries', *EDP Analyzer*, Vista, CA.

CODASYL Data Base Task Group (1971) *DBTG Report*, New York: ACM.

Codd, E.F. (1972) 'Further Normalisation of the Data Base Relational Model', *Courant Computer Science Symposia*, 6, *Data Base Systems*, New York: Prentice Hall.

Gane, C. and Sarson, T. (1977) *Structured Systems Analysis*, New York: IST Data Books.

IBM Corporation (1975) *Business Systems Planning: Information Systems Planning Guide*, White Plains, NY.

Meadow, C.T. (1967) *The Analysis of Information Systems*, New York: Wiley.

Vickery, B.C. (1960) *Faceted Classification*, London: ASLIB.

CHAPTER 8

System Integration Using IBM's 'Database' Computer

by George Berrich (The Reo Stakis Organisation)

INTRODUCTION

The application referred to in this sub-section concerns a large multi-company group. The companies are diverse in nature: one is a casino and another is a wholesale meat company. The problem involved communicating information up, down and across the group structure using a common approach such that data may be understood and referred to in a uniform fashion. The solution adopted was to use a single company database which spans the whole organisation.

THE ORGANISATION

Stakis Public Limited Company (PLC), formerly known as The Reo Stakis Organisation Limited, comprises many smaller diverse companies, e.g.

- Stakis Hotels and Inns Ltd
- Stakis Casinos Ltd
- D. and A. Haddow Ltd (an off-license chain)
- James Ferguson and Sons Ltd
- Apollo Leasing Ltd

There are also many smaller trading companies in the group. However, they do not attract any additional data processing (DP) requirements. One small separate company is called Stakis Group Services. This is the DP department. Apart from the main board of directors of Stakis PLC, only three sub-groups have activities which span the whole group of companies. These are:

- Stakis Group Services (the DP department)
- Group Accounting/Treasury
- Audit Department

EVOLUTION OF THE DP DEPARTMENT

The DP department of Stakis PLC went through the same evolution as other DP departments that traversed the computer era. Visible record computers, batch processing, on-line data capture and then database techniques were used in turn. From a highly staffed department of a mainly clerical nature it evolved into a small, professional unit in which the work-load is handled by computers rather than DP personnel. Batch processing still remains an integral part of the operation but is not used to the extent to which it was. On-line data entry by end-users has replaced use of many keypunch operators. Communications facilities provide answers to users directly via terminals. Database software has given end-users immediate access to their own and other users data and has provided them with the means to format that data to meet their own requirements. End-users have also assumed a large part of the analyst/programmers role.

CHOICE OF SYSTEM

Probably the first and most important constraint in choosing a computer system is cost, not just the capital cost which is usually depreciated over a number of years, but also, and perhaps more important, the running costs. Running costs include hardware maintenance/rental, staffing, accommodation and so on. These costs may be offset in several ways. For example, by a general management charge to end-users or by a charge to end-users based on a computer usage calculated by rates applied to units of computer resources used. Resources would include CPU, disk space, etc. The closer the cost can be related to the end-user, the easier it is to justify the expenditure.

The next constraint on choice of system concerns the extent to which the new system is similar to the old. Its minimum level of output should be comparable to the existing level of service. The change to the user interface should be as transparent as possible. All new features should be gradually introduced at a pace that can be absorbed by the end-users. Programs and files must either be portable to the new system or must be convertible using standard conversion utilities supplied by the manufacturer. System conversion should be as fast, simple and efficient as possible. This is usually 'guaranteed' by the manufacturer but is not always the case in practise.

The growth path from the existing to the new system should be as trouble-free as possible. This means that critical applications, such as payroll, should be transferred quickly with minimal end-user impact. It is also important to recognise that a larger and faster machine is not always the answer. Horizontal rather than vertical growth may be required. Perhaps, more stand alone intelligent systems linked in a network is a more appropriate solution.

If other systems are used within the organisation, then it is important that data should be transferable to and from the new system. Once again, the manufacturer's claims have to be viewed with scepticism. For example, many manufacturers claim to be 'IBM compatible'. However, the meaning of compatible in this context should be taken at its widest.

In addition to the constraints described above, an additional factor was taken into account when choosing a new system. This factor concerned the extent to which the new system supported state of the art developments such as database software and communications facilities.

After all factors had been considered, an IBM System/38 was chosen as the solution to Stakis PLC data processing requirements.

SYSTEM/38

System/38 was announced by IBM in 1978 as the long-awaited replacement for the highly successful but ageing System/3 range of computers. The machine architecture is a complete break from anything which has appeared from IBM previously. It includes database and security support operations in the machine instruction set and comes equipped with a truly interactive operating system. It is capable of running batch and interactive work from up to 80 local work stations and 8 communication lines, and can accommodate 5000 mega-byte of disc store. System/38 offers a radical alternative to machines up to the power of an IBM 370/148. It provides large system facilities at the price of a minicomputer. The cost of a relatively small System/38 configuration is slightly over US$100 000 (£50 000).

The most striking feature of System/38 is the total integration of hardware and software. The hardware logic and organisation, microcode features, operating system and all compilers and utilities including the query language were all designed by the same team working at one location. Features of the system include:

(a) Object oriented addressing. The operating system is unaware of the physical location of data items and program statements in the machine. All data is referenced by name and the machine automatically provides instructions to create and manipulate data in the physical address space. As example, the machine instruction set includes a 'create program' instruction. When a high level language such as COBOL, RPG, or CL (Control Language) has produced an intermediate code from the source statements, it issues a 'create program' instruction and the machine creates a micro-code version of the program, assigns a virtual address to it and finds space on the disk to store it. None of this is apparent to the compiler or programmer. The machine memorises the name and address of the created object program and can locate and activate the program on subsequent instruction.

(b) Security. For every object it creates, the machine stores the owners name and the mode of use which has been defined for this and other users. For example, any request for a database file causes the machine to check to see if the person requesting the file is authorised to use it and by reference to another object called the 'user profile' determines exactly what mode of use is allowed. This hardware implemented authorisation mechanism provides System/38 with an extremely powerful security feature.

(c) Built-in database facilities. One of the most useful aspects of System/38 is its orientation towards database management. The machine stores collections of records in objects called *data spaces* which are presented to the programmer as database files. The machine can build and maintain several indexes over a file as required by the user. It can also store external descriptions of the format of records. High level language programmers treat data spaces as traditional disk files but without needing to define the required record structure or access structure.

The System/38 database system may be regarded as one of the first practical designs capable of handling large volumes in relational-like structures.

(d) Micro-coded operating system. The System/38 machine contains the basic elements of a complete operating system in micro-code. Facilities such as queue management, task management and data management are implemented as micro-code routines and form the lowest interface to the machine. This interface is equivalent to the System/360 assembler level.

The 'visible' operating system, called the *Control Program Facility* (CPF), presents a simple, easy to use interface to the application programmer and end-user through a single consistent control language called CL. This language provides around 300 interactive commands which may also be compiled into CL programs. DO loops, IF . . THEN . . ELSE logic, string manipulation and arithmetic statements are also available in CL.

SYSTEM/38 FILES

PHYSICAL DATABASE FILES

A System/38 *physical file* is a file which contains physically stored records. As such it is similar to a disk file in a conventional system. A single physical file contains a set of fixed length records all of which have the same format.

The content of a physical file is specified by means of a *physical file description*. This description consists of file name and record format. The set of physical file descriptions constitutes the database schema.

Records are stored in physical files in arrival order. Records may be accessed in this order or in key sequence or by record number.

LOGICAL FILES

A *logical file* is a file which is defined over one or more physical files. See fig. 8.1. Any number of logical files may be defined over the same set of physical files. A logical file contains a definition of how to retrieve and format fields taken from records from one or more physical files. This definition includes statements which:

- specify which fields are to comprise the record of the logical file
- rename fields

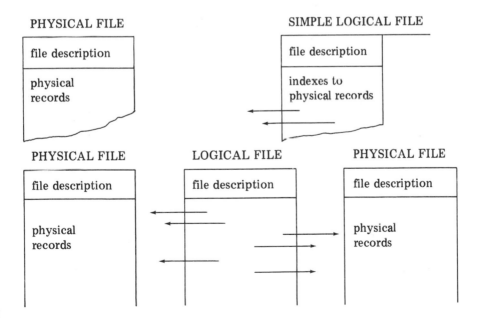

Fig. 8.1 Physical and logical files.

- create new fields by concatenation of fields taken from physical records. For example DATE = MM+DD+YY
- specify the order in which the fields are to appear in the logical records
- specify the key fields of the logical records

Changes to the record format of physical files have no impact on application programs which use logical files defined over the modified physical files. The mapping information used to create logical files from physical files is automatically updated by the system.

The availability of logical files allows users to view the database in a way which is most appropriate for a particular application. Any change to the record format of a logical file only affects those application programs which use that logical file. In this respect, the system is highly data-independent.

An additional feature of logical files is that a single logical file may be defined over two or more physical files and may 'logically' contain records of different type and length. This results in a simpler file logic than in more conventional systems in which one is normally constrained to make different record types appear to have the same length thereby requiring the application program to block and de-block records as the file is processed.

Data may be accessed through logical files or from physical files directly, no distinction is made as far as the application programs are concerned.

SYSTEM/38 UTILITIES

SOURCE ENTRY UTILITY (SEU)
This utility helps the programmer to enter and maintain source statements in RPG III, COBOL, CL as well as statements specifying the database schema (i.e. the physical and logical file specifications).

The syntax of each statement can be checked as it is entered. When CL statements are issued, the command selection menus and parameter prompting facilities can be used in the same way as they are when the SEU utility is not used.

The major function of the SEU is to allow programmers to:

- add, delete, move, copy and change parts of a source file
- copy lines from one source file to another
- search for a specific string in a source file
- edit a source file
- allow two source files to be viewed on the screen simultaneously. This is accomplished by segmenting the screen.

DATA FILE UTILITY (DFU)

The data file utility provides functions for data entry, file maintenance and display. Specifically, the DFU allows the programmer to:

- create data entry, maintenance and inquiry programs quickly. The programmer names the file concerned and the utility creates application programs using default parameters for record layout on the screen etc.
- tailor a file definition (physical or logical) so that only selected fields are accessed

The DFU also provides an audit trail of all data which is entered using a DFU constructed application program.

QUERY UTILITY

This utility allows the programmer to sequence, summarise and/or tabulate data from a database file. Results may be displayed on the screen or printed. Query differs from inquiry (see DFU above) in that inquiry is essentially concerned with the selection of single records whereas the query utility allows sets of records to be selected, sequenced and summarised.

The query utility allows the programmer to:

- select records
- sequence records
- sample records
- define fields whose values are based on computations involving other fields
- define tables containing summary information
- specify the presentation of data in two-dimensions
- specify the format of reports including report headings

The utility is self-documenting, thereby saving a great deal of effort. Query applications may be run interactively from a work station, in batch mode, or as part of a larger job stream. Reports can be created in minutes using the query utility and the common approach minimises the support required for maintenance. In the Stakis PLC, end-users have been trained to create, maintain and request execution of query applications.

APPLICATIONS SOFTWARE

Applications software can be acquired in a variety of ways:

(a) In-house development. The in-house development of applications software is greatly helped by use of the utilities described above.

However, such development is probably the most draining of DP resources. The average staffing level for a System/38 is about 9. This includes data entry personnel, operators, programmers and management. Typically, little manpower is available for in-house development. On the other hand, the advantage of in-house development is that the end-user will generally be provided with programs tailored exactly to his or her requirements.

(b) Off-the-shelf packages. This is an approach which is becoming more common. Many companies are now marketing packages for a variety of applications. Maintenance costs are typically ten per cent of purchase price. Packages often include training programs together with user and reference documentation. Although modifications may be made, they are generally quite costly and most users tend to modify their own procedures to conform to the requirements of the package. Source code is not normally available, however, many packages act on user defined physical files and these files may be readily accessed by in-house developed programs. This facilitates the interfacing of off-the-shelf packages with the rest of the system.

(c) Custom packages from a software house. This is typically a very expensive method of obtaining software. However, user satisfaction is generally high. This approach is often used when the application is of a very specialised nature and/or when the time-scale rules out in-house development.

SYSTEM INTEGRATION — AN EXAMPLE APPLICATION

In theory, DBMSs offer great potential for system integration. In practice, integration generally only occurs to a limited extent. There are a number of reasons for this. For example: (i) the provision of several user views of the same data is sometimes more complicated than would first appear, (ii) the implementation of several access paths through some data is often only possible if some paths are implemented with low efficiency, and (iii) end-users are often reluctant to allow other end-users access to their data unless a high level of privacy control can be guaranteed.

Fortunately, System/38 overcomes these problems to some extent. The provision of various end-user views is possible by use of logical files and several different access paths through the same set of records may be implemented efficiently due to the machines micro-coded addressing mechanism. Also, as mentioned earlier, System/38 provides very robust security control.

An example application which demonstrates these features is now described. The application concerns the personnel and salary administration function within Stakis PLC. The integrated database for this application may be regarded as consisting of three types of data: payroll data, personnel data and sickness data.

PAYROLL DATA

Payroll data for a single company is held in three physical files as illustrated in fig. 8.2. Updating of these files is accomplished by an assortment of key-to-disk batch, online data entry and batch, and real time depending on the critical nature or volatility of the data. All updates come from a central location which controls the payroll administration for what is typically a geographically dispersed company.

PERSONNEL DATA

Personnel data for a single company is held in a physical file structured as illustrated in fig. 8.3. Update is accomplished primarily through the use of the data file utility (DFU). This allows records to be added, changed and deleted from the file. Although the personnel data is mainly used to supply information to the payroll system to satisfy both statutory and company requirements, it is also used to compliment the traditional manually maintained personnel file.

PAYROLL MASTER FILE

KEY 1   KEY 2

BRANCH	EMPLOYEE #	various YTD and static items

WEEKLY/MONTHLY SUMMARY FILE

KEY 1   KEY 2

BRANCH	EMPLOYEE #	various weekly/monthly items

TABLE FILES (one for each area, division etc.)

KEY

BRANCH	DESCRIPTION

Fig. 8.2 Payroll files.

PERSONNEL MASTER FILE

KEY 1   KEY 2

BRANCH	EMPLOYEE #	personnel detail items

Fig. 8.3 Personnel files.

SICKNESS DATA

Sickness data for a single company is held in a single physical file with a structure as illustrated in fig. 8.4. Update of this file is carried out by a combination of use of DFU and RPG III programs in a real-time mode, and batch programs. Transfer of data from the sickness file to the payroll system is achieved by use of a transaction file which is processed as part of weekly and monthly runs.

SICKNESS MASTER FILE

KEY 1   KEY 2

BRANCH #	EMPLOYEE # sickness YTD details and balances

SICKNESS RECORD FILE

KEY 1   KEY 2   KEY 3

WEEK #	BRANCH #	EMPLOYEE #	weekly sickness details

Fig. 8.4 Sickness files.

SECURITY

Security is handled in a variety of ways. Batch updating is controlled through traditional means, however, the operator who processes the batch updates is treated as a user of the database and has to be explicitly granted authority to access relevant data items. Online data entry by end-user departments is controlled by use of passwords and menus. A password, as well as determining access rights to specified files also has an initial program attribute which is effective as soon as the user signs on to the system. From this point on, the user is presented a series of functions specific to his or her requirements and no more.

Real-time updating is also restricted by use of passwords and logical views which are implemented by use of logical files. In general, real-time updating is limited to data items which are of a semi-permanent nature and require infrequent change.

Although the end-users may be thought of as the owners of the data, it is the responsibility of the DP department to provide the 'police' protection to ensure accuracy, integrity and privacy. To some extent, this control is necessary to protect end-users from themselves. The age-old proverb 'a little knowledge is a dangerous thing' applies to database technology and it would be quite wrong to allow end-users to have full control over the specification of privacy controls and so on.

The personnel and salary administration system described above is replicated for each company in the Stakis PLC. Minor changes were necessary, for example: data-items were renamed and various different reports were required. However, the main structure was adhered to. This ensured a consistency of approach and allowed all files to be regarded as comprising one large database. Staff interchangeability is less traumatic and happens frequently between similar departments of different companies.

CONCLUDING COMMENTS

Systems integration using IBM's System/38 is greatly facilitated. All data, for many applications involving several companies is held in one large database. Access to data is only limited by the security function. This is largely a consequence of three features of this system:

- the ability to provide logical views by use of logical files
- the ability to access records efficiently in a variety of ways
- the robust security mechanism which is available

CHAPTER 9

Design of End-user Interfaces

By G. McLeod (Grampian Police)

INTRODUCTION

This chapter looks at factors influencing the design of an end-user interface in the context of a patient information system. First must be defined what is meant by the term *end-user interface*. The end-user is the person who makes ultimate use of the information stored in the computer. In this particular case it means the doctors who use the information to assist in the care of their patients. Confusion arises because the term *user* is often applied loosely. For example, the software programmer supporting a database management system might consider the applications programmer as a user of his system. Another way of looking at it, is that the end-user is not usually a computer professional. For him the computer is just another tool to help in his day to day work.

The end-user *interface* is the method by which information can pass between the computer system and the end-user. At the time of writing, video terminals are perhaps the most popular device, though of course there are much more sophisticated peripherals available. Indeed, as is shown later, the humble printout cannot be forgotten. It is up to the designer to choose the most effective means of communicating the stored information to the end-user.

The man—machine interface is probably the weakest link in most computer systems. It is certainly the hardest to research, involving as it does wide ranging disciplines from electronics to psychology and from systems programming to work study. In the end a compromise is usually reached, often simply depending on budget and available hardware and software. An effective end-user interface will meet the needs of the end-user, providing the required information in a timely manner and in an acceptable form. The interface should be straightforward for a non-computing person to use, in the current jargon, *user-friendly*.

Most computer systems require information flow in both directions across the interface: in other words, data input as well as data output. There are exceptions but in most cases acquisition of data *from* the user is as important as dissemination of information *to* the user. In the field of patient information there are particular difficulties in data entry which are discussed later.

There are a number of basic issues which confront the designer of an end-user interface. Perhaps the most obvious is whether the system should be an interactive one. The alternative is batch and the value of such a system should not be underestimated. It is possible to write very effective batch systems where the data is punched up and entered into the computer and output for the user is produced at a later date. The so-called 'real-time' system offers many advantages, particularly when part of a database system, but the user's requirements may only justify the cheaper batch system.

If the system does support interactive terminals what sort of screen handling software is appropriate? Should specialised peripherals be considered e.g. touch-sensitive terminals or bar-code readers? What level of security can be provided to restrict unauthorised access? As far as the user is concerned there are three major factors to consider.

- presentation of the data
- response time
- reliability and resilience

Finally the most important question — how does it all fit together with the database? In what way does the choice of database affect the design of the end-user interface? These and other issues are considered later in the context of the patient information system.

THE APPLICATION : A PATIENT RECORD SYSTEM

The broad aim of the application has been defined as '. . . to improve and facilitate the transfer between doctors, or clinically important information about high-risk patients' (Petrie *et al.*, 1982). In fact when the application was first conceived in the early seventies the aim was much less clear — it was simply an experiment into using computers in hospital medical records. Much has been learned in the intervening ten years particularly in the area of the end-user interface. Indeed there is still much to be learned but it is hoped that this account will give some insight into some of the problems along the way.

A good place to start in medical records is the manual record — sometimes called the patient's case-note. This is a hospital file which contains all the bits of paper about the patient which have accumulated over the years. It includes correspondence, results of lab tests, summaries by clinicians and it tends to be bulky and cumbersome to use. It is difficult and time-consuming to extract the required information. This was particularly true at out-patient clinics. Here doctors must see a large number of patients at any one clinic and valuable time can be wasted searching through a disordered case-note. Indeed if some piece of information is overlooked, e.g. a drug allergy, the result could well be hazardous for the patient.

Two solutions present themselves. The first is a major effort to tidy up the manual record. This includes splitting the notes into various sections and sorting each section into chronological order. The second is to use the computer to assist information retrieval. The former has enjoyed considerable success in a local records office (Wilson *et al.*, 1978). The latter forms the basis for the present discussion.

It was decided that it was unrealistic to attempt to computerise the entire patient record, at least at this stage, and instead to hold a summary of clinically important information. This includes:

- patient identification: name, address, date of birth, sex, marital status, maiden name
- general practitioner: name, address
- list of problems: diagnoses, operations
- list of drugs: current and historical, with dose, route and may include particular drug warnings
- episodic data: in-patient stays, out-patient attendances

In addition, particular specialties hold selected information important to that specialty, e.g. blood sugar levels are stored for diabetic patients.

All this information can be printed on two or three sheets of A4 paper, see fig. 9.1. A copy is placed in the front of the patient's case-note. This can then act as a 'key' into the rest of the manual record. In fact, in some instances, notably at out-patient clinics, the summary can provide enough information to eliminate need for the manual record. The summary information is also available to the general practitioner together with comments from the hospital clinician.

Information is input to the system by the medical secretary of the consultant in charge of the patient. This information can come from a number of sources. When the patient is first entered into the computer, administrative data, such as name and address, are transcribed from the manual case-note. The clinician may supply further written information and may also use a dictaphone. The medical secretary uses a visual display unit (VDU) which is situated in her

PATIENT RECORD SYSTEM	Hospital Unit Number	123456

PATIENT SUMMARY as at 12 . 4 . 82 N.B. This list may be incomplete.	Surname SMITH	Forenames John
	Address 2 Main Street Aberdeen	Date of birth 5—7—17

No.	Year	Active	Inactive
1. 1. 1	75 75	Infarction, myocardial Failure, ventricular — Lt	
2.	30		Tonsillectomy
3.	75	Osteoarthritis	
4.	74		Smoking
5.	77	Hypertension	
6.	79	Embolus, pulmonary	

Current Medication as at 12. 4. 82

Start mth/yr	Prob. no.		Dose		Route	Freq.	Finish (if Date known)
2/75	1.1	Digoxin	0.125	mg	Oral	x1	
2/75	1.1	Frusemide	80	mg	Oral	x1	
2/75	1.1	Slow K	600	mg	Oral	x3	
5/77	5.0	Propranolol	40	mg	Oral	x3	
4/79	6.0	Warfarin	10	mg	Oral	x3	

(Fig. 9.1)

*** DIGOXIN *** CAUTION IN ELDERLY PATIENTS, RENAL INSUFFICIENCY,
             HYPOKALAEMIA (DIURETICS) ***

*** PROPRANOLOL *** CAUTION IN AIRWAYS OBSTRUCTION, CARDIAC
             FAILURE, PERIPHERAL VASCULAR DISEASE, DIABETES
             MELLITUS ***

*** WARFARIN *** CAUTION IN PEPTIC ULCERATION, LIVER DISEASE, RENAL
             INSUFFICIENCY, HYPOALEUMINAEMIA ***

Fig. 9.1 The computer produced summary. (All data is fictitious.)

own room and connected to the central computer either by a private wire or through the telephone system.

The software driving the VDU is fairly simple but includes a number of important points. Each prompt for data can be answered 'HELP' by the user. So if at any time the secretary is unsure what the system is asking for, then the system itself will help out. At the other end of the scale an experienced user can choose a number of 'short-cuts' which greatly speed up the rate of data entry. This concept of catering for a wide range of experience in the user is very helpful. The system also confirms at regular intervals as to whether the user wishes to carry out a set of updates. This, together with a facility to 'break-out' of an update by pressing a control key, reduces errors creeping in.

When a patient is discharged from a hospital ward, the secretary uses the system to produce a structured letter to the general practitioner from the clinician. The system then updates the database with any new information about the patient. A slightly different procedure allows the secretary to 'register' a patient who has not been through the ward.

When a patient comes to an out-patient clinic a summary, or patient-profile as it is known, is printed. This document provides the doctor with the information he requires about the patient and also acts as a 'turn-around' document. This means that the same piece of paper which supplies data to the user also acts as a data-entry form for new information to go back to the computer. The doctor simply writes any changes in the patient's condition or medication, includes any follow-up information, and then passes it back to his medical secretary for entry into the system.

Use is also made of the system for research and preventative care. Doctors have access to the data via an interactive 'browsing' program. This is discussed in more detail later.

We can identify the end-user interface in this system as:

- printing of patient summaries
- doctors updating these documents manually

- data entry by the medical secretary
- browsing for research purposes

THE ENVIRONMENT

Some six thousand patients are currently registered in the database (late 1982). In fact the policy has developed to use the system only for the care of the so-called 'high-risk' group i.e. chronically sick patients, rather than to attempt to computerise records for the entire population — around 600 000 in the area. The system is used in three medical units, their associated out-patient clinics, and a large hypertension clinic. In addition, patient follow-up care is shared with general practice and two hundred local practitioners participate in the scheme.

The system was originally developed on a CTL Modular One — a medium sized minicomputer. This was installed in 1974 and has since been replaced by the new range CTL 8046. The data occupies around eighteen Mbytes. There are five remote VDUs used by the medical secretaries who can enter data for around forty patients an hour.

The system has been well received by clinicians and their secretaries alike. It is clear that the success of the system beyond a few enthusiastic doctors is dependent on how well it can meet the information needs of its users. This, in turn, is dependent on the effectiveness of the end-user interface.

DATABASE MANAGEMENT

As early as 1973 it was agreed that the patient record system should be developed using database management techniques. In particular the CODASYL DBTG approach was favoured. There were a number of reasons for this:

(a) CODASYL was beginning to formulate a standard for database management. If this standard was then implemented across many different computers — in much the same way as COBOL is — this meant that systems developed on one computer could be transported to another. This is an important consideration.

(b) The medical data being considered was fairly complex particularly in its inter-relationships. There were a number of many to many relationships. For example, a patient may have a number of diagnoses or problems. On the other hand any particular problem, e.g. hypertension, is found in the problem list of many patients. So there exists a many to many relationship between patient and problem title. CODASYL DBTG offered a chance to model these relationships in a well-defined manner.

(c) Many complex programs would have to be written. Instead of writing many lines of program to handle files, CODASYL offered a high-level language with which to access the data. In a business where the most expensive commodity is people, any saving in time to produce programs is worth considering. For example a piece of program to display a patient's history might look like:

```
DISPLAY "ENTER PATIENT NUMBER".
ACCEPT PAT-NUMBER.
FIND PATIENT USING PAT-NUMBER.
PRIOR-CARE.
FIND PRIOR CARE RECORD ACCEPTING 0307.
IF DBMERR EQUAL 0307 THEN GO TO END.
GET CARE.
DISPLAY "WARD =" CARE-WARD.
DISPLAY "ADMISSION =" CARE-ADM-DATE.
DISPLAY "DISCHARGE =" CARE-DIS-DATE.
GO TO PRIOR-CARE.
END.
```

Here the appropriate patient is found and his set of care episodes is traversed in reverse chronological order. The program is succint, readable and all pointers are safely hidden from the programmer.

(d) It seemed likely that the patient record system would be one of many systems sharing different items of data. These might include patient administration, pharmacy stock control, chemical pathology, waiting-lists, out-patient clinic bookings. All these systems overlap at different points. Most would require some form of patient index for identification purposes, pharmacy could share a drug title dictionary with the patient record system and so on. This possibility also indicated that database had a positive advantage.

It is perhaps worthwhile looking at these reasons with the benefit of hindsight. The transportation concept is sound. Much Health Service work is now done on ICL computers. ICL market IDMS which is a database management system to CODASYL DBTG standards. We could transfer our database to an ICL IDMS-X environment with little or no change. Unfortunately little else of the system could be transported, in particular much of the software which drives the end-user interface.

It *has* proved easier to model the relationships in a database and it is certainly easier to write programs. The database structures have proved flexible enough to meet changing needs and to reflect our deepening understanding of the complex relationships between things in the real world. New programmers joining our project team have quickly picked up the concepts involved and are soon writing programs carrying out complex functions.

The shared-data idea is the most often quoted advantage of database systems but in our case has yet to be proven. It can be demonstrated that sharing data is technically sound but it is much harder to convince users working in different departments that it is worth doing. People are reluctant to let someone else use the data which, traditionally, is their responsibility. It is easy to make assumptions and confuse different uses of an apparently common data item. A good example is address. The family practitioner's understanding of a patient's address is the home that he visits. A hospital, on the other hand, may hold the address that the patient is discharged to — this could well be a relative who lives in the same town. It is clear that two different data items exist and cannot be shared. Only now, some ten years on, is the Health Service beginning to explore the concept of shared data.

Having decided that database was essential the next problem was that there were no database management systems available at that time on minicomputers. The first version of the patient record system was written to use a pilot database management system developed jointly with Aberdeen University. This was written in FORTRAN and implemented a subset of the original CODASYL DBTG specification. It was limited in facilities and in size but valuable experience was gained and it paved the way for the next stage.

By 1976 there were still no CODASYL systems for minicomputers so it was agreed to develop a large subset of CODASYL as a production system. This took some eight to ten man-years to design and develop and is still in use in 1982. Security, transaction processing software and the screen handling system were also developed in-house. Most of the systems software was written in CORAL 66 which is an ALGOL-like procedural language.

ROSIE, our database management system, implements both schema and sub-schema levels and the DML includes FIND, GET, STORE, MODIFY, DELETE, INSERT, REMOVE, IF, OPEN ALL and CLOSE ALL. Database-marks are available and checkpointing can be done automatically or under program control. This means if a program fails or if the programmer chooses then the database is rolled back to last known good state or checkpoint. Sets can be chained or pointer-array and may own more than one record-type. The pointer-arrays are implemented using balanced 8-tree indexes. Record indexes are used at the top level as CALC is not implemented. With this exception the system is very similar to IDMS-X.

Despite the success of our database system there is little to recommend anyone developing their own database management system. Large-scale systems software is best left to the computer manufacturer or the systems house to develop. Even once developed the system requires on-going improvement to keep it up to date with current user needs. This can prove very expensive in person resource.

EXPERIENCE

Earlier an effective end-user interface was defined as one which meets the needs of the users. This apparently obvious statement cannot be over-stressed. It is vital that the users' needs are well researched, not forgetting that what the user *says* he needs may be very different from a realistic approach to his requirements. The user may insist that an interactive terminal is essential when in actual fact a monthly printout or micro-fiche may be quite sufficient.

Unfortunately the opposite may well hold and it may be impossible to meet the requirements with the available technology. Very often budget is the limiting factor. In the end a compromise must be reached. It can be shown that database offers the end-user some significant advantages.

When VDUs first came into vogue it seemed that the ideal solution to medical records was to place such a terminal on the doctor's desk. This has been tried with varying degrees of success in other projects but in our experience doctors in general do not like the idea of a terminal on their desk. This is partly irrational, fear of something new, or 'will I have to learn to type?' but it is also true that it could well interfere with the doctor—patient rapport.

A very simple alternative is to use an encounter document. This carries all the information from the computer to the doctor in a clear structured fashion with important sections such as drug warnings highlighted. This same piece of paper carries information back to the computer in the form of the doctor's hand-written additions.

In the early days the next stage was to transfer this new data to punched cards to be read by the computer. This gave rise to a number of problems. Punching was long and laborious, and many errors appeared even with experienced staff. It was very hard to read the complicated medical terms and very easy to get them wrong.

This problem was solved by giving a VDU to the medical secretary. This has been immensely successful for two reasons. Firstly, there is knowledge. The secretary is trained in medical matters. She may not understand it all but at least she is used to dealing with the unpronounceable medical terms and she has a better than most chance of reading the doctor's writing! Secondly, the terminal allows the secretary to interact with the computer. It is in this area that the database has proved vital.

The database allows fast on-line access to all the data held on each patient as well as to extensive dictionaries of consultants, drugs and problem titles. This offers comprehensive validation of all data entered into the system. Because the data for a patient can be displayed, only new or modified data need be entered. The user — in this case the medical secretary — can visually check what she is doing and any validation errors can be notified at that time. There is a good chance that the originator of the data, the clinician, is nearby and can be asked to correct any errors so discovered.

One of the difficulties in using computers in the medical records field is the 'softness' of the data. It may be complicated and lengthy to calculate an employee's pay but it is usually well defined how to do it. Such data is 'hard'. Medical data, on the other hand, is frequently much more difficult to pin down. Clinicians themselves may differ in opinion of how best to structure the data. Data analysis reveals a rich variety of relationships between different items. So it is essential that a sufficiently detailed data analysis is carried out before designing the database schema.

The advantages of a CODASYL database are (i) that an attempt can be made to model these rich structures, (ii) that it permits efficient navigation of the data structures and (iii) that such navigation is readily programmed.

There exist standard data analysis techniques which result in an entity-relationship model of the real world. It is relatively straightforward to map this kind of model on to a network of records and sets which make up a CODASYL schema. Sometimes alterations are made for speed or efficiency but generally entities (i.e. things such as patients and doctors) map to records and relationships map to sets.

If the structure of records and sets is necessarily complex then it is important that the appropriate linkages and traversals of these linkages are carried out as efficiently as possible. By assigning these tasks to the database management system this assists the programmer in making a program both efficient and error-free.

It is these underlying advantages that permit the end-user interface to function adequately. Good screen-handling software is important to make best use of the terminal but is in fact complementary to the database system.

It is worth noting here that a database system used in this way makes heavy demands on the hardware resources of the computer. These should be adequate to ensure a realistic response time at the terminal. There are also a number of other software techniques which we use but which are not immediately relevant to this discussion.

These include soundex coding of surnames, intelligent phrase matching, checkdigits.

It is our experience that user discussion is vital. It is after all the user that uses the end-user interface and the system can only be a success if the user is intimately involved in its design and its on-going development. It helps if some particular person on the user side, in our case a doctor, can be nominated to attempt to bridge the gap between computer person and user. We have a group meeting on a regular basis which includes representation from both users and computer people.

It is often surprising what makes the difference as far as accept-ability is concerned. From the start we have insisted on using both upper and lower case letters, and on printing on A4 size plain white paper. Apparently the sprocket holes down each side of the paper caused much lack of credibility and our recent acquisition of a letter-quality printer and sheet-feeder resulting in typescript output have done much to boost our success. It must be stressed that a system stands or falls on its end-user interface. An apparently good system which is hard for the user to accept will never be extended beyond a few enthusiasts.

We have proved that much can be done with standard VDUs but it is important to consider the wide range of peripherals now on the market. Bar-code readers are proving very popular for stock control applications. One medical application (Petrie, 1979) utilises a touch-sensitive VDU. A number of options are displayed on the screen and the user simply touches the appropriate part of the screen to select one of the options. The keyboard is only used when it is required to type in some new alpha-numeric data.

An interesting situation has developed in one of our user depart-ments. Next to the patient records terminal in the secretary's office is a second terminal which is linked to another computer running a chemical pathology system. The possibility of sharing the same terminal was investigated, but it became apparent that information was required from both systems concurrently. In reality this is a distributed database which would require a fairly complex end-user interface in order to access both systems at the one terminal.

Earlier 'browsing' was discussed. A powerful interactive program is available to clinicians in order to access the database in many different ways. The interface is simple to use and basically allows the user to navigate his way around the database, fig. 9.2. This facility is used for research and for preventative care studies. The program was developed for debugging purposes but it was realised how useful it was and it now has a very easy-to-use interface. The doctor must have some idea about the structure of the database but only at a

INTROG

TASK: *FIND PATIENT UNITNO 123456*
123456   SMITH   John   5/ 7/17 M MA

TASK: *LIST PROBLEM*

1.0	1975	AC	Infarction, myocardial
1.1	1975	AC	Failure, ventricular − Lt
2.0	1930	IN	Tonsillectomy
3.0	1975	AC	Osteoarthritis
4.0	1974	IN	Smoking
5.0	1977	AC	Hypertension
6.0	1979	AC	Embolus, pulmonary

TASK: *FIND DRUG*
TITLE: *WARFARIN*
TITLE FOUND   Warfarin
NUMBER OF PATIENTS   26

TASK: *LIST OWNER*
100000   JONES   Mary   12/ 4/31 F WI
123456   SMITH   John   9/12/48 M MA

Fig. 9.2 An example of browsing.

general level and the program can offer help and advice at any stage.

Queries which would be too lengthy to run interactively, e.g. 'give me all the female patients under 60 years old who suffer from hypertension and are being treated with drug X', are handled by a batch program. The doctor simply fills in a form stating his requirements and a generalised search program is run, usually overnight.

An online system like ours can be divided into a number of different parts:

- database management
- application programs
- user-interface software
- transaction processing
- security, integrity and recovery

These are all inter-related to make up the complete system. CODA-SYL provides standards in database management and in the parts of the application programs which deal with the database. Standards are important for many reasons. They mean that programmers can move between systems and systems can move between different computers. COBOL may not be the best theoretical language available but the fact that it is so widely used makes it very useful practically. Lack of standards in the other parts — particularly in the end-user interface area — is a real deficiency.

It has been said that a system is only as good as its parts and this is certainly true of the end-user interface. It is also essential, however, that each part of the system fit together properly. This is especially true of recovery. When a system breaks it is vital that the service is restored as quickly as possible and with the minimum disruption to the user. This means close cooperation of the recovery software with the database management system, the transaction processing software and the user interface.

To conclude, the end-user interface is the 'shop window' of the system. Whether we like it or not we are in the business of 'selling' computer systems to the uninitiated, often ill-informed, and sometimes openly hostile, potential user. Despite, or perhaps because of, the media, the public is still very sceptical and very often a little scared of computers. It is up to the designer, particularly of the end-user interface, to ease the transition into making computers an acceptable tool in today's society.

REFERENCES

Allen, K.F., McLeod, G., Petrie, J.C. (1980) 'Does a database really help health care?' *Annals World Association of Medical Informatics*, 207—212.

Lindsey, D.C., Meredith, A.L., Petrie, J.C. (1977) 'An experimental database for clinical and administrative use', *Medcomp 1977*, 725—39.

Petrie, J.C., McIntyre, N. eds. (1979) *The problem oriented medical record — its use in hospitals, general practice and medical education*, Edinburgh: Churchill Livingstone.

Petrie, J.C., McLeod, G., *et al.* (1982) 'A computer-assisted patient record system', *Medical Informatics Europe, Dublin*.

Wilson, L.A., Petrie, J.C., Dawson, A.A., Marron, A.C. (1978) 'The new Aberdeen medical record', *Brit Med J.*, 414—16.

CHAPTER 10

Data Integrity and Security

By P. Prosser (formerly with Alcan Plate Ltd)

INTRODUCTION

This section discusses integrity and security of databases. Integrity is defined to be entireness, wholeness: the unimpaired state of anything; security is defined as state, feeling or means of being free from danger.

There is a certain duality of security and integrity. There is little point in having a secure system (data that is free from the danger of being destroyed or lost) that cannot be said to have 'integrity' (that is the information held within the database or files is known and believed to be correct).

Security of a system tends to be an operational function, but of course must be a designed feature of a system. The system's security to a large degree depends on the discipline of computer operations staff, an external factor. Integrity is a feature designed into the application programs that act upon a database and the structure of the database itself; internal factors.

In engineering the maxim is to design in simplicity and lightness. This is true for software engineering. In terms of security the operations to be performed must be light, as they have to be performed manually, by operations staff, religiously. If the task is complex and lengthy it becomes susceptible to errors and security is lost. The design of integrity should be simple and well understood so that the system can be implemented, and once implemented, successfully run.

This topic is discussed, loosely, in the context of a system which was designed and implemented for Alcan Plate Ltd in Birmingham (the system is described later in some detail). The system was developed in stages and gradually integrated. The system itself will never be complete because by nature a production environment constantly changes as new production techniques become available and market trends change. The system described here will continue to change to meet those requirements. As described in other parts of this book, system flexibility is a feature enhanced by the database approach.

THE APPLICATION

Alcan Plate Ltd (APL), formerly James Booth & Co, have been manufacturing quality aluminium plate since 1938. Throughout the years the works have been continually modernised. APL is at present undergoing an investment program for the 1980s. The major investments are in the development of an advanced heat treatment furnace controlled by an on-line computer system and in a complete management information system (MIS).

THE MANUFACTURING PROCESS

APL produce high quality aluminium plate for the aero-space industry and aluminium armour plate (Chobham armour) and painted products (for the likes of caravan bodies). The manufacturing process is briefly described below.

Casting

Process scrap, raw aluminium ingot and the necessary alloying elements are combined together and melted in one of three large casting furnaces. After the molten metal has been fluxed and cleansed it is cast into slabs or billets by the semi-continuous Direct Chill (DC) method; that is the metal is cast between jets of water without a mould. At stages in the casting, samples are taken for chemical analysis. The slabs and billets are uniquely identified by a cast number. A slab is typically 3000 mm long, 1200 mm wide, 325 mm thick and weighs approximately 3000 Kg. Billets are cylindrical and are of similar weight. Immediately following casting, slabs are lifted by overhead crane to a work station called the High Bay Scales (HBS), there the metal's cast number is recorded as is its alloy, dimensions and weight.

Homogenising

Slabs and billets of specific alloys require homogenising or stress relieving. This is a batch process, slabs and billets requiring the same heat treatment are loaded in a furnace together. Homogenising takes between three and twelve hours.

Sawing

Slabs and billets that have a recognised flaw (either physical such as cracking or crazed surface or chemical) may have that flawed area sawn off. The new length of the slab is reported.

Scalping

The scalper resembles a giant milling machine. Slabs are machined to remove the outer skin from the two major surfaces. The scalper machines both surfaces at the same time to a high engineering finish. Up to 20 mm may be taken from each surface. After scalping the slab is ultrasonically tested to ensure freedom from internal flaws. Slabs are then weighed and graded according to their surface quality.

Chemical analysis
The samples taken from the DC casting units are spectrographically analysed and their composition compared to internationally accepted limits. If the alloy falls outside of its expected limitations then it is scrapped and the shop floor is informed. The slab may then later be re-melted.

Delivery
Slabs that have been scalped and have successfully passed chemical analysis can now be transported by fork lift truck to a holding area, the Amazon Bay, ready to be used in the hot rolling process.

Soaking pits
The soaking pits are furnaces which are used to raise the temperature of slabs before hot rolling. The heat in the pits is controlled so that all slabs are raised to their correct rolling temperature. On reaching that temperature they are left for several hours to soak so that they assume a uniform temperature. Between 10 and 20 slabs will be in a pit together. Operators are given log sheets informing them what size and alloy of slabs to load into pits and the temperature settings for that pit. The slabs are selected from stock in the Amazon Bay and are lifted into and out of the pits by an overhead crane (namely the Amazon).

Hot mill
Slabs that have completed their soaks are unloaded from the soak pits onto the hot line where they are rolled into plates of required dimensions. The plates may be sheared into lengths on the hot line. Plates are identified by a unique plate number and then loaded onto pallets, again by crane.

Cropping
The hot rolled plates tend to crack at the edges during the rolling operation. These cracked edges are cropped off.

HHT furnace
After cropping the plates are heat treated in a Horizontal Heat Treatment Furnace. This is a continuous process. The furnace is about forty metres long and is made of a series of furnaces and baths linked

by a conveyor belt. Plates progress through the furnace, are brought up to temperature, held there for a specified period of time and then quenched in water. This quenching freezes the plate's crystalline structure. Plates requiring similar treatments progress through the furnace together as envelopes. An envelope is by definition a group of similar plates. The furnaces, temperatures and conveyors speeds are controlled by a Siemens R30 computer. This computer is linked to the shop floor reporting system (SFR) computer (an HP3000) via a MRJE link. Plate/envelope information is passed from the SFR systems computer to the furnace controller.

Controlled stretch
After HHT the plates are subjected to a controlled stretch. The plates are submitted to a maximum pull of 4000 tonnes to stretch them by about 2% of length. This stretching operation is performed by hydraulic rams. The stretch fulfils two objectives: to remove distortion after HHT, stress relieve the plate. If plates had not been edge cropped prior to this operation then the edge cracks would propagate and the plate break. This would not only lead to the loss of the plate but also the possible damage to the hydraulics of the stretcher. The releasing of such energy from the rams within a short period of time (milliseconds) destroys the ram's seals. This is not an uncommon event.

Ultrasonic testing
Plates are immersed in tanks of water and scanned ultrasonically in the x–y plane. Flaws in the plate are displayed on a TV monitor. Flaws on the plate are marked and if they cannot be cut out then the plate is scrapped.

Final sawing
The plates are sawn into the dimensions required by the customer.

Packing
Sawn plates are packed as per customer requirements. Plates may be oiled and wrapped in plastic to protect their surface prior to being loaded onto wooden pallets. At this stage invoices are produced.

Until the start of the project, APL's use of computers was limited to bureau services running scheduling systems as batch jobs. The scheduling system attempted to maximise the utilisation of one critical resource, the heat treatment furnaces. Plates are processed through these furnaces as batches, each batch receiving the same heat treatment. This scheduling system alone caused a significant reduction in the cost of plate production. The scheduling system was far from ideal as the data it used was picked up from hand written log sheets produced on the shop floor.

This data was then entered into the system. The scheduling system run once a week typically, and was using untimely (and therefore sometimes inaccurate) data and could not respond quickly to changes in the Work In Progress (WIP).

Computers can be used in factory environments in essentially two roles:

(a) Real-Time control of machines or processes. Typically microprocessors or robots perform these tasks. APL have a Siemens R30 computer to control the HHT furnace.
(b) Shop Floor Reporting. The work force on the shop floor report on the progress of work. The system is collecting and distributing information. The computer stores a representation of the state of the shop floor, Work in Progress.

The HP3000 was used to support an interactive shop floor reporting sytem, maintaining a WIP database. The SFR system is only a part of a factory wide Management Information System. That system is made up of 5 parts namely: (i) Order Entry Handling, (ii) Process Planning, (iii) Scheduling, (iv) Shop Floor Reporting and (v) Invoicing. These systems reflect the normal production cycle. Customer orders are the start of the cycle. The Order Entry Handling (OEH) system processes customer orders from the time of receipt until they are shipped and the customer invoiced. The other functions of an OEH system are to process customer enquiries, provide price quotations, interface with commercial and accounting system and interface with process planning.

Process planning is the next step in the cycle. Customer orders are selected and these orders are planned; that is a set of instructions are derived on how to produce the order. Material requirements are stated. The route the work is expected to take through the factory is described. The process of selecting orders may be a first stage of a scheduling system.

The third step is scheduling. Given a batch of planned orders that have not yet been released onto the shop floor a scheduling process proposes a sequence for releasing that work into production. The objective of that scheduled sequence will be to maximise the utilisation of resources. Resources are always a combination of the four Ms: Men, Money, Materials, Machines. The scheduling system may try and maximise only one of these, whichever is the most critical resource. Secondary objectives of the scheduling system may be to minimise the value of the WIP, to minimise production times thus improving delivery dates and increase cash flow.

The scheduling system derives its data from a number of sources such as the order book (OEH system), planned orders (interim state of Work in Progress), the state of the shop floor and the materials available (WIP). The work is then released onto the shop floor. This is the fourth step in the cycle.

The shop floor reports against the progress of work. There are three points in time that the status of work will be reported back to the OEH system. These points are (i) when production starts, (ii) when production is complete and (iii) optionally when production has been scrapped for some reason.

The OEH system produces an invoice when the order has been completed. If the order has been scrapped then that order will again re-enter the production cycle at the planning stage.

Therefore we have a closed loop system made of four integrated components: Order Entry Handling (OEH), Process Planning (PP), Scheduling (S), and Shop Floor Reporting (SFR, sometimes called (WIP)). The scheduling system should be designed to loosely integrate with the other systems. The reason for this is that scheduling systems change in time as production techniques change and costs of resources vary.

FEATURES OF A SHOP FLOOR SYSTEM

The shop floor is a dynamic environment affected by a large number of random events such as the breakdown of machines, absence of key workers, non-availability of materials, scrapping of production.

For efficient control of resources management have to be aware of the up to date status of the WIP. Therefore it is necessary to monitor the actual condition of the activities that have been planned. Most manual WIP control systems are inadequate, and the flow of information is often delayed with the result that decisions are made in the absence of relevant information. A computer based SFR system can be used to keep accurate track of the very large volume of data involved and quickly highlight events that require management attention. The preparation of a realistic work sequence to be released onto the shop floor, produced by the scheduling system, is dependent on the availability of information on the current state of the shop floor activities. Inadequate or inaccurate data will only result in the creation of an unrealistic schedule that cannot be executed on the shop floor.

The shop floor is divided into machine centres (sometimes called work stations). A machine centre is an area where work is executed and reported to the SFR system via a shop floor terminal. The action of reporting to the system immediately updates the WIP database.

Typical information reported by the operators at machine centres are (i) arrival of work, (ii) the starting of work on a job, (iii) successful completion of work or (iv) the scrapping of work due to failure to pass quality control, (v) departure of work from this machine centre. From this information the following statistics are derived for each machine centre:

(a) Service Rate: the amount of work processed by this machine centre today.

(b) Arrival Rate: the amount of work arriving at this machine centre today (note if arrival rate is greater than service rate there is a queue building up).

(c) Recovery Rate: the percentage amount of good production leaving this machine centre compared with that arriving.

(d) Average Queuing Length: on average the number of jobs waiting at this machine centre at any given time. This gives an indication of the amount of storage/buffer space required at this centre.

(e) Average Queuing Time: the average time a job waits at this centre prior to processing beginning. This information is used to estimate the amount of lead time for a specific job with a predicted route through the shop floor.

(f) Average Processing Time: the average time to perform the operation at this machine centre (same use as (e) above).

(g) Transportation Time: average time a job takes from leaving previous machine centre to reaching this one (same use as (e) above).

(h) Energy Consumption: the amount of energy consumed per task. Energy is broken down into: gas, oil, electricity, oxygen.

(i) Down Time: the down time in a period that the machine centre was unavailable, categorised by reason for breakdown or type of maintenance.

(j) Accumulated Costs: overheads for this machine centre per unit time; a combination of rates, wages, depreciation etc.

The above statistics are derived from the action of reporting on the movement of work on the shop floor and are a by-product of secondary importance. The most useful information is the location and states of items of work. This information is used to drive the scheduling system and the clerical side of the production cycle.

REASONS FOR CHOICE OF SYSTEM

Alcan Plate Ltd (APL) chose to purchase Hewlett Packard equipment. There are a number of reasons why this came about. Initially APL considered a design of the OEH system existing on a separate processor. The SFR system would be split over two smaller data capture machines. These satellite machines were to be connected to the OEH system machine with data being down loaded to the SFR system and the OEH system being updated by the SFR system. The loss of the OEH system would not immediately affect the SFR system and the SFR system could be run in a degraded mode if one of the satellite machines was lost.

Hewlett Packard's range of systems appeared to meet the requirements of the above design. It was envisaged that a HP 3000 would support the OEH, scheduling and process planning functions. HP1000 would support the SFR system. The machines would be linked by HP's communication software DS (Distributed Systems). It was decided that Database Management System (DBMS) would be used to implement the data structure. The HP3000 and HP1000 use compatible versions of IMAGE. High level programming languages were also a requirement. It was hoped that PASCAL would be used.

HP had a full range of data entry terminals, specifically rugged shop floor reporting terminals that could be connected to the HP1000 via a twisted pair wire, in multi-drop mode (as opposed to point-to-point). For APL's future process controlling requirement HP's 1000 range and modules were most suitable.

A further attractive feature of HP equipment to APL was that there was a local OEM company newly set up dealing in HP hardware and eager to develop the OEH system. Being a young company it was hoped that APL would get that company's loyalty and attention. This proved to be the case; a good working relationship developed to the benefit of both companies.

Things did not go as planned. APL took delivery of their HP3000 and development of the OEH system proceeded on this machine. Two HP1000s were ordered. This took place at a period of industrial unrest with APL working a three day week and loosing foreign orders to their competitors. The order for the HP1000s was cancelled and development of the SFR system proceeded on the existing HP3000. At that time the shop floor terminals were not compatible with the HP3000 in multi-drop mode. This was cause for concern.

Eventually the climate changed for the better. Industrial problems were solved. The order book began to fill up again. A second HP3000 was purchased to support the SFR function and use as a development machine. Hewlett Packard developed MTS (Multi Terminal Software) to allow the shop floor reporting terminals to be compatible with the HP3000.

DATABASE MANAGEMENT SYSTEM USED

The SFR system maintains a Work in Progress database. This database was implemented and maintained using the HP3000 database management system IMAGE. IMAGE is a collection of related products as follows:

(a) *The schema processor:* following the design of the database it is described using the database description language. This external description is called the schema. The schema processor checks the syntax of the schema and compiles it into a root file.

(b) *The creation of the database:* this process takes the root file produced in (a) above and creates a database from it. The database is initially empty.

(c) *Library procedures:* a collection of library procedures, callable from high level languages, is available for maintaining the database. Typically the procedures are used to store, modify, retrieve and delete data from the database.

(d) *Maintenance of the database:* utility programs may be used to maintain back-up copies of the database and perform functions such as recovering or restructuring the database.

(e) *Query language:* an interpretive language used for accessing an IMAGE database without the use of purpose built application programs.

IMAGE relationships, within a database are as follows:

(a) The database is made up of related DATA SETS (similar to files).

(b) Data sets contain DATA ENTRIES (similar to records within files).

(c) A data entry is made up of one or many DATA ITEMS (similar to fields within a record).

(d) Data sets may be related. There are three types of data sets:

   (i) DETAIL data sets: sets that contain information and are references via MASTER data sets.

   (ii) MANUAL MASTER data sets: an index to possible many DETAIL sets. A MM data set contains information additional to that relating it to a DETAIL data set. Entries within a MM data set must be explicitly created prior to creating a relative entry in a DETAIL data set.

   (iii) AUTOMATIC MASTER data set: an index to one or many DETAIL data sets. Entries in the AM set are created and deleted automatically by IMAGE. When a new entry is produced in a DETAIL set that is referenced by an AM set, and no similarly related entry exist, then a related entry is created automatically in the AM set. The converse is true with deletions from related DETAIL data sets.

IMAGE only allows implicit relationships to a depth of one. That is MASTER sets cannot reference sets other than DETAIL sets and DETAIL sets cannot reference any other sets. There is only a MASTER to DETAIL relationship. More complex relationships must therefore be *explicit relationships* implemented by a combination of the structure of the database and the application programs that act upon it. Therefore any relationship can be implemented but may not be immediately apparent from study of the database schema; additional supportive documentation may be required.

One characteristic of the database language is that all data item names must be declared before declaration of data sets. This restriction should be thought of as a discipline. The declaration section of the schema should be structured as a simple data dictionary. Data items should be declared in alphabetic order and their meaning and use commented. Similarly, data sets should be commented and any explicit relationships described.

A naming convention was adhered to in the development of the system. Data sets within the database were named as follows: Automatic Master sets were given names A01 to A99, Manual Master sets were named M01 to M99 and Detail data sets were named D01 to D99. Within the schema the meaning of the data sets were fully commented. Data item names were given more colourful names, that is their names reflected their meaning. Data items were basically of only three types: character (B), integer (I) or double integer (D). Data items could be multiples of these types, such as B6 (six characters).

Within the application programs, data items within data sets were referenced by variables with names that fully described their meaning. For example variable B6'ALLOY'D21 is the data item ALLOY in detail data set D21 and is of type 6 characters; I1'LENGTH'M01 is data item LENGTH in manual master data set M01 and is of type 1 integer. This convention was the basis for development of application programs that were both robust and easily understood.

Segments of code, be they procedures or programs, were also subject to a naming convention. The source code for segments were held in editor files named SEG01 to SEG99. The source code was then compiled and prepared into a segmented library with corresponding names (SEG01 to SEG99). Within the code after each call to an IMAGE library procedure, a procedure was called to test the result of the most recent IMAGE call and produce a suitable error message and diagnostic if in error. Essentially that test routine was called as follows:

DTEST(STATUS,512);

The routine DTEST produces a diagnostic message if STATUS is not zero, implying a database error has occurred. The IMAGE routine DBINFO is called by DTEST to produce this diagnostic. Following this a QUIT routine is executed, displaying DTEST's second parameter, and then terminating the process. The second parameter is of the following form: divide it by 100 to get the segment in which the error occurred (therefore the source for above error would be in SEG05), the remainder of the division gives a position within the segment.

The value of naming and coding conventions cannot be over estimated. Well thought out conventions give programmers a clearly defined environment to work in thereby reducing communication problems. Program errors are easily recognised and therefore quickly remedied. The development of conventions must proceed at the design stage of a project and should be thought of as the basis of a robust, secure system.

INTEGRITY AND SECURITY MECHANISMS

Some of the mechanisms available to improve security and integrity of a system are now discussed. The mechanisms have been divided broadly into four parts. The first of these parts is a description of some of the simplest techniques currently used to enhance integrity of databases (and all computer systems generally). There's little new in this but its always worth reminding ourselves of the simpler things in life! The next part deals with the concept of a transaction and how locking affects integrity of a transaction. The third part deals with integrity health checks. A very useful trick (technique) is described. The last part deals with the mysteries of transaction logging and recovery. Forward recovery is compared to backward recovery.

SIMPLER TECHNIQUES

The simplest techniques for providing security and integrity tend to be the most fundamental and valuable. It must be remembered that security/integrity maintenance must be a routine task performed religiously and that the more easy it is to perform the more likely that it will be done correctly.

The most common technique used is to take day end copies of the database. On the HP3000 the DBMS, IMAGE, provides a utility

DBSTORE to perform this task. DBSTORE copies the database to magnetic tape. In other systems a copy of the database may be written to disc. There is no point in copying the database, for security reasons, and then keeping the copy in an insecure environment. The copied database must be kept in a secure environment, preferably away from the computer system. The copy should be kept in a fire proof safe away from the computer, the reason being that this would minimise the catastrophic effect a fire could have on the computer system. At least the copy could be taken to another machine.

The medium that data is copied to should be frequently renewed. Magnetic media (tape in particular) does degrade with use and with time. To copy data to poor quality tapes and discs is tempting providence. As may be appreciated, replacement of recording media is not cheap but it must be compared with the cost to a company of the loss of its data (imagine losing an order book; records of all the stock items in an inventory control system; all the flight bookings for an airline; a country's tax records!). As a rule of thumb, tapes should be replaced once a year, and the old tapes should be destroyed to avoid being 'dangerously' used or passed to some lower security application (to be used by program development teams for example).

Finding time to perform the back-up procedure can be a particularly difficult task. The copying of the database must take place on a quiescent system; nobody can be accessing that database. In the SFR system, production on the shop floor is executed by continuous shifts (overlapping) 24 hours a day, seven days a week. Production cannot be stopped merely to allow a database to be backed-up. Production is paramount. Therefore, reporting of production to the system must be arrested for that back-up period. In such an environment, the time to perform the back-up must be minimal to avoid the catch up time required by the reporting users when the system becomes available again. This catch up is the effort required to enter the data produced whilst the system was unavailable. Also consider that operations staff may have to be present whilst back-up is performed; this may mean shift working or at least overtime. Back-up is expensive!

Once a week the entire system should be backed-up, that is the database, the application programs acting on it and all the software that makes up the computer system. This is done in case of catastrophic damage to a disk leading to loss of system and data. This back-up takes the greatest time. System back-up is of particular importance in the development environment where the system (its application programs) is changed or developed as the database is modified.

TRANSACTIONS AND LOCKING STRATEGY

A transaction on a database is the modification of one or many data sets at the completion of which the database is in a logically consistent state. For example in a stock control system the selling of stock to the customer may be thought of as a transaction consisting of:

(a) In the INVENTORY data set, for this item: decrement the quantity on hand, increase the quantity sold this period, and accumulate the value of sales of this item.

(b) In the SALES ledger data set (if a credit customer): put an entry for this customer.

(c) In the AUDIT data set: put summary information.

The transaction is complete if, and only if, steps (a) (b) and (c) above have been performed. The transaction may be complete as above but leave the database in an incorrect state. This can occur if another process reads the same item in data set INVENTORY above immediately before it is updated in (a), and then proceeds to perform steps (a) through (c) after the other process. This is explained more fully below:

Step	Process A	Process B
1	READ (ITEM 'X)	READ (ITEM 'X)
2	INC (QTY' OF 'X)	INC (QTY' OF 'X)
3	WRITE (ITEM 'X)	WRITE (ITEM 'X)

In the example above assume two processes, A and B, which read the same data entry from the same data set, ITEM 'X in step (1) above.

The quantity sold of item X is then increased to step (2) (increment QTY' OF 'X). After incrementing the quantity, the data entry is written back to the data set. If QTY' OF 'X has a value of 10 and processes A and B start at the same point in time and proceed at the same rate then at the completion of step (3) QTY' OF 'X will have a value of 11. It should have a value of 12. How is it ensured that this is the case? Processes A and B must be made independent of one another by being forced to run sequentially through this critical section, not concurrently.

Processes A and B must communicate with each other. One process must tell the other that it is about to enter a critical state and the other process must then wait until that process signals that it is no longer critical. On getting this signal the waiting process can proceed. The mechanism that allows this is universally referred to as *locking* (the basis of inter-process communication). A successful locking strategy is a prerequisite of data integrity as demonstrated below.

The example would have to be modified as follows:

Step	Process A	Process B
1	LOCK (ITEM 'X)	LOCK (ITEM 'X)
2	READ (ITEM 'X)	READ (ITEM 'X)
3	INC (QTY' OF 'X)	INC (QTY' OF 'X)
4	WRITE (ITEM 'X)	WRITE (ITEM 'X)
5	UNLOCK (ITEM 'X)	UNLOCK (ITEM 'X)

The construct LOCK (ITEM 'X) has the effect of forcing a process to suspend if another process has currently a LOCK in effect. The suspended process is re-awakened when the active process performs an UNLOCK. The constructs LOCK and UNLOCK are indivisible operations; that is an attempt to perform two LOCKS simultaneously by separate processes will be forced into a chronological sequence. Successful locking strategies are essential to the integrity of data as demonstrated.

The IMAGE database management system (DBMS) allows locking at three levels: data item level, data set level and database level. Locking at the data item level allows concurrent processes to modify the database so long as they do not access the same items, thus allowing a high degree of concurrency. Locking at data set level allows concurrent processes to modify the data base so long as they modify mutually exclusive data sets. Locking at the database level only allows one process to modify the database at one time; processes queue up in chronological order to modify data.

As the level of locking becomes more detailed (the ultimate detail being data item locking) the amount of work the DBMS must perform to apply these locks increases; more time is spent comparing lock items to determine if they are mutually exclusive. This is the cost of high concurrency.

Another complex matter worth thinking of (it is only mentioned and no conclusions are offered) is that in most computer systems only one process can actively possess the CPU at any instant in time. If the database resides on one disc drive it can safely be said that only one process can have the present disc I/O pending. Therefore it may be more efficient, if transactions are short, to allow processes exclusive access to the database to perform modifications and save complex locking strategies.

One consideration when designing a locking strategy is that of *dead lock* avoidance. Dead lock occurs when two concurrent processes, A and B, are simultaneously suspended waiting on a resource that the other process has locked. This can only occur if processes are allowed to lock multiple resources. If processes become deadlocked at the very least one of these processes will have to be aborted; generally the system will have to be brought down in as orderly a fashion as is possible. This obviously affects database integrity.

To avoid deadlocks when locking multiple resources, a hierarchical locking strategy should be adhered to. There should be an accepted sequence in which resources are acquired and locked. Assume that a database application locks at the data set level and each lock must be explicitly called. Further assume that data sets are referred to by number. A workable locking strategy might be that data sets are locked in increasing order of set number and released in decreasing order of set number. This is demonstrated in the example below, with processes A and B not impeding each other:

Step	Process A	Process B
1	LOCK (1)	LOCK (4)
2	LOCK (8)	LOCK (7)
3	UNLOCK (8)	LOCK (8)
4	UNLOCK (1)	UNLOCK (8)
5		UNLOCK (7)
6		UNLOCK(4)

In the example below if process A moves faster than process B such that A reaches step 2 before process B reaches its step 3, when process B reaches its step 3 it is suspended, waiting on data set 8. When process A reaches its step 3 process B is re-awakened and allowed to proceed to its step 3, LOCK (8).

Step	Process A	Process B
1	LOCK (1)	LOCK (4)
2	LOCK (8)	LOCK (7)
3	UNLOCK (8)	LOCK (8)
4	UNLOCK (1)	UNLOCK (8)
		UNLOCK (7)
		UNLOCK (4)

The hierarchical strategy can be proved by mathematical induction to avoid deadlock. It is worth noting also that if it can be proved that in the strategy each process always locks a common resource (lets say data set number 4 is always locked) then processes will proceed in chronological order and we are as well locking at the database level.

INTEGRITY HEALTH CHECKS

The database should be subjected to regular 'health' checks by application and system programs that diagnose 'disease'. In this instance 'disease' should be thought of as loss of integrity, an incidence of errors.

Errors can only be defined subjectively in the environment in which they are detected. Therefore the environment they occur in must be defined. It can be said that an 'erroneous system, given a set of triggering conditions, will cause a set of undesirable effects'. The object of the health check is to detect the errors before the triggering conditions occur. This is an extremely difficult task for anything but a trivial system as it presupposes that all triggering conditions are defined. This can never be the case. A good diagnostic system should analyse the behaviour of the system under a meaningful subset of the total condition space.

Integrity tests should be carried out on the database at regular intervals and after a system failure of any kind. Integrity tests fall broadly into two areas; tests of *logical* integrity and test of *structural* integrity.

Logical integrity

Essentially, tests of logical integrity confirm the correctness of data. In the simplest of forms such an integrity test might be to confirm that the processed transactions agree with trial balances, or that check digits agree with their corresponding data. In a database transaction a logical transaction might consist of a number of corresponding PUTs (creation of records, writes) to different data sets. The integrity checker should test that such pairs co-exist.

The integrity test procedure should produce a report detailing any inconsistencies. The integrity test procedure should be well documented, and each test explained fully. A function of this report should be to advise remedial action to be taken for specific diagnosed problems. There is no point in diagnosing a problem without (i) letting it be known what the problem is and (ii) suggesting a remedy for that problem. It must also be realised that an integrity test system must be nasty and sadistic by nature. It has as its primary objective to find errors (secondary to advise a cure), not to certify a system as being error free. A good diagnostic system fails if it does not detect any errors.

Do not underestimate the effort required to check logical integrity nor underestimate its value. It turns out that Zeno's paradox applies equally well to finding errors as it does to shooting arrows: finding the first half of the errors present takes a unit of effort, finding half of the remaining errors takes a unit of effort, and so on ad infinitum. There is something akin to a half-life situation for errors.

In the SFR system a trick was devised to implement a first stage integrity test (Zeno's first arrow!). This trick is applicable to any system. The purpose of the first test is to determine if, after a failure, any processes terminated in mid-transaction leaving the database in an inconsistent state. The trick is now described.

Within the database a data set was set aside to represent users. As a user logs onto the system he puts a new data entry into the data set, corresponding to himself. The data entry consists of his identification (ID) and a flag (FLAG). Initially the flag is given a value of zero. All transactions on the system take the following form:

```
LOCK(ITEMS);
SETFLAG(ID);
<< modify database as required >>
UNSETFLAG(ID);
UNLOCK(ITEMS);
```

Routine SETFLAG reads the data entry with key ID from the USER data set, sets the corresponding FLAG to one and over-writes the existing data entry (an update). Therefore if a user flag is set to one he is in a critical section; a lock is currently in effect. Routine UNSETFLAG does as SETFLAG but zeros FLAG for an ID. As the user logs off, his data entry is deleted from the USER data set.

When the database is in a quiescent state (such as at the end of day when all users have logged off, or following a system failure), if any entries exist in the USER data set then a process failed to log off. If any of the USER's FLAG's are set to one then their process must have aborted in mid-transaction leaving the database in a corrupt state. If the database is indicated to be corrupt further checking may be performed by the integrity checking routines or (if transaction logging has been used) the system can be recovered from the log files.

If after a system failure all the USER flags are zero then the system went down without having any transactions on the fly; the database should have maintained its logical integrity. In that case no recovery is required and the system can be safely handed back to the users after clearing out all entries in the USER data set. This is of increasing value as the cost of recovery increases.

Structural integrity

Structural integrity has to do with the way that the data is physically stored by the DBMS. For example IMAGE allows chains of data, like items linked together. Records must therefore have backward and forward pointers to allow chain traversal. In the event of a failure as a data entry is being written to disk these pointers may become corrupted. A chain may be broken (traverse it and you fall off the edge of the world!) or may contain a loop (you traverse it for ever!).

Detecting such weaknesses in the structure of the data should not be the user's responsibility but the DBMS's responsibility. It is too technical and usually beyond the scope of average applications. In any event what remedial action could a user take on diagnosing a structural failure? Manipulation of structural elements of a database not only allows flexibility in repairing damage but allows infinite scope in producing errors.

Generally avoid developing such systems. Use systems that have been tried and tested by the DBMS vendor or some third party source. Do not use unsupported software to perform such tasks.

TRANSACTION LOGGING AND RECOVERY

FORWARD RECOVERY

On completion of a transaction, a summary of all processing that took place on the database to perform that transaction is written to the log file. Given a transaction as below:

```
DBLOCK
DBBEGIN                 << 1 >>
   DBDELETE(    )       << 2 >>
   DBUPDATE(    )       << 3 >>
   DBPUT(    )          << 4 >>
DBEND                   << 5 >>
DBUNLOCK
```

All statements nested within the DBBEGIN/DBEND pair make up the transaction. The statements (1), (2), (3), (4) and (5) with their parameters are written to the log file. Items (1) and (5) contain process identification. To perform a recovery the last DBSTORE of the database is DBRESTORE and a recovery procedure is run that executes all statements on the log file that make up complete transactions. A complete transaction is a collection of database modifications nested between DBBEGIN/DBEND pair, both with same process identification.

TRANSACTION LOGGING/BACKWARD RECOVERY

In this method the object is to back out incomplete transactions from the current database after a corruption of the database. The example below is used to illustrate the technique:

```
DBLOCK
DBBEGIN                 << 1 >>
   DBDELETE(    )       << 2 >>
   DBUPDATE(    )       << 3 >>
   DBPUT(    )          << 4 >>
```

DBEND $<< 5 >>$
DBUNLOCK

The log file to be used in a backward recovery is significantly different from that required for forward recovery. In backward recovery what is written to the log file is the *a priori* image of the data entry and the action about to be performed on it. In statement (2) above an image of the data entry about to be deleted is stored on the log file with information regarding (a) the set it belongs to and (b) a code representing the action performed on it (a deletion). In statement (3) the pre-updated image is written to the log file with a code representing an update performed on this data set. In (4) what is written to tape is the entry that was created, the data set it was created in and a code to represent a PUT. A beginning and end of transaction marker is written to the log file, nesting the above instructions. Therefore there are log images for (1), (2), (3), (4) and (5) above in that order.

If the database has been corrupted, or there is a possibility that a transaction has not completed, then a backward recovery may be performed using the log file described above. The recovery routine starts at either end of the log file and works towards the other end of the file. The recovery routine does as follows:

(a) On encountering a DBDELETE code the *a priori* image is DBPUT'ed — as in (2).
(b) On encountering a DBUPDATE code the *a priori* image overwrites the current image in the database — another DBUPDATE is performed as in (3).
(c) On encountering a DBPUT code, the entry written to the log file is deleted from the database — DBDELETED, as in (4).

The above actions (a) to (c) are only performed for INCOMPLETE transactions, that is database modifications without matching DBBEGIN/DBEND pairs. Complete transactions are ignored. This process terminates when the log file has been exhausted.

COMPARISON BETWEEN FORWARD AND BACKWARD
RECOVERY PROCEDURES
It should be noted that processes can inter-leave transactions in time implying that the log file may contain sequences as follows: (assume concurrent processes (x) and (y))

```
DBBEGIN(x);
DBBUPDATE(x);
DBBEGIN(y);
DBPUT(x);
```

```
DBUPDATE(y);
DBEND(x);
DBEND(y);
```

The recovery procedures must therefore be capable of deferring modifications belonging to a transaction until reaching that transaction DBEND.

A design principal when using transaction logging is that applications must adopt a strategy such that transactions logged are truely independent of any other presently incomplete transaction.

The basic overhead of both transaction logging techniques is the production of the log file. Both logs contain roughly the same information (note that the backward recovery log file requires either variable length records or records the size of the maximum data entry of all the sets in the database).

During recovery the backward technique is significantly faster. This is because (a) no DBRESTORE is required, (b) less work is done as only incomplete transactions are operated upon (all others are ignored). The disadvantage of backward recovery is that if the database cannot be recovered, (may be due to a physical fault in the disc), then one can only DBRESTORE from the previous DBSTORE and manually re-enter the transaction. In the forward recovery technique the DBSTORE is used regardless; physical disk faults are not such a serious problem.

To summarise, the comparison between forward and backward recovery systems:

(a) In forward recovery a database restore is required. In backward recovery database restore is not required.
(b) In forward recovery all complete transactions on the log file are performed on the database. In backward recovery all incomplete transactions are backed out.
(c) The forward recovery technique is tolerant to hardware disc faults. Backward recovery is not hardware fault tolerant.

Forward transaction logging can be used to maintain a duplicate system and avoid the database restore costs in the event of a recovery requirement. The technique about to be described also allows a system to operate with minimum interruption; that is no back-ups of the system are required, allowing nearly 100% system availability.

For instance assume an environment exists such that two identical processors exist. Processor A maintains the live (or production system). Processor B is essentially a secondary machine supporting functions such as development and other non-critical systems.

On day one a copy of the live database (identical) exists on A and

B with copies of the required software. The live database on processor *A* is updated interactively and transaction logging takes place on a log file *AT*1. At a suitable time the transaction log file is closed and a new one opened *AT*2. This requires the production system to be unavailable during transaction log change over. This should be a relatively short period of time. The old log file *AT*1 is carried to processor *B* and a recovery procedure performed on the copy database using this log file. The copy database should then be identical to the database on processor *A* at the time of transaction log change over.

In the event of the production system crashing on processor *A* the current log file is taken to machine *B* and the recovery procedure performed. A new log file is started on machine *B*. All terminals from machine *A* must be swapped to machine *B*. Processor *B* has effectively become the live system. The data base has been recovered without a restore being performed. Stores of the database are unnecessary allowing high system availability.

Essentially one system is updated immediately by interactive sessions and the back-up system is updated in batch. The live system produces the batch data in its log files to update the back-up system. This technique can be taken one step further.

A secure system can be designed that does not rely on database back-ups or transaction logging. Such a system requires two identical processors connected together; processors *A* and *B*. Interactive users are connected to machine *A* interacting with its database. Updates to *A* are transmitted to processor *B* immediately. A duplicate database on *B* is updated on receiving transaction data.

In the event of machine *A* crashing users are connected to machine *B*. This switch over may be performed automatically by a heart beat system. The heart beat is essentially a box of electronics that communicates with processor *A* and processor *B*. The heart beat could be thought of as reading and writing to a program in *A* and to an identical program in *B*. If an unacceptable wait occurred in reading from the program in *A* then the heart beat could assume that processor *A* had died (its heart, the program, stopped beating). The heart beat, which also controls the data lines between the terminals and the processor, swaps the lines to processor *B*. Obviously this system could be extended to include many processors. This type of system is not uncommon in banking and military applications.

Systems that allow high availability are costly. Transaction logging takes up machine resources (the transaction log file and the writing to it). Transaction logging systems on the HP3000 using IMAGE logging, are typically 30% slower than comparable systems without logging. When logging it must be to a device other than that supporting the database (to avoid having all one's eggs in one basket, lose that disk and you've lost everything), and to spread the I/O's over different disks (avoid high disc activity on the one disk). Therefore there must be one disk and a magnetic tape drive, or two disk drives minimum.

The ultimate in secure systems is the ultimate in cost; that it duplicate hardware and software using the heart beat technique above.

CONCLUSION

As J.K. Galbraith said 'There ain't no such thing as a free lunch'. Secure systems cost money and effort. The amount of effort (money) spent on security and integrity should be in direct relationship to value of the data being protected. If your data is money or peoples' lives then security costs should be irrelevant; go for the most secure system.

In the application described here, the DBMS IMAGE itself has made a considerable contribution to integrity maintenance.

IMAGE, as described earlier, is a collection of programs and system procedures. IMAGE facilitates transaction logging by including procedures in the system library. Support programs DBSTORE (save a copy of the database), DBRESTORE (restore a copy of a database produced in DBSTORE) and DBRECOVER (recover the database DBRESTORED by processing complete transactions on the named transaction log file against the current database) allow sophisticated database integrity with little operational or design effort by the user or developer. The IMAGE program QUERY allows the developer and maintenance team to go into the database and take a look and possibly fix a problem that has been diagnosed.

Another feature of IMAGE that is worth mentioning is that it is widely used throughout the world and is well understood and well supported. There is a User Contributed Library of programs some of which are database tools. A number of software companies have spun off from the HP3000 development such as Alfredo Rego's company REGO SOFTWARE PTY. Rego designed IMAGE for HP. Rego now markets a number of software products the most popular being ADAGER (adapter manager) for the maintenance of IMAGE databases. Bob Green's company ROBELLE markets amongst other things database performance measurement tools.

To conclude, it is worth remembering that a system is only as secure as its weakest component. The following questions should be considered. Is the computer system operating off a protected power supply? When was the last time you renewed your disk packs, magnetic tape, cleaned the read/write heads on your disks and tape drive? Are you saving money by reducing your maintenance costs? Is your computer room an open house and is it a clean environment? Do you have a well documented change control procedure, recording all changes that have occurred in your system? Can users store things on the wrong set of tapes, clobbering whatever data was on the tapes with the follow up that people will attempt to restore the wrong data from the correct tape? Do you keep a well organised tape library? Keep asking questions!

Security and integrity are essentially disciplines for dealing with problems that are IMPORTANT but not URGENT. The naive person waits until a problem has become IMPORTANT, URGENT and IMPOSSIBLE to solve before any action is taken.

CHAPTER 11

Data Manipulation Using a Relational DBMS

By W.A. Gray (University College Cardiff)
and R.C. Welland (University of Strathclyde)

INTRODUCTION

This chapter is based on experience using a relational database management system. Between 1977 and 1980 the United Kingdom Social Science Research Council (SSRC) funded a project at University College Cardiff to investigate the role of the relational data model in social science research (Churchhouse, 1981). In this project a variety of social science data which had previously been analyzed by other techniques — not necessarily involving computers — were reanalyzed using two relational database management systems to store and process the data (Bell, 1980a; Charitou, 1979; Eskioglou, 1979). The application used to illustrate this chapter was one of these applications. The financial support of the SSRC during this project is gratefully acknowledged, as is their support of W.A. Gray with a Senior Fellowship on Database Management between 1979 and 1981.

AVAILABLE RELATIONAL SYSTEMS

When the project started in 1977, relational database systems were in their infancy, being based on a mathematical model of data proposed by Codd (Codd, 1970). There were a number of experimental systems available — a full list of these is given in Chamberlin (Chamberlin, 1976). Most of these systems were in the public domain having been developed by research workers at universities and similar institutions, although two computer manufacturers, IBM and Honeywell, were actively involved with developing relational systems. Honeywell were offering MRDS (Multics Relational Data Store) on their Multics computer range (Honeywell, 1980a, b) as a customer product, while IBM had a number of experimental systems which they were investigating at that time (Schneidermann, 1978; Todd, 1976; Astrahan, 1976). IBM were not alone among the computer companies in such investigations but they were the leading company and two of these experimental systems, System R and QBE, have since become customer products.

As MRDS was available through a local network at the Avon Computing Centre of Bristol University it was chosen as one of the database systems for the project. Its interface language, LINUS (Logical Inquiry and Update System) was based on the relational algebra approach. As a contrast to this the other relational system chosen, INGRES (Interactive Graphics and Retrieval System) had a predicate calculus *query* *l*anguage (QUEL), and was one of the experimental systems which were available in the public domain (Stonebraker, 1976). INGRES had been developed by a team of research workers at the University of California, Berkeley. In 1979 it was referred to as representing 'the state of the art' in minicomputer based relational systems (Kim, 1979). This statement agreed with our feelings in 1977. However, there were a number of other reasons why INGRES was chosen, namely:

- it would run on locally available hardware (the Departmental PDP 11 minicomputer)
- it appeared to be the most widely used relational system at that time
- it had a predicate calculus query language

The 1977 situation has to be contrasted with the position in 1983. Currently a proposal is under consideration for adoption as the relational database standard by ANSI (American National Standards Institute). There are now a large number of commercially available relational systems — the leading fourteen relational systems for mini and mainframe computers are compared in Schmidt and Brodie (Schmidt, 1983). A number of relational systems have been implemented on microcomputers, see for example (Ashton-Tate, 1981; Condor Computer Corp., 1981). In fact, any file management system now claims to have relational capabilities.

THE APPLICATION

In an earlier SSRC funded project at University College Cardiff, Professor Coxon (Department of Sociology) had collected and analyzed data about the careers of clergymen in South Wales (Coxon, 1978; Fowler, 1979). The aims of this study were:

- to determine the basic components of clergy careers
- to investigate the inter-relations of individual careers
- to relate life histories to a range of sociologically relevant factors
- to explore the relevance and impact of Welsh culture and language on conception of the ministerial role

Two types of data were collected for this study: biographic data, fig. 11.1 and career data, fig. 11.2. For each clergyman there is one set of biographic data and one or more sets of career data. A set of career data refers to an appointment held by the clergyman and thus corresponds to a segment of his total career to date. A segment describes the position held, when the appointment started and, by

Data Item		Description
Full Name	Name in INGRES Model	
clergyman identifier	clident	number uniquely identifying clergyman
year of birth	yrbirth	year of birth, e.g. 1922
highest degree	hidegree	code showing level of the highest degree (1 doctorate . . . 7 diploma, 8 other, 9 missing)
discipline of degree	discipline	name of degree's subject (e.g. theology, arts, history)
institution	inst	code showing institution which awarded degree
theological college	theocoll	code showing the theological college attended
year made deacon	yrdea	year in which clergyman was made a deacon
year ordained priest	yrpr	year in which clergyman was ordained as a priest

Fig. 11.1(a)   Description of biographical data.

clident	yrbirth	hidegree	discipline	inst	theocoll	yrdea	yrpr
535	1934	2	history	11	5	1959	1961
536	1909	8	not applic		5	1930	1933
540	1929	2	theology	20	5	1952	1954
543	1927	8	theology		20	1957	1960
544	1915	8	theology		19		1941
545	1911	3	arts	7	17	1934	1937

Fig 11.1(b)   Examples of biographical data.

the value of the segment number, where this appointment is in the clergyman's total career structure. The segment numbers are assigned in numerical order to correspond to the time order of the appointments. A subset of this data was reanalyzed using two relational database systems, MRDS and INGRES (Charitou, 1979).

Data item		Description
Full name	Name in INGRES Model	
clergyman identifier	clident	number uniquely identifying clergyman
career segment number	carsegno	sequence number in clergyman's career of this segment
career description	career_ des	name of position referred to in segment (e.g. curate, priest)
diocese	diocese	name of diocese
parish	parish	name of Welsh parish (blank for others)
start of appointment	styr	year in which appointment started

Fig. 11.2(a) Description of career data.

clident	carsegno	career des	diocese	parish	styr
535	1	staff (theo coll)	Canterbury		1966
535	2	staff (theo coll)	Canterbury		1967
535	3	school teacher	Bath and Wells		1971
535	4	staff (theo coll)	Canterbury		1976
535	5	rector	Llandaff	Whitchurch	1976
536	1	assistant curate	Birmingham		1934
536	2	assistant curate	Llandaff	Radyr	1940
536	3	vicar	Birmingham		1942
536	4	army chaplain	Bath and Wells		1944
536	5	vicar	Llandaff	Roath	1946
536	6	vicar	Llandaff	Llanishen	1949
536	7	cathedral deacon	Birmingham		1952
536	8	assistant bishop	Llandaff	Llandaff	1957

Fig. 11.2(b) Example of career data.

In the original project the software used in the computer analysis required the data items to be coded. Where appropriate this data has been decoded in this section to aid the reader's comprehension. This was not done in Charitou's reanalysis of the data.

The types of analysis performed on this data included:

- frequency counts of career descriptions, highest degrees, diocese names and colleges
- determining the average age of clergymen overall and the year when they took up certain appointments for the first time
- crosstabulations of types of career against college and education
- tables showing the number of years clergymen spend at each career level

In order to undertake this last type of analysis, the career data sets had to be augmented by a level code which gave the level corresponding to the appointment. This level code was added to the data after the initial database had been created.

Although at first sight this appears rather an obscure application, it has similarities to applications in personnel management, analysis of census data and analysis of time series data. Effectively we have a situation where there is static descriptive data about an object or person, the biographic data, and time varying data about the same object or person which is recorded every time there is a change in the data values.

DEVELOPING THE RELATIONAL MODEL

The data for any application exists originally in the real world. Before this data can be stored and processed in a computer using a database system, a model or schema must be constructed which can be mapped into a representation appropriate to the schema of the database system to be used and suited to the analysis to be performed on it. This model construction is known as data modelling and fuller descriptions of the processes can be found in (Open University, 1980; Feorey, 1982; Vetter, 1981; Martin, 1981). The essential stages in this modelling process are shown in fig. 11.3. There are a number of different ways of tackling data modelling and one method is described.

Fig. 11.3 Stages in constructing a data model.

In the diagram (fig. 11.3) there are three mapping stages between: the real world and the conceptual model; the conceptual model and the logical (or database) model; and the logical model and the physical model.

It should be realized that this modelling process occurs when any application is computerized in any way and is not peculiar to the use of database software. For instance, the example given in fig. 11.3, might be for constructing a FORTRAN program to process the marks and list the students in descending order of their average mark for all the subjects sat. In this case the real world and conceptual models are as stated in fig. 11.3 and the logical model is the FORTRAN array in which the marks are held. This is the programmer's view of his data in the computer. The FORTRAN compiler then maps this array into its own internal representation of the data in the computer's memory, the physical model. Thus it can be seen from this analogy that the first two mappings are essentially the designer's responsibility while the final mapping can be automatic or semi-automatic if the user is allowed to choose between alternative physical representations. In a database management system it is normally the database administrator who decides on the mapping between the logical and physical models, although in a late bound system such as INGRES this responsibility may be undertaken by the user to improve the efficiency of his model for the particular application.

The construction of the conceptual model is essentially a paper and pencil exercise. During this stage the entities of the data and the relationships between these entities are identified and used to construct a series of entity relationship diagrams representing the conceptual model. This is an iterative process. In each iteration a different operation that will be performed on the data is considered, for example, determine the average age of the clergymen who are bishops. The data required to support this operation is determined, in the present example age and career description, and the current conceptual model is modified if it cannot support the operation. This process is repeated until a check of all the operations against the data model shows that it is capable of supporting them. An initial model is usually constructed to start this iterative process either by analyzing the first operation or by examining the real world representation of the data. Throughout this process at each iteration are being determined the data items or attributes of the conceptual model and their groupings into entities as well as the relationships between the entities.

For the clergy career application, the model or schema shown in fig. 11.4 was developed. In this model there are two entities 'clergy-

man' and 'career' linked by the relationship 'has'. This is an example
of a one to many relationship; given a clergyman he has one or more
career segments but given a career segment it only refers to a single
clergyman. The attributes which make up the entities are shown in
the boxes of this figure.

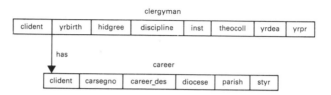

Fig. 11.4 Conceptual model for clergy database.

Due to the nature of our application the conceptual model in fig.
11.4 is relatively simple. It is more usual for there to be several
entities in the conceptual model linked by several relationships.
There are three basic types of relationship: one to one, one to many,
and many to many. In a conceptual model relationships are shown
by lines linking entities with an arrowhead on the many side of the
relationship.

Our data analysis might have revealed that clergymen attended
several theological colleges in the course of their training (which is
not the case in our simpler model) and each theological college
obviously trains more than one student. This is a many to many
relationship which implies the need for a more complex conceptual
model such as that shown in outline in fig. 11.5. The many to many
relationship 'attended' links the new entity 'theocollege' to the
'clergyman' entity. (Essentially the 'theocoll' attribute has migrated
from the entity 'clergyman' to become a separate entity.) This
modification would be necessary if there was additional information
about the colleges, such as the type of training given and location,
and it was required to use this additional information in the operations that were to be performed on the data. It is important to
realize that the exact form of the conceptual model depends on the
data and on the operations expected to be carried out on the data.

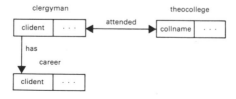

Fig. 11.5 Modified conceptual model.

In the construction of the conceptual model the frequency with which it is expected to perform operations has not been taken into account, nor the existence conditions for entities, attributes and relationships. This information should be determined as it will be used in the next stages. The existence conditions cover such things as:

(a) If there is an occurrence of a clergyman entity; must he have attended a theological college or are there clergymen who did not attend theological colleges?
(b) If there is an occurrence of a career segment; must all the attributes have a value or can some have a missing value? For example, in the clergy database if the diocese is not Welsh then the entity for parish was left blank, indicating an unrecorded value.

A logical model (or database schema) is then created by mapping the structures of the conceptual model into the structures supported by the schema of the database management system. It is the resulting model which can be realized in the schema which is known as the logical model. A conceptual model can be mapped into a number of logical models which are appropriate for a CODASYL (network), hierarchical, or relational database management system, or for an application program written in a conventional programming language. For a particular database management system there may be several alternative logical models. It is in choosing among these alternative models for the same database system that we consider the extra information about frequency and existence to help decide which logical model is most appropriate for our application. For all database systems the entities of the conceptual model are usually mapped directly into the logical model as records, segments or relations in CODASYL, hierarchical or relational systems, respectively, with the subdivisions of these structures representing the data-items or attributes. The difference between the three database models is much more apparent when examining how relationships are represented.

Hierarchical systems have an inbuilt hierarchy or tree structure which can represent one to many relationships. The relationship between two segments (entities) is shown by their positioning in the tree, so that the 'has' relationship of fig. 11.4 would be represented by making the clergyman segment the parent of the career segment in a tree. This tree structure is exploited by the retrieval language and it is a very efficient way of representing data which has a natural hierarchy. However, if the data has a many to many relationship it is difficult to represent this without duplicating data unnecessarily which can lead to problems with consistency and integrity (Date,

1981). Thus in this model the links between entities shown by the relationships are built into the schema structure by the positioning of segments in trees, and to exploit other links at a later time, the trees must be reconstructed.

CODASYL systems represent the entities as records and the relationships as CODASYL 'sets'. By representing a relationship as a set, the link between the entities (records) is again built into the structure of the logical data model, and it is these inbuilt links which are used by the retrieval language. As with the hierarchical systems, to exploit new links between records at a later time the logical model must be recreated, if they are not present.

In a relational database system, the entities and relationships of the conceptual model are held as relations, or tables, in the logical model. A 'one to many' or 'one to one' relationship between two entities is represented by a common data item (attribute) in the two relations. Such an attribute must be created if it does not already exist. In the example of fig. 11.4 the attribute 'clident' can be used to represent the 'has' relationship. The tables involved are stored separately with no system links between them. A user affects the link through his retrieval language by joining the tables on an attribute with common values. Thus the link needed for a relationship is not built into the logical model but is effected at retrieval time by joining on common attribute values.

To represent a 'many to many' relationship between two tables (for example, 'attended' in fig. 11.5), it is necessary to create a separate table 'attended' which has the identifying attributes from the two entities being linked by the relationship (in the example, 'clident' from 'clergyman' and 'collcode' from 'theocollege'). Any other information concerned with this relationship can also be stored in this table, for example the number of years spent at the college and the date of starting. This 'attended' table can be joined with either of the other two tables by the user when interacting with the retrieval language, so effecting the many to many relationship dynamically. Because these links are effected at retrieval time through attributes having common values, new links between other attributes which have common values can be used without changing the logical model even though the use of these links was not anticipated when the logical model was created.

Having decided on the logical model, a mapping between it and the physical data model which supports it must be determined. In an *early bound* system this mapping is defined when the logical model is compiled by the database system, as a separate stage before the data is stored in the database. If the system allows the user to select appropriate physical representations to improve the efficiency of the application this must be done at this stage. However, if the system is *late bound* then the user can enter a logical model with minimal information about the physical model requirements. The system then takes the default physical representations, which can be changed dynamically at a later time to suit particular operations.

THE DATABASE MANAGEMENT SYSTEM

The original version of INGRES was produced by a research team at the University of California, Berkeley (Stonebraker, 1976). It was one of the first relational database systems available in the public domain and was therefore popular with British universities who often find it difficult to obtain funds to purchase commercial software which is not of widely applicable use in the university. The other main reasons for the popularity of INGRES was that the first version was designed to run under the UNIX operating system (Bell Laboratories, 1978) on the DEC PDP-11 range of machines — this combination is widely used in Computer Science Departments in the United Kingdom. UNIX is an operating system developed at Bell Telephone Laboratories.

The work described in this section was undertaken using the version of INGRES available in the public domain. More recently a commercial version of INGRES has been developed which runs under VMS on the DEC VAX range of machines; any comments on our experience of using INGRES do not necessarily apply to any such more recent implementations. A comparison of the commercial system with System R and Oracle, two other relational systems, is given by Dieckmann (Dieckmann, 1981).

The INGRES system provides an interactive terminal interface via a language called QUEL which has strong similarities to the query language interfaces provided by other relational database management systems such as System R, ORACLE and MRDS (Schmidt, 1983). However, QUEL is a strictly *predicate calculus* type of query language unlike, for example, System R which includes some features of the relational algebra approach. The query language QUEL is described in some detail later. A full description of QUEL and INGRES can be found in the INGRES Reference Manual (Woodfill, 1982) and its companion tutorial (Epstein, 1977a).

The version of INGRES used also provided a single host language interface via EQUEL (Embedded QUEL) and the UNIX system programming language 'C'. The more recent commercial version of INGRES supplied by Relational Technology Inc. provides additional host language interfaces to Pascal, FORTRAN and C (Dieckmann, 1981).

The designers of INGRES chose to build their original system on top of the UNIX operating system. This gave the twin advantages of:

- portability, as UNIX is a very popular operating system, especially in the research and university communities
- fast development, as UNIX was originally designed to be an operating system that was particularly helpful during development of software

However, the price paid for this was the building of a relational database system using a filestore structure which was far from ideal for storing relational format data with a further disadvantage in the way that the operating system and database had to be interfaced.

For readers unfamiliar with UNIX some features which are relevant to the discussion in this section need to be described briefly. The UNIX operating system provides a tree structured filestore where the terminal nodes of the tree are data files and the non-terminal nodes are directories containing references to other directories or data files. Each file is divided into blocks of 512 bytes and the UNIX system transfers blocks from backing store into buffers in main store as required. The blocks currently in the buffers are replaced by incoming blocks using a 'least recently used' algorithm. The INGRES system for handling relations therefore has to be built on top of this block transfer and buffering system.

The unit of work in the UNIX system is the *process* which on the smaller PDP-11 machines is limited to an address space of 64 Kbytes. Processes can communicate via *pipes* which are one-way links allowing one process to write data to be read by another process. The UNIX system manages the swapping of processes and the synchronization of pipes.

INGRES is a large system which has to be broken into five basic processes:

- the interactive terminal monitor (24K)
- command analyzer (53K)
- query decomposition (49K)
- one value query processor (51K)
- utilities

The figures in brackets show the approximate size of each process in bytes. When using the host language interface via the 'C' programming language the first process above is replaced by the EQUEL object program.

The remainder of the chapter describes the facilities of QUEL. A user interacts with QUEL through the interactive terminal monitor. This monitor manages a workspace, or query buffer, in which the user prepares QUEL statements before sending them to the command analyzer for processing. There are a series of monitor commands which help a user to control interaction with INGRES through QUEL. A user types QUEL statements at a terminal, these statements are held in the workspace until the user issues a monitor command which sends the contents of the workspace to the command analyzer. Other monitor commands enable a user to clear the workspace. drop out of INGRES into the UNIX text editor and edit the contents of the query buffer before returning to INGRES; print the contents of the query buffer; save the contents of the query buffer in a file and recall them at a later date; and evaluate macros.

In the examples of QUEL interactions given later, the monitor commands and system prompts are omitted, as they are not essential to the understanding of the process. Whenever a query stored in the query buffer is ready for processing the user must type the monitor command:

\g or \go

which sends the contents of the query buffer to the command analyzer. By judicious use of these monitor facilities a user can build a complex query gradually out of less complex parts.

The work described here was undertaken on a PDP 11/34 with 96 Kbytes of store and three R K05 disk drives, each with a capacity of 2.5 Mbytes. Thus the main store available was marginally larger than the minimum (64 Kbytes) required to run INGRES. However, it was not sufficiently large to allow two INGRES processes to be in the main memory concurrently, so there was little gain in efficiency by having 96 Kbytes as opposed to 64 Kbytes of memory. This meant, particularly if the query was complex, that there was continual process swapping when INGRES was evaluating a query between the query decomposer and the one variable query processor processes. This can be avoided on computers with more than 110 Kbytes of memory as the two processes can exist in memory simultaneously. Performance evaluations of INGRES have been done by Bell (Bell, 1980b) and Hawthorn (Hawthorn, 1979). Bell in particular investigated the interaction between INGRES and UNIX while Hawthorn's was a more general evaluation.

CREATING THE INGRES DATABASE

In INGRES a database having the logical model shown in fig. 11.4 was created by issuing the UNIX command:

creatdb clergydata

which created an empty database with the identifying name 'clergy-data'. This command can only be issued by users who are allowed to create databases. After creation the database is then available to authorized users through the QUEL or EQUEL interfaces, one of these users is regarded as the owner of the database and he is regarded as the database administrator. He is the only user who can destroy the database. Any of the authorized users can create and access relations in the database but they can only destroy their own relations.

A logical model equivalent to the conceptual model of fig. 11.4 was created using the following QUEL commands:

create clergyman (clident = c3, yrbirth = i2,
 hidegree = i2, discipline = c10, inst = i2,
 theocoll = i2, yrdea = i2, yrpr = i20)

create career (clident = c3, carsegno = i2,
 career_des = c20, diocese = c15, parish = c15,
 styr = i2)

Execution of these commands created two relations called clergyman and career with the attributes (domains) shown. The physical structure of each of the domains is shown by a format statement after the equals sign. Allowable formats are 'i' for integer of length 1, 2 or 4 bytes; 'f' for floating point of length 4 or 8 bytes and 'c' for character of any length between 1 and 255 bytes. Thus when a relation is created the physical structure of its attributes must be defined but not the structure of the relation. It will default to a heap structure. In the logical model we have assumed that the users will effect the 'has' relationship in the conceptual model by dynamically linking the two relations over the 'clident' attributes when formulating queries. It is not necessary for the linking domains in a logical model to have the same identifying name.

In an INGRES logical model, entities are called *relations* and attributes *domains* and these names are used in the remainder of this chapter.

All database management systems have utilities for bulk data capture and export from and to the supporting operating system filing system. These are needed to allow the database to be dumped for backup purposes and to allow the database to be recreated, after a system crash, from the backup copy. In INGRES this is achieved by the *copy* command which can transfer data from a relation into a standard UNIX file and vice versa. While this command is not necessarily ideal for the initial capture of data it can be used in this role provided the data can be prepared in UNIX files to correspond to the relations. For our example database the data was first stored in a UNIX file, it was then split by program into two separate files corresponding to the two relations: clergyman and career. This data was then imported into the database using the *copy* command.

QUERIES

The basic QUEL command for extracting data from a database is the *retrieve* command. The simple form of this command, which displays data on the user's terminal, is:

retrieve (target-list) [where qualification]

The target-list specifies the domains which are to be involved in the final set of data retrieved and the qualification, if any, indicates what conditions are to be imposed on the retrieval.

In order to be able to formulate target-lists and qualifications a method of uniquely identifying a particular domain of a given relation is required. The same domain name may appear in two, or more, different relations and therefore a domain name alone is not necessarily unique. Therefore, in QUEL a *tuple variable* is associated with each relation which is being manipulated. The user chooses the names of the tuple variables using the *range* statement. This has the general form:

range of tuple-variable is relation-name

At any point in time the ten most recently issued range statements are in force. Thus a range statement remains in force from the time of specification until the end of the INGRES session unless a new range statement redefines the association of a particular tuple-variable with a relation or more than ten range statements are issued. However, in the examples given, range statements are included in all queries to avoid any confusion over the association of tuple-variables with relations.

In the application described above, the following range statements could be used:

range of m is clergyman
range of c is career

A particular domain of a relation can now be uniquely identified by using a specification of the form:

tuple-variable.domain-name

Therefore in our example the following could be used:

m.clident   m.theocoll
c.clident   c.diocese

There is also a special 'shorthand' notation to allow specification of all domains in a relation:

tuple-variable.all

Having considered how to identify a particular domain of a relation, now consider how to formulate queries using the retrieve command. A simple example of the use of retrieve is:

range of m is clergyman
retrieve (m.all)

which would display the entire contents of the relation clergyman, because m is associated with the relation clergyman and there is no qualification. This statement would present the retrieved data on the user's terminal in the form shown in fig. 11.6.

clident	yrbirth	hidgree	discipline	inst	theocoll	yrdea	yrpr
535	1934	2	history	11	5	1959	1961
536	1909	8		0	5	1930	1933
540	1929	2	theology	20	5	1952	1954
543	1927	8	theology	0	20	1957	1960
544	1915	8	theology	0	19	0	1941
545	1911	3	arts	7	17	1934	1937

Fig. 11.6 Sample output from retrieve command.

To reduce the amount of data presented on the screen the target-list can specify only the domain or domains of interest. For example:

range of m is clergyman
retrieve (m.discipline)

lists only the values in the domain discipline of the relation clergyman.

Suppose that details are wanted of all clergymen who attended a particular college (say, St. Augustines, Canterbury); this can be achieved using a suitable qualification. For example:

retrieve (m.all) where m.theocoll = 5

would print all the domains of the relation clergyman where the value in the domain college is 5, the code for St. Augustines.

The simplest form of qualification is a condition of the form:

$$\text{domain-identifier comparator} \begin{Bmatrix} \text{domain-identifier} \\ \text{constant} \end{Bmatrix}$$

where the comparators are:

$<$ (less than) $<$ = (less than or equal to)
= (equal)   ! = (not equal)
$>$ (greater than) $>$ = (greater than or equal to)

To retrieve the details of all career segments relating to appointments before 1945 the query could be formulated:

range of c is career
retrieve (c.all) where c.styr $<$ 1945

To restrict the amount of data presented on the screen the target-list can be more selective. Suppose that there is interest only in the year in which the clergymen from college 5 became deacons and priests then the query could be formulated as:

range of m is clergyman
retrieve (m.yrdea, m.yrpr)
    where m.college = 5

Simple conditions can be combined using the operators 'and' and 'or'. Thus to find the career designation and location of all clergymen appointed between 1945 and 1960, inclusive, the following query could be used:

range of c is career
retrieve (c.career_des, c.diocese, c.parish)
    where c.styr $>$ = 1945
    and c.styr $<$ = 1960

So far the queries illustrated have involved the manipulation of data within a single relation but the real power of the relational model comes when the data in two or more relations is combined. For example, suppose that a list is required of the identifier and year of birth of all clergymen appointed as bishops in the year 1960. This could be formulated as:

range of m is clergyman
range of c is career
retrieve (m.clident, m.yrbirth)
    where c.clident = m.clident
    and c.yrappoint = 1960
    and c.career_des = 'bishop'

The effect of this command can be visualised as creating a new tuple, combining the contents of clergyman and career, for each value of clident in career, with styr equal to 1960 and career_des equal to 'bishop', which matches a tuple in clergyman with the same value of clident. From this combined tuple the domains clident and yrbirth are then selected for display on the user's terminal.

All the queries illustrated so far have simply produced raw data but INGRES includes a number of aggregation operators which allow simple arithmetic functions to be carried out. Suppose that a count was wanted of the number of different colleges represented in the database, then it would be possible to write:

range of m is clergyman
retrieve (num = countu(m.theocoll))

where countu is an aggregation operator which counts the unique occurrences of a particular value in a relation. Therefore this query would return a single value representing the number of different college names occurring in the relation clergyman.

It is possible to combine aggregation with qualification and the number of vicars recorded for a particular diocese could be retrieved using the query:

range of c is career
retrieve (num = count(c.clident))
    where c.diocese = 'Llandaff'
    and c.career_des = 'vicar'

The above examples of the use of the aggregation operators count and countu are obviously rather artificial as the more likely type of query would be, in the first case, count the number of clergymen who attended each theological college and, in the second case, draw up a table of the number of vicars recorded for each diocese. INGRES provides a powerful facility for partitioning the tuples in a relation, using a 'by list', and applying the aggregation operator to each partition.

The following query could be used to list the codes of all theological colleges and the number of clergymen who attended each college:

range of m is clergyman
retrieve (m.theocoll,
    num = count(m.clident by m.theocoll))

To list the name of each different location and the number of vicars associated with it we could use:

range of c is career
retrieve (c.diocese,

num = count(c.clident by c.diocese))
    where c.career_des = 'vicar'

The available aggregation operators in QUEL are:

count   — count of occurrences
countu   — count of unique occurrences
sum   — summation
sumu   — summation of unique values
avg   — average (sum / count)
avgu   — sumu / countu
max   — maximum
min   — minimum
any   — 1 if any tuples satisfy qualification,
           0 otherwise

When matching character variables the following characters extend the power of the matching algorithm by taking a special role:

*   matches any string of zero or more characters
?   matches any single character
[ ]   matches any character enclosed in the brackets

The identifiers and year of appointment of all incumbents of parishes, in the diocese of 'Llandaff', the names of which begin with a letter between 'N' and 'Z' can therefore be retrieved by using:

range of c is career
retrieve (c.clident, c.styr)
    where c.diocese = 'Llandaff'
    and c.parish = '[N—Z] *'

INTERACTIVE DATA MODIFICATION

Data can be interactively added to the database using the *append* command. For example:

append to career (clident = 536, carsegno = 9,
    career_des = 'bishop', diocese = 'Bangor',
    styr = 1960)

would enter a new tuple recording the promotion of clergyman 536 in 1960; the parish domain being given the default value of space. Interactive amendments can also be achieved using the *replace* and *delete* commands. These have the general form:

delete tuple-variable [where qualification]
replace tuple-variable (target-list) [where qualification]

The delete command is used to remove specified tuples from a relation and the replace command to amend domain values in specified tuples.

Thus to delete all clergymen born before 1900 from the clergyman relation, use:

range of m is clergyman
delete m where m.yrbirth < 1900

Alternatively, the name of a diocese can be changed from 'Llandaf' to 'Llandaff' by:

range of c is career
replace c (diocese = 'Llandaf')
    where c.diocese = 'Llandaff'

With these commands any required modifications of the data can be effected.

SCHEMA MODIFICATION

In early bound database systems, the logical data model or schema of the data is pre-compiled before any processing is performed. This pre-compilation is a stand-alone process which cannot be undertaken while people are interacting with the database. Change to logical models stored in such systems is not a simple task. All users must be logged out; the data exported out of the database into external files; the new schema created; and all the data re-imported into the database. Such systems are said to have static data models. MRDS is a relational DBMS with a static model and most CODASYL systems have static data models.

INGRES is a late bound system. Its logical model is very dynamic and flexible. New relations can be created by users while they are processing their data. There are two ways of creating new relations: by issuing a *create* command or by using another form of the *retrieve* command which places the retrieved data in a new relation instead of displaying it on the user's terminal.

Since the actual structure of the conceptual and logical models depends on the data and the processes to be performed on the data, it follows that if the processing requirements change then it may also be necessary to alter the logical model. Such a change is much more easily effected in a late bound system. The price for this flexibility is that a late bound system is usually less efficient with respect to retrieval time than an early bound system.

In the clergy career application it was realised that the logical model needed to be modified by adding information about the level of the appointment in the career structure of the clergymen. This level was to have value zero for low-level appointments, like curate, rising to nine for high-level appointments like bishop and archbishop. To make this amendment a new domain level had to be added to the career relation. In some relational systems, particularly those having a physical structure of transposed files, for example, RAPID (Schmidt, 1983), this is achieved by adding a new domain to the existing relation. In INGRES the information had to be retrieved into a new relation which had the extra domain by using:

```
range of c is career
retrieve into carlevel (c.all, level = 0)
    where c.career_des = 'curate'
    or c.career_des = 'assistant curate'
```

This created a new relation 'carlevel' which had all the domains of career and an additional domain level. As *retrieve into* can only be used if the relation does not exist already, the other level numbers had to be added by using the *append* command to add the tuples to this relation, for example:

```
range of c is career
append to carlevel (c.all, level = 1)
    where c.career_des = 'vicar'
    or c.career_des = 'rector'
    or c.career_des = 'priest'
```

A similar append command was used for each value of level added to the data. When all the data has been transferred to the new relation, the old relation can be deleted from the database by:

```
destroy career
```

This deletes the relation and its data from the database.

INTERFACE MODIFICATION

It is often desirable to be able to tailor the user interface to suit a group of users. This may be done to give the commands more meaningful names or because some query is used very frequently with only the value of one or two parameters changing each time. Tailoring is achieved in INGRES by using the QUEL macro facility. A macro allows the association of a meaningful name with a group of instructions which perform some task. Suppose it is frequently required to list the vicars in a specified diocese, then a macro 'list-vicar' could be defined which expects a diocese name as a parameter, as follows:

```
define; listvicar $d;
    range of c is career
    range of m is clergyman
    retrieve unique (c.clident, m.yrbirth, m.theocoll)
        where m.clident = c.clident
        and c.career_des = 'vicar'
        and c.diocese = '$d')
```

After this macro has been defined and stored in INGRES, a user could type:

listvicar Llandaff

to get a listing of all vicars in the diocese of Llandaff. The unique phrase is an option in retrieve which suppresses duplicate values of the rows in the retrieved table, so that in this case only one entry for each clergyman is obtained even if he has held several appointments as a vicar in the diocese.

EFFICIENCY FACILITIES

In any database system facilities are usually provided for tuning (improving) the performance of the system for a particular application. These facilities usually allow the physical structure of the database to be changed. In an early bound system these changes are usually made by recompiling the schema to restructure the data representation. However, in a late bound system, when the logical model can be changed in the query interface, it must be possible to restructure the physical model as well through the query interface if the system is to achieve any acceptable level of efficiency. In INGRES this is done by the *modify* command in QUEL.

INGRES relations can be held in one of the eight formats shown below:

- isam,   cisam   — indexed sequential access method
- hash,   chash   — random hash storage structure
- heap,   cheap   — unkeyed and unstructured
- heapsort, cheapsort   -- heap with tuples sorted and duplicates removed.

There are four basic formats and each format has a normal version and a compressed version. A 'c' preceding the name indicates the compressed version. The only compression used is space suppression. For the isam, hash and heapsort formats a primary key which is one of the domains or a set of domains must be specified. It is only possible to have one primary key in each of these organizations.

By default in INGRES the tuples in a relation are stored in heap format. This assumes no structure is present and the tuples are stored in arrival order. It is an appropriate structure if all operations on the relation need to examine every tuple. However, certain types of query only need to retrieve identifiable tuples, for example:

range of m is clergyman
retrieve (m.all) where m.clident = '536'

This query is to locate only the single tuple referring to clergyman 536. If this type of query dominates then the relation's structure can be modified to hash or isam on the domains involved. This reorganisation can only be done for one set of domains at a time; either

modify clergyman to isam on clident

or

modify clergyman to hash on clident

but not both simultaneously.

If the query identifies a range of values in a domain then it is better to modify the structure to isam. For instance:

range of m is clergyman
retrieve (m.all)
    where m.clident > '530'
    and m.clident < '550'
    and m.theocol = 5

This query retrieves biographical details of clergymen with identificaton numbers between '530' and '550' who went to St. Augustines, Canterbury.

Thus a user has to balance the cost of restructuring data against the extra cost of retrieving it from an inappropriate structure.

If a relation needs to be retrieved regularly using more than one identifying key then secondary indexes can be created on a relation. Fuller descriptions of these efficiency commands and their use can be found in Epstein (Epstein, 1977b).

OTHER FACILITIES

As the example application only involved a single user analyzing data there was no need to consider giving different users different views (subschemas) of the database. INGRES provides such a facility although it imposes some constraints on the users. Also there was no need to use integrity constraints as the data had previously been corrected and checked before it was imported to INGRES where it was a completely static database.

There is a fairly useful *help* command, which can be used in a variety of ways. It can list parts of the INGRES manual (Woodfill, 1982) which is stored on-line. Information about the relations in a database can be displayed, as can the details of the domains within a relation, by accessing a limited data dictionary. *Help* can also be used to display integrity constraints and views if required.

INGRES allows the owner of a relation to grant various levels of access to a particular relation via a *permit* statement. Again, this did not prove useful in the clergy career database because of the single-user nature of the application.

PROBLEMS

Some types of queries are difficult to formulate in QUEL. For example: locate bishops with the same career structure, that is identify each pair of bishops with the same number of career segments and where the corresponding career segments are at the same level. This query is made easier using the modified career relation 'carlevel', introduced earlier. However, it is still very difficult to formulate this query using predicate calculus alone. The natural solution is to want to use a nested loop structure to systematically compare the careers of each pair of bishops in the database. As INGRES does not have any looping construct an alternative solution must be found and this is left as a challenge to the reader! This is a general problem with any relational query language (calculus or algebra based) which is not embedded in a host language.

Each domain in an INGRES relation has a fixed format which leads to problems in handling variable length text. In general, data capture is a problem because the format required for data in the relational model may be very different from the form in which the data is actually received. The most convenient logical model for data capture is often very different from the logical model for data processing. In the clergy career application the interface between these was implemented using a special program to re-format the data.

The user's control over the presentation of results from INGRES is poor. The basic form of output is tabular, as shown in fig. 11.6, and there is very little control for sophisticated report generation. In general, little attention seems to have been paid to the output requirements of the users of relational systems. INGRES also lacks straightforward links to other packaged software such as statistical analysis, cross-tabulation and graphical display packages. This is not an inherent problem of relational systems; since looking at MRDS, for example, there are good links to report generators and other software tools.

Another problem is the inefficiency of data access. The relational calculus does not allow the user to control the way in which relations are accessed or combined. The relational algebra, as typified by MRDS, allows the user much more control because he has to specify the operations on the relations. INGRES allows the user to specify some access control which would probably be considered part of the DBA's role in a CODASYL system.

The weakness of the public domain version of INGRES is that it is built on top of the UNIX filing system which is page structured, using 512 byte pages, and cannot be easily 'tailored'. The commercial version of INGRES uses a better filing system but still cannot avoid the problem that standard filing systems are not suitable for implementing the relation model efficiently. This is a general problem caused by the mismatch between the relational DBMS software and current hardware together with its controlling software. There are encouraging signs of advance in the evolution of hardware and associated system software, such as IDM (Epstein, 1980) and CAFS (Carmichael, 1981; Crockford, 1982).

REFERENCES

Ashton-Tate (1981) *dBASE II User Manual*. Ashton-Tate, Culver City, California 90230.

Astrahan, M.M. *et al.* (1976) 'System R: A relational approach to database management'. *ACM Transactions on Database Systems* 1, 97–137.

Bell, A.J., Gray, W.A. and Speck, W.A. (1980a) 'Analysis of 18th century pollbooks'. *2nd International Conference on Databases in Social Sciences*, Madrid.

Bell, A.J., Gray, W.A. and Fiddian, N.J. (1980b) 'Performance evaluation of a relational database management system'. *IUCC Conference*, University of Exeter.

Bell Laboratories (July–Aug. 1978) 'UNIX time-sharing system'. *Bell System Technical Journal* 57(6) part 2, 1897–2312.

Carmichael, J.W.S. (1981) 'Personnel on CAFS: a case study'. *ICL Technical Journal* 2, 244–252.

Chamberlin, D.D. (1976) 'Relational database management systems'. *ACM Computing Surveys* 8, 43–66.

Charitou, O.G. (Dec. 1979) *Comparing High Level Interfaces to Relational Database Management Systems*, Dissertation in partial fulfillment of MSc, University College Cardiff.

Churchouse, R.F., Gray, W.A., Albrow, M.A. and Read, M.W. (1981)

Investigating a Relational Data Base Management System in Social Science Research. Final report on Grant HR5158 to SSRC, University College Cardiff.

Codd, E.F. (1970) 'A relational model of data for large shared data banks'. *Communications ACM* 13, 377—397.

Condor Computer Corp. (1981) *Condor Series 20 rDBMS User's Manual*. Condor Computer Corp., P.O. Box 8318, Ann Arbor, MI 48107.

Coxon, A.P.M. (1978) *Clergy Career Patterns and Social Change in South Wales*. Sociology Department, University College Cardiff.

Crockford, L.E. (1982) 'Associative data management systems'. *ILC Technical Journal* 3, 82—96.

Date, C.J. (1981) *An Introduction to Database Systems*. 3rd edn. Addison-Wesley.

Dieckmann, E.M. (Sept. 1981) 'Three relational DBMS'. *Datamation* 137—148.

Epstein, R. (Dec. 1977a) *A Tutorial on INGRES*. Electronics Research Laboratory, University of California, Berkeley.

Epstein, R. (Dec. 1977b) *Creating and Maintaining a Database Using INGRES*. Memo no. ERL-M77-71, Electronics Research Laboratory, University of California, Berkeley.

Epstein, R. and Hawthorn, P. (1980) 'Design decisions for the intelligent database machine'. *AFIPS Conference Proceedings* 49, 237—241.

Eskioglou, P.G. (Sept. 1979) *A Database System for Historical Research in Accountancy*. Dissertation in partial fulfillment of MSc, University College Cardiff.

Feorey, T.J. and Fry, J.P. (1982) *Design of Database Structures*. Prentice Hall.

Fowler, R.C. and Coxon, A.P.M. (1979) *The Fate of the Anglican Clergy*. Macmillan.

Hawthorn, P.B. (Nov. 1979) *Evaluation and Enhancement of the Performance of Relational Database Management Systems*. Memo no. UCB/ERL M79/70, Electronics Research Laboratory, University of California, Berkeley.

Honeywell Information Systems (1980a) *Multics Logical Inquiry and Update System (LINUS)*. Reference Manual AZ49.

Honeywell Information Systems (1980b) *Multics Relational Data Store (MRDS)*. Reference Manual AW53.

Kim, W. (1979) 'Relational database systems'. *ACM Computing Surveys* 11, 185—212.

Martin, J. (1981) *An End-User's Guide to Data Base*. Prentice Hall.

Open University (1980) *Conceptual Modelling; Logical Modelling*. Course M352, Block II, Open University Press.

Schmidt, J.W. and Brodie, M.L. eds (1983) *Relational Database Systems*. Berlin and New York: Springer-Verlag.

Schneidermann ed. (1978) *Data Base Management Language in Databases: Improving Usability and Responsiveness*. Academic Press. Zloof, M.M. 'Design Aspects of Query-By-Example', 29—56.

Stonebraker, M. *et al.* (1976) 'The design and implementation of INGRES'. *ACM Transactions on Database Systems* 1, 189—227.

Todd, S.P. (Aug. 1976) 'Peterlee Relational Test Vehicle: a system overview'. *IBM Systems Journal* 15, 3.

Vetter, M. and Maddison, R.N. (1981) *Database Design Methodology*. Prentice Hall.

Woodfill, J. *et al.* (July 1982) *INGRES Version 6.3 Reference Manual*. Electronics Research Laboratory, University of California, Berkeley.

PART 3
In Conclusion

CHAPTER 12

Concluding Comments

By R.A. Frost (University of Strathclyde)

BENEFITS

The benefits which derive from the successful implementation of a database system can be very great. They include:

- improved access to data
- reduced cost of data processing and storage
- improved control over integrity and privacy of data
- reduced cost of system expansion especially in a data-independent system

However, it should also be recognised that the cost of an unsuccessful attempt to introduce database techniques can be very high. This cost includes:

- the cost of the DBMS and any additional hardware purchased for the database project
- the effort in man-power which includes effort on the part of management and end-users
- the reduction in credibility of the DP department
- the savings which would have been made had the project been successful

Project failure can occur for a number of reasons. Some of the most common of these reasons are:

- lack of management commitment and end-user co-operation
- underestimation of the effort required to implement the database system
- failure to appoint staff who are experienced in database techniques
- purchase of an unsuitable DBMS
- lack of DBMS vendor support

The change from conventional data processing techniques to the use of a DBMS should be regarded as analogous to the introduction of a new plant in a manufacturing concern, the introduction of a new management structure in an accounting department, or the introduction of a new commission structure in a marketing organisation. It is not a simple task. The mechanics may be reasonably straightforward but this is only one aspect of the problem. Many people are likely to be involved and without the support of the majority of these people, the project could fail. For this reason, the introduction of a database system should be a well planned gradual process. The main ingredients for success are: (i) support from management and end-users, (ii) time and (iii) documentation. To improve the chance of success, the designer should *always* carry out the following tasks:

(a) Identify failings of the existing system which affect management and other end-users. Factors such as storage efficiency are unlikely to be of interest to anyone outside the DP department. End-users are more interested in response times, accuracy and availability of data.

(b) Interview management and other end-users and *ask them what they want the new system to do*. Specify these requirements formally and obtain users *written* agreement that the formal specifications are correct.

(c) Perform a data analysis study and construct a data-dictionary and a tentative database schema *before any thought is given as to what DBMS is to be purchased*. The unconstrained network view could be used for the tentative schema.

(d) Produce complete documentation of requirements before the short-list of DBMSs is drawn up.

(e) Appoint a database administrator (DBA) as soon as it is possible to do so.

(f) Allocate a good deal of time to the requirements study and DBMS appraisal. This could be of the order of 2 to 5 man years. Remember that you are likely to use the DBMS for at least 5 years. If it is a reasonably comprehensive system for a mainframe computer, then the DBMS and associated software could cost between US$20 000 (£10 000) and US$120 000 (£60 000). Even in a relatively small company, two or three application programmers may be employed. The choice of an inappropriate DBMS could reduce their effective productivity drastically.

Unless there is an urgent need to implement a database system in a short time, gains will be made by spending a good deal of time on the requirements study and data analysis.

The appointment of a database administrator (DBA) at an early stage of the project will improve the chance of success. The position of DBA is one of great managerial responsibility and candidates should not be judged on technical knowledge alone. The DBA is responsible for liaison with end-users and management, and a good deal of tact and diplomacy is required for this aspect of the job. The DBA will also be responsible for, or part responsible for, negotiations with DBMS vendors. Computer sales personnel are well-paid, well-trained and tend to be good at their job — which is selling hardware or software. The DBA needs to be able to see through the sales patter to negotiate a good deal for his company. This requires experience which technical DP staff rarely have had the opportunity to acquire. On the other hand, management of data security, privacy and integrity often requires a technical knowledge of the DBMS which professional managers are unlikely to be able to assimilate as easily as candidates with a computing background. Choice of an appropriate DBA is possibly as difficult and as important as choice of an appropriate DBMS.

PROBLEMS

Some of the problems which might be met when attempting to implement a database system are now discussed. The order in which they are presented is not related to their importance which will vary from situation to situation:

(a) Some end-users may not appreciate the need for a change to database techniques. Such people may only see the exta workload involved in learning about the new system. It is more important to attend to these users than to those who are obviously going to benefit from the change. Some end-users may be very wary about having a computer terminal on their desk, for example, and if they see no benefit and have not been involved in any discussion or training, they can become openly hostile to the project. In certain circumstances such seeds of discontent can germinate and hostility can spread throughout a department. If this happens, the success of a project can be seriously jeopardised.

(b) Some of the DP staff might resent the appointment of a DBA. Because of the importance of the job and the fact that the DBA is responsible for a project which is likely to require cooperation from most members of the DP department, the appointment should be at a level which is equivalent to the DP manager. However, this could lead to obvious difficulties if the DP manager feels threatened. Different circumstances require different solutions but in all cases the chain of command should be well-defined.

(c) Management may not recognise the need for a detailed requirements study and data analysis. This could be overcome by
presenting figures indicating the cost of premature decisions.
Referring management to a book such as this one may make
them more aware of the difficulties of database work.

(d) The 'functional' sub-division of data categories may prove difficult.
An attempt to produce a rationale for the sub-division of data
categories is likely to fail. Many people have tried to produce a
universally acceptable classification of data items but none have
yet succeeded. A categorisation which is suitable for one organisation may be totally inappropriate for some other. Be satisfied
with a working categorisation which is acceptable to most users.
The seven sub-divisions presented in chapter 7 may be a reasonable
starting point for a manufacturing concern.

(e) Data-item definition may also prove difficult. This is much more
important than the classification of data-items. It is vitally important that definitions are found which are acceptable to *all* users.
The data which one user enters as a value of data-item type X
must be of type X. If not, the database will be in error as far as
other users are concerned. All must have the same understanding
of what type X means.

(f) Construction of the database schema should not be too difficult.
In the first instance, the database schema could be defined using
the unconstrained network view. This will give a clear picture of
what data is to be stored and what access paths are to be provided
and this should help in the appraisal of DBMSs in the selection
process. After selection, the schema can be re-defined using the
view of the DBMS chosen. However, there may be difficulty in
determining which 'things' should be regarded as entities and
which things should be regarded as attributes. An employee is
'obviously' an entity and his height is 'obviously' an attribute
to most people. A department is an entity but what is the head
of the department: an attribute of that department or an entity
related to the department? The answer is not clear and depends
to some extent on the usage of the data as mentioned earlier, in
Chapter 4. If we are never interested in the head of a department
in his or her own right, i.e. if we never want to ask questions such
as 'what is the age of head H?', then head is an attribute. If,
on the other hand, we are interested in the person who is head of
some department then head is an entity. The distinction is really
an implementation consideration. Entities map to records and
attributes map to fields within records in many DBMSs. The
'key' of the record typically identifies the entity which is represented by the record. If the relational view is used no distinc-

tion is made between entities and attributes. All 'things' are regarded as entities. For example, consider the following tuple:

Manager	dept.	age	nationality	hobby
Man = 11	D1	29	British	fishing

each of these values identifies an entity which may itself be involved in other tuples:

dept.	head	successor number	relation number
D1	J. SMITH	29	30

The simplest approach is to regard all things as entities in the first instance and to construct a database schema accordingly. Entity types (sets) which never have arcs (access paths) leaving them (and are never likely to) may be regarded as candidates for categorisation as attributes. There is no real need to make the distinction until individual DBMSs are considered. At this stage if it is necessary to think about record structure then decisions will have to be made. If a relational DBMS is being considered, then the problem does not arise.

(g) Many of the problems which can occur during DBMS selection have been discussed in chapter 5. One in particular concerns vendor demonstration. Do not allow suppliers to stage sales-oriented demonstrations. They are a waste of time for you and could influence non-technical management. Demand *facts* and demonstrations of *relevant* applications. If the supplier cannot provide such demonstrations then ask them for the names of their existing user base. Do not be content with one or two names — they are likely to be the most successful installations. If the supplier will not meet these requests, then they have something to hide. Before committing yourself to a product, make sure that you have a contract which includes details of:

- cost
- delivery date
- installation dates
- training dates
- size of database which can be stored on your system, max. size of database schema, etc.
- availability of vendor support
- details of access to source code
- cost of modification to source code

- the right to make copies of the software for use within the organisation
- the right to sell software which has been developed using the DBMS package

(h) Having selected the most appropriate DBMS, the next set of problems concerns the use of this DBMS — problems in creating the database schema, in sub-schema sub-division, in designing the privacy mechanism, in designing a back-up and recovery policy and in constructing application programs. One 'additional problem which has not really been covered concerns loading the database. A great deal of effort may be required to convert traditional files and copy them over to the database. Adequate time should be allocated for this task. The time required is frequently underestimated and this results in a chaotic start to what should be an improved DP service.

(i) The next problem concerns the way in which the DBMS should take over from the old system. Four methods are available: (i) direct changeover, (ii) parallel running, where the old and new systems run in parallel until the new has been validated, (iii) pilot running in which the new system is run at a later time (say the weekend) using the same input data as was used by the old system and (iv) phased changeover which is the same as parallel running except that only sample data is used at first, e.g. a subset of the sales ledger.

Direct changeover should only be used where it cannot be avoided e.g. in certain real-time systems. Parallel running should always be used if resources permit. Pilot running and phased changeover are better than direct changeover and can be used where resources cannot support parallel running.

(j) When the system has been running for some time, inevitably there will be a request to mount new applications. After all, that is why end-users helped to implement the database system. If the system was chosen correctly and if foresight was used in the construction of the database schema, then many new applications can be mounted with little effort. However, if an early-bound DBMS were chosen and if the database schema was designed only to support those access paths which were identified as being of immediate use, then there could be trouble. In some systems even the addition of an extra field to a record can require a great deal of system re-organisation. Imagine telling an end-user that he will have to wait three months for you to add a discount code field to customer records. He or she will wish that they still had their ancient visible record computer which could probably be re-programmed in less than one hour.

(k) Another serious problem which could arise when the system is running is that of hardware or software failure. Failure of a database system can be catastrophic. Be well prepared. As mentioned in chapter 10, the security of a system is highly dependent on the attitude of the operators. Do not fail to impress upon them the importance of the back-up procedures.

TO DO

A list of things to do to help avoid some of the problems mentioned above is now presented. The list is not comprehensive. Its purpose is to be a reminder of some of the more important points. The order is not significant:

(a) Do find out about the organisation for which the database system is being built. Identify the decision makers. Mount a thorough systems analysis study.

(b) Identify objectives of the new system and obtain user's written agreement to these objectives. Analysts could use questionnaires as well as free-format documents and should interview end-users from the top down *and* from the bottom up.

(c) Sell database concepts within the organisation. Identify and expose the shortcomings of the conventional system. Do not talk to end-users about inefficient use of storage and so on. They will not be interested unless they are affected by *late, incorrect* or *unavailable* data. You need users who are dissatisfied with the old system to obtain commitment to the new system. Cost-justify the database approach to your bosses. Remember to include factors such as reduced cost of new application development, improved availability of data and so on.

(d) Obtain management commitment and involvement at the beginning. Arrange for them to visit an installation using a DBMS. Without management commitment you stand a good chance of failure.

(e) Draft the DBA's remit and appoint a DBA early in the project. One of the DBA's first tasks is to form a committee with representatives from all end-user departments and/or groups. This committee should be chaired by the DBA who should be given sufficient authority to take decisions when the representatives are unable to agree.

(f) The staff training program should commence as early as possible. Before a particular DBMS is chosen, analysts, programmers and end-users should be sent on courses and/or given material to read on general aspects of database management. It may also be possible to buy a micro-based DBMS for in-house training. MDBS and dBASE II are examples of packages which run on micro-computers.

(g) Invest considerable effort in the initial requirements analysis and data analysis. Establish standards for data-item description *well before* the data analysis starts. A difficult question is whether or not to purchase a stand-alone data dictionary system before the DBMS is selected. If you can afford to, then do so. If not, then you can use pre-formatted forms which can be maintained manually. The contents of these forms could be that listed in chapter 3.

(h) Create an unconstrained network conceptual schema before discussing detailed data requirements with end-users. Use this schema to make sure that you have a complete and correct understanding of the organisational structure.

(i) Create a detailed requirements book which should constitute an implementation independent specification of what the system is required to do. This book can be used to help you create the database schema.

(j) Create an unconstrained network database schema. Validate this schema by checking that all end-user requirements can be accommodated by it. Ask users for predicted future requirements and test the database schema against these requirements. Modify the schema appropriately. This schema can be used to help you evaluate the various DBMSs considered. When one has been chosen, the database schema can be re-written according to the view of the universe used by that particular DBMS.

(k) Assign responsibilities for data, specify the privacy constraints and establish the back-up and recovery requirements *well before* the DBMS selection process.

(l) Consider future requirements carefully. What increases in volumes are likely? What new end-user requirements are possible? What additional communications facilities might be required in the future?

(m) Determine what sort of end-user interface is required. You know what data the end-user wants, now find out how he or she wants access to it. Pay attention to detailed requirements. The colour of paper and the type-face can be very important to an account-ant who wants to present a trial-balance at a board meeting.

(n) Choose the DBMS carefully. Talk to other DBMS users. Talk to programmers, operators and end-users not just to management or the DBA who is unlikely to admit that he or she made the wrong decision in purchasing a particular DBMS. Keep up-to-date in what is available. Perform a detailed resource requirements/performance study for each of the DBMSs on the short list. Remember that the cost of a wrong decision is very much more than the cost of the DBMS package. The DBMS also represents a substantial investment in manpower and opportunity. Consider all costs when evaluating a DBMS: cost of package, end-user involvement, cost of software and hardware to support it, cost of training, data conversion, development of application programs and testing. Do not forget the on-going costs: DP personnel, software and hardware maintenance, back-up, communications costs and so on. Estimate costs over five years to give a better indication of the cost of the various alternatives. Also consider end-user requirements, if they are likely to change then a data-independent DBMS is a must.

(o) Implement the database system gradually. The *first application should be regarded as an experiment*. However, it should be stressed that the choice of DBMS should be made with respect to all applications.

(p) Allocate plenty of time for all aspects of the project.

NOT TO DO

There are many things that shouldn't be done because they could jeopardise a database project. Three are presented which are often cited as the cause for project failure or near failure. To improve the chance of success remember these 'don'ts':

(a) Don't underestimate the time and manpower required.
(b) Don't forget to encourage management commitment and end-user co-operation.
(c) Don't start evaluating DBMSs until there is a complete, implementation independent, detailed specification of requirements.

A FINAL REMARK

Deliberately very little has been said about the operating environment and communications requirements of database systems. This subject is still poorly documented. In particular, the discipline of 'distributed databases' is in its infancy. However, interest in it has been encouraged by the recent proliferation of distributed computing networks.

It is most important that database techniques are not seen to be valid only in the context of a central processing facility. The physical storage mechanism is of secondary importance compared with the advantages which can be gained from the use of a conceptual schema, data dictionary, database schema and the establishment of well defined controls for integrity, privacy and back-up. The distribution of the physical database over components of a computer network should be seen as a technical problem concerning storage media. Much of the database approach is just as valid in a distributed computing environment as it was 2000 years ago when data was stored centrally using the clay and papyrus of Babylonia and Egypt.

Index